MEN OF PROPERTY

MEN OF PROPERTY

The Canadian Developers Who Are Buying America

SUSAN GOLDENBERG

PERSONAL LIBRARY

TORONTO

Personal Library, Publishers
Suite 439
17 Queen Street East
Toronto, Canada M5C 1P9

Publisher: Glenn Edward Witmer
Editor: Marion E. Raycheba
Design & Layout: First Image/Michael Gray

Distributed to the trade in Canada by:
John Wiley and Sons Canada Limited
22 Worcester Road
Rexdale, Ontario M9W 1L1

Distributed to the trade in the United States by:
Everest House
P.O. Box 978
424 Raritan Center
Edison, New Jersey 08817

Canadian Cataloguing in Publication Data
Goldenberg, Susan
Men of property

Includes index.
ISBN 0-920510-46-9

1. Real estate development–United States. 2. Investments, Canadian–United States.
3. Corporations, Canadian–United States. I. Title.

HD255.G62   333.77'0973   C81-094864-8

Printed and bound in Canada by
T. H. Best Printing Company Limited, Don Mills, Ontario

To My Parents

Contents

Foreword

Many of the developers profiled in this book have rarely been interviewed in depth before. None of the developers had any influence over the content of this book, nor did they request any. However, in cases of complex transactions, dates and dollar figures have been reviewed with the firms.

In addition, this book is based on interviews with company directors, business associates, banks, insurance and pension companies, accountants, lawyers, investment analysts, government officials, architects, and major tenants.

Current and historical annual reports, Ontario Securities Commission documents, and newspaper and magazine articles were used for background information. Some people were also kind enough to let me read their personal records.

Since real estate development is constantly changing and growing, it should be kept in mind that this book went to press in July 1981.

9

Chapter One

WHY THE CANADIAN DEVELOPERS GOT SO BIG

"Leverage is the name of the game."
POPULAR EXPRESSION AMONG DEVELOPERS

"Inflation makes heroes of developers."
MICHAEL SPOHN
VICE-PRESIDENT
T. EATON REALTY CO.

If you live in Erin Mills near Toronto, Indian Springs in Palm Beach, Crow Canyon in San Francisco, or Four Lakes Village in Chicago, you are living in a house or apartment developed by Canadians.

If you work in Doulton House in London, England, the Omni International in Atlanta, Denver Square, New York's Chemical Bank, the Minneapolis City Center, the Edmonton Centre, First Canadian Place in Toronto, or Place Ville Marie in Montreal, you are working in an office tower developed or purchased by Canadians.

If you shop at the Galleria in White Plains, the Clockamas Town Center in Portland, Toronto's Eaton Centre, or Vancouver's Pacific Centre, you are shopping in centers developed by Canadians.

If you vacation at the Mayo Hotel in Tulsa, the Hyatt Regency in Vancouver, the Four Seasons Hotel in Toronto, or the Brunswick Square Hotel in Saint John, you are staying at hotels owned by Canadians.

Starting with almost no money, the top ten Canadian developers have, within 30 years, planted the Maple Leaf throughout Canada, the United States, and England and are now scouting opportunities in South America, Europe, and Hong Kong. In the process, they have become the world's largest real estate developers with combined assets of more than $16 billion. This amount is expected to at least double by 1985.

The $16 billion figure, however, gives only a glimpse of what the developers are worth. They list the value of their assets according to the price at the time of purchase or development. With inflation, the *true market value* of their assets would be at least three to four times higher.

In 1973, the Canadians had virtually no assets in the U.S.A. By 1982, at least half of their assets will be south of the border. By 1985, 75 percent of the assets of many of these firms will be in the U.S. They are not neglecting Canada, but the United States' larger population (ten times that of Canada) and its older cities yield many more development opportunities.

Their success in Canada not only made the developers tough, but also very, very rich. So rich, in fact, that they were ready, willing, and able to overpay for U.S. property in their eagerness to snap up land.

"When land was at $7,000 an acre and owners were asking for $11,000, Canadians were paying $19,000," says Richard Metler, executive director, Homebuilders Association of Central Arizona. "That drastically increased the price everybody was paying for awhile. The Canadians were ready to pay a premium because they felt the land would rise in value. And they were right — it's now worth $25,000 an acre."

The largest Canadian developer is privately owned Olympia & York Developments Ltd. with assets estimated at $3.5 billion. Next is publicly owned Cadillac Fairview Corporation, the result of a merger, which has assets of $3 billion.

Although Trammell Crow Co. of Dallas, the largest U.S. developer, has developed 100 million square feet — double the total square feet built by Olympia & York — its assets of $3 billion are slightly less than Olympia & York's $3.5 billion. Trammel Crow's assets are derived from industrial properties, which appreciate in value more slowly than office buildings, Olympia & York's specialty.

There is about a billion dollar difference in assets between Trammell Crow and the number two U.S. developer, Gerald D. Hines Inc., which has estimated assets of between $1.5 billion and $2 billion.

By contrast, in Canada, despite its much smaller population, a pack of developers is snapping at the heels of the leaders in the field.

There is a trio near $2 billion: Trizec Corp. ($2.1 billion), Nu-West Group Ltd. ($1.98 billion), and Daon Development Corp. ($1.6 billion).

Four firms are clustered at the $1 billion mark: Oxford Development Group ($1.4 billion) and Bramalea Ltd. and Campeau Corp., both at $1 billion.

Genstar Corp. has real estate assets of $597 million. But its activities in such other widely diverse businesses as marine transportation and cement and lime production raise its total assets to $2.4 billion.

Being precise about the assets of the top ten developers is impossible because they are constantly changing through the sale — or much more likely — the acquisition of property.

Developers use three phrases to account for their success. One is "location, location, and location." If they choose a site in a high growth area with a strong business base, they can be assured of a good market. The second is that "Inflation makes heroes of developers." The third is "leverage," in which existing buildings are used as leverage to borrow money for future projects.

Without a developer's building anything new, the value of his property and the rents he can charge will soar, thanks to inflation. On the other hand, real estate is mostly a business of borrowing, using existing property as leverage for more funds. The higher interest rates are, the more it costs developers to borrow.

Unlike heads of companies in many industries, developers have a kind of immortality because they are survived by their projects. Their houses, office towers, and shopping centers have changed the face of the earth. In the opinion of critics, the developments have not always been for the better, but they have certainly brought mankind a long way from the first real estate ventures of cave dwellings.

"It's not like a car that becomes obsolete in a few years," says John Daniels, chairman of Cadillac Fairview. "We build for a span of centuries."

Each of the top ten Canadian developers has a different personality. Olympia & York specializes in office buildings. Cadillac Fairview does everything — housing, office towers, new communities, and redevelopment projects. Genstar is a pioneer in diversification, with other interests in transportation, financial services, construction and cement.

Trizec concentrates on office buildings and shopping centers and is the only one developing nursing homes and mobile home parks. Nu-West and Carma specialize in housing. Carma is the only cooperative in the top ten. Daon pioneered condominium conversion.

Oxford's key interest is multi-use redevelopment projects. Bramalea built North America's first new town. Campeau concentrated on eastern Canada, while the other developers moved west. Based in Ottawa, Canada's capital, Campeau has extremely good ties with the federal government for which it has built several office buildings.

Although they are among the world's wealthiest men, with personal fortunes, through their stock holdings, of $50 million or more, these men of property are little, if at all, known by the thousands of Canadians and Americans who work or live in their buildings.

Few are listed in *Who's Who* or belong to the exclusive business or social clubs. Their main interests are work and family life. They live comfortably but not ostentatiously.

Because of their far-flung empires, their travel schedule is horrendous. At any given time, at least half of the senior executives will be flying to operations in Texas, California, Florida, Missouri, Washington, Georgia, New York, New Jersey, Oklahoma, New Mexico, Arizona, Colorado, and Minnesota, as well as throughout Canada.

Many of these companies are owner-run by their founders who are now in their fifties. Most were not well off in their youth, although nearly all of them attended university, primarily studying engineering.

Three of the companies are based in Toronto — Olympia & York, Cadillac Fairview, and Bramalea. Campeau operates out of both Ottawa and Toronto. Three firms are headquartered in Calgary — Trizec, Carma, and Nu-West. Oxford is in Edmonton, Daon is in Vancouver, and Genstar operates out of Vancouver and San Francisco. They all have divisional offices throughout Canada and the U.S. and make a point of hiring American talent in the U.S.

But while they are low-key in their personal lives, these developers share common characteristics: they are gamblers, risk-takers, entrepreneurs, willing and eager to give the go-ahead instantly for multimillion dollar developments that will take years to pay off. They are not afraid to borrow or to use leverage.

Often, there are no contracts or written instructions. Deals may be finalized on napkins or pieces of foolscap. They are backed up, though, by bound volumes of master plans, which detail every minute step.

"Real estate developers are every bit as good, and maybe better, than any underwriter in the world of finance because financing is such a big part of their business," says William Corcoran, a director of Daon and president of his own investment house, W.J. Corcoran Ltd. of Toronto.

"At the same time, they also understand population growth and the development process. When most of us look at grass, we see grass, but developers visualize buildings. Real estate is a very visual business, unlike financing. Developers first have models of projects, then you tour buildings as they are under construction and are completed."

Developers may compete on one project, then link forces for a joint venture on another. They are also a clubby group, willing to share the nuts and bolts of their successes and failures with their counterparts at other firms and to give advice.

The siege mentality they acquired as a result of the anti-develpment sentiment of the late 1960s and early 1970s remains to a degree, but learning to compromise with ratepayers' associations has muted much of that early criticism.

"It's a fad that has passed to a very great degree," says Albert Reichmann, president and co-founder of Olympia & York, the world's biggest developer. "Developers had to answer a lot of questions and create an environment. Also, they're slowing up in tearing down buildings."

The pre-eminence of the developers is a reversal of the typical situation in which much of Canadian industry is dominated by multinationals. How did the Canadian developers get so big? There are six principal reasons.

1. The Canadian population is thinly scattered along the U.S. border, forcing developers to expand across Canada and to widen their product lines from residential to commercial.
2. The fierce rivalry in Canada forced them to build innovative projects. This brought them international renown and assisted them in winning competitions in the U.S.
3. Unlike the U.S., Canada has a national banking system. The banks are among the world's largest and have branches worldwide. They have given wholehearted support to the developers.
4. The collapse of the U.S. real estate market in the mid-1970s enabled the Canadians to buy property at dirt cheap prices. (Perhaps the most famous purchase was Olympia & York's acquisition in 1976 of eight New York City skyscrapers for $350 million. Today, they are worth more than $1 billion. The simultaneous collapse of the British real estate market allowed Canadian subsidiaries, such as Bramalea, to repatriate themselves. In other cases, British-owned subsidiaries were bought by different Canadian firms.)

5. Tough Canadian zoning regulations schooled developers in dealing with red tape, an education which served them well later in the U.S. In many U.S. cities, the regulations are much less rigorous than in Canada.

6. To counteract the traditional peaks and valleys of real estate demand, the Canadians have boldly diversified into unrelated fields, primarily natural resources. This diversification provides a cushion against any potential softness in the real estate market.

Unlike the U.S., which has clusters of large cities, most of Canada's population is strung along the U.S.-Canadian border. Moreover, the entire Canadian population is equal to that of California alone.

"The distances between major cities in Canada are greater than in the U.S., but the administrative challenge is simpler because there are fewer centers," says Michael Galway, executive director of the Canadian Institute of Public Real Estate Companies (CIPREC), the industry's trade association. "Therefore, it's not unusual for developers to have offices across Canada and the developers are used to traveling to expand, and then oversee, their business."

Because the Canadian market is smaller, the developers, in order to grow, had to broaden their product line. The natural progression has been from houses to apartments, warehouses, office buildings, shopping centers, and multi-use redevelopment projects covering blocks and blocks in the downtown core.

"Since the Canadians are in many areas geographically, as well as in multiple product lines, they would phase down one area of activity and step up another depending on demand," says Mac Campbell, senior vice-president and chief financial officer at Daon. "U.S. developers haven't done this and, therefore, are more vulnerable to cycles in demand."

The limited demand in Canada, as compared with the U.S., for housing and office buildings pushed the Canadians into developing superior projects and made them tough competitors. "With a number of very capable people competing against one another in a small community, a developer had to be good to survive," says Kenneth Field, president of Bramalea.

"This environment produced a survival of the fittest syndrome. With first class office buildings across the street from each other, developers had to try to outdo one another to draw attention and tenants to their project. Canada has been a fabulous school where you were either good or got knocked out."

A lot of top Canadian real estate firms have either been knocked out, bought out, or merged. Of the top ten publicly owned Canadian developers in 1973, only five are in the top ten today.

Two of those, Cadillac and Fairview, merged in 1974. One of them,

Oxford, went private in 1979.

The two others were Trizec, then the top firm, and Campeau, then second in size. They no longer hold these prestigious spots. Cadillac Fairview is now number one among the publicly owned firms, Trizec is number two, and Campeau ranks sixth in terms of assets.

Fewer than a dozen of the 43 real estate companies that went public in 1968 and 1969 when they were listed on the Toronto Stock Exchange are around today on the TSE. The rest have gone private or gone out of business or been acquired by competitors. Going public enabled the developers to raise the necessary capital base for going to their bankers and borrowing more money.

Expansion would have been impossible, though, without financial support and the developers have always had enthusiastic backing from the Canadian banks. The importance of this help cannot be over-estimated.

Unlike the U.S., Canada has a national banking network of only 11 banks, compared with the regionalized system of 15,000 banks in the U.S. Some U.S. banks have only one branch in one city.

But the Canadians have branches across the country, and so they can easily fund the Halifax, Montreal, Winnipeg, Calgary, Edmonton, and Vancouver projects of a Toronto developer. Moreover, with branches around the world, they can assist developers when they enter foreign markets.

Canadian banks are among the world's largest, because Canadians' strong saving habits have placed Canada's so-called Big Five banks among the top 75 worldwide.

The Big Five are the Royal Bank of Canada (No. 34 in the world with assets at year end October, 1980, of $62.8 billion); Canadian Imperial Bank of Commerce (No. 41, assets, $55.4 billion); Bank of Montreal (No. 54, assets, $48.8 billion); Bank of Nova Scotia (No. 62, assets, $43.2 billion) and Toronto Dominion Bank (No. 74, assets, $33.8 billion). Because of their size and their intimate knowledge of the market value of the developers' property (few developers divulge this to shareholders, preferring to give book value), the banks willingly provide corporate financing.

In other words, the developer can ask for a pot of money and use it for whatever projects he wants. In turn, the banks take a floating charge against all of the developers' assets.

The banks regard the real estate industry as a safe borrower because assets (offices, houses, shopping centers) cannot be moved if a developer runs into debt and because property values keep rising due to the constant demand for shelter.

The banks were also able to judge the true financial status of the developers since the industry instituted new clarifying accounting practices in 1970. Before then, a developer could sell a parcel of land for $1 million, with five percent — $50,000 — down and a promissory note for the remaining $950,000.

If he had paid $250,000 for the land, he would then declare a profit of $750,000, even though he was still owed $950,000. This practice worried both the securities commissions and accounting profession, as well as many developers, because it gave a misleading impression of profits.

Consequently, the industry adopted new rules calling for a minimum cash down payment of 15 percent and for the balance to be paid in stages as development progressed.

There is also little risk in the banks' lending heavily to well-run development companies because, unlike other industries where assets depreciate as time passes, real estate companies benefit from inflation, which raises the value of property. The difference between what the developer paid for a property and its inflated value is called the surplus appraisal. Whereas other companies that sell some of their assets lose value, real estate firms can sell off assets and, due to inflation, bounce back to the same level of assets, even though they have fewer holdings.

"If a company with $400 million in surplus appraisal sold off 20 percent at $80 million, the next year what would be left would be back up at $400 million," says Stephen Moore, real estate analyst at Burns Fry Ltd., a Toronto investment dealer.

In addition, developers are able to defer taxes for years because capital cost allowances yield them substantial write-offs. Consequently, the developers pay very little tax each year. For example, Cadillac Fairview, Canada's largest publicly owned developer, paid only $2.1 million in taxes in its fiscal year ended February 29, 1980. Deferred taxes in 1980 were $19.4 million and Cadillac Fairview's total deferred income tax, up to February 29, 1980, is $131.4 million.

By contrast, the localized U.S. banking system lends on a project by project basis. The system drives the Canadians crazy, and so they prefer to deal with the U.S. branches of their Canadian banks.

"In the U.S., the bank gets the building if a project goes broke," Kenneth Field of Bramalea says. "As a result, the U.S. bank builds up a team of people to control the developer. Because they would be stuck with the building if you go broke, they determine how much should be spent for mechanical systems and plumbing, or even how many bathrooms there should be. It drives developers nuts.

"By contrast, the Canadian banks never get that involved. If they have had confidence in the people they're dealing with, they believe the building will be a success."

The close ties between the developers and the banks have another advantage, too. In a battle for status, each of the banks has built a head office monument to its success. Those quarters were built by the developers.

In addition, the banks have become co-partners in several major ventures in Canada, putting up much of the funding needed. The keeping-up-with-the-Joneses game has also benefited the developers in Calgary where every oil company has erected its own tower.

When the Alberta oil boom struck in the mid-1970s, following the Arab oil embargo, Canada's style of corporate financing enabled the developers based in eastern Canada to follow the banks west. It also allowed developers in western Canada to do their banking in Calgary and Vancouver instead of flying to Toronto for major transactions.

Their expansion across Canada and their pipeline to assured financing from the Canadian banks put the Canadians in a strong position to purchase prime U.S. property in the mid-1970s when the U.S. real estate market collapsed.

The 1973 to 1976 real estate slump in the U.S. was the worst the industry had suffered since the Depression of the 1930s. Many developers went bankrupt.

In 1975 the country had a five year oversupply of office buildings. Many projects were 50 percent empty. The vacancy rate in others was as high as 80 percent. Commercial and industrial building in 1975 was 40 percent of the record 184 million square feet in 1973.

What went wrong in the U.S. is that developers overbuilt because too much financing was available. They would build regardless of the economics and whether their financing was short-term or long-term.

At the same time, U.S. tax laws allowing individual investors to write off part of their ownership in buildings created a surge of investor-owned properties.

Lots of money was available because Real Estate Investment Trusts (REITS), pools of capital invested in mortgages and real estate, had been established in the U.S. in the early 1960s. By 1973, the U.S. REITS industry had $21 billion in funds.

The pressure to invest that money was so intense that many REITS ignored normal lending and appraisal standards and backed poor projects. When the developers were unable to meet their mortgage payments, the REITS tumbled.

In addition, the U.S. REITS were buffeted by a setback in residential construction. U.S. housing starts declined from 2.4 million in 1972 to an annual rate of only 1.5 million in 1974.

The loan portfolios of the U.S. REITS left them overexposed to this slowdown in housing construction because, at the end of 1973, more than 55 percent of their outstanding loans were short-term construction and development or land loans. This represented 22 percent of the total construction and development loans in the U.S. — a vulnerable proportion considering the deteriorating market conditions.

By contrast, the Canadian REITS were in a healthy state both because the Canadian real estate industry was stronger and because REITS were more stringently regulated.

While U.S. housing starts fell drastically from 1972 to 1974, Canada had a record number during that period. The structure and investment policies of Canadian REITS were also more tightly governed by securities and tax laws than U.S. REITS.

REITS leverage in Canada was kept to a 5:1 debt/equity ratio compared with an 8:1 ceiling in the U.S. Canadian REITS were also required to hold at least half their mortgage portfolios in well-secured first mortgage loans, and sponsorship of Canadian REITS was more stringently regulated than in the U.S.

The sponsor of a Canadian REITS had to have net assets of at least $2 million and invest at least $1 million in the equity of the REITS, thus ensuring that large Canadian financial institutions would take a continuing interest in their REITS. No such stipulations existed in the U.S.

The small number of public Canadian REITS in 1973 — only four compared with more than 200 in the U.S. — eliminated the cutthroat competition existing in the U.S. That competition forced some U.S. REITS to sacrifice quality for volume in order to maintain earnings growth when construction activity slackened.

Canadian developers, unlike their U.S. counterparts, did not face an oversupply situation, partly because of their number one gripe — government red tape in approving zoning changes and its slowness in providing the sewers, water mains, and roads needed for land development.

But that very foot-dragging meant that development could not proceed unchecked in Canada. And because there was an undersupply of office and housing space, developers could charge more than if there had been a glut.

The tottering state of the U.S. real estate industry in the mid-1970s created a vacuum that the Canadians rushed to fill. They snapped up prime pieces of land for housing, rental apartments that they converted into condominiums, office towers, and large rundown tracts in the inner city cores for future redevelopment.

The prices were rock bottom, but the property was blue chip. Today, close to 50 percent of the profits of many of the Canadian developers come from their U.S. operations.

There was nothing wrong about the Canadians heading south. It made sound economic sense. But the developers were sensitive about possible charges from Canadians that they were taking profits made in Canada to the U.S. for building projects there, using U.S. labor. On the other hand, they did not want to look like vultures invading the ailing U.S. market.

So, instead of saying they were going to the U.S. because prices were cheap and the market was ten times larger, the developers initially said that the attraction in the U.S. was the lack of zoning regulations compared with the bureaucratic mountain of red tape in parts of Canada. It is perfectly true that zoning regulations are tougher in Canada, but it should not be forgotten that the real reason the Canadians headed south was the larger U.S. market. In addition, the developers regarded newly introduced rent controls as a dampener on profits they could make from rental housing.

At first they flocked to the so-called "sunbelt" — Florida, the southwest, and California — to which easterners in the U.S. have been migrating heavily. As a result, Jack Poole, president of Daon, calls the "sunbelt" the "moneybelt."

The Canadians have also gone to the Pacific Northwest, home of natural resource expansion, as well as of the aerospace and military industries, which are being enlarged under the administration of President Ronald Reagan.

Some statistics bear out the wisdom of the Canadians' selection of location. Population growth in San Diego County in California in the 1970s was three times the national average. Los Angeles, Orange, and San Diego counties now have 13 million people, making them the second largest concentration outside the Boston-New York-Washington corridor. Moreover, those 13 million people are equal to about three-fifths of Canada's total population. Growth in Florida has been 2½ times the national average. The Canadians are also moving east into areas around Washington, D.C., and the commuter belt outside New York City.

The zoning regulations were vastly lighter in the U.S., at least when the Canadians first headed south. The comparison that the Canadians most liked to make was between zoning free Houston and zoning heavy Canada.

In Houston, developers can bring a project on stream in 18 months. In Canada, it can take 18 months just to clear all the government authorities at the municipal and provincial levels.

Too much of a good thing can be bad, however, the developers have found. Because Houston has no zoning restrictions, anybody and everybody has built houses and, consequently, there is a four year glut. That means the developers must charge half the price they do elsewhere and often they must assume part of the mortgage in order to sign up buyers.

But Houston is an exception. Zoning restrictions in the rest of the U.S. can be just as tough as in Canada.

Careful tax planning, leading to hefty tax breaks, has accompanied the southward expansion of the Canadian developers. They started by establishing branches because the startup costs would result in those branches recording losses. These losses could then offset profits in the more mature Canadian operations.

As activity bloomed in the U.S., separate U.S. entities were established. This limits liability in case of lawsuits. In addition, setting up a U.S. operation enables the companies to say that they are good American citizens, should there be objections to foreign investment.

Once they are in the U.S., the developers establish offshore companies in the tax havens of the Netherlands or Antilles. Any surplus taxable income flows out of the U.S. to the Netherlands or Antilles, both of which have low tax rates. In turn, the overseas company lends money to the U.S. operation, which then writes off the interest it must pay on those loans. Such a tax benefit is possible only if the developers are in at least two countries other than Canada.

The success of the developers has resulted in their shares trading at all-time highs. Activity in the real estate index on the Toronto Stock Exchange strongly outpaces the performances of the gold, oil, and gas indices. But investors face the problem of ascertaining the true value of the companies, since, with the exception of Daon, they do not give their true value in the balance sheet.

There is no obligation for the industry to give the so-called surplus appraisal — the difference between the cost and current value of its property. But it can be substantial. Daon's surplus appraisal in its 1980 fiscal year exceeded its book value by $469 million. After allowing for taxes at 50 percent on the excess, the shareholders' equity in Daon at market value increased during fiscal 1980 to $394 million from $312 million.

Both the Canadian Institute of Chartered Accountants and the developers are trying to work out guidelines to provide a better picture of the current appraisal value of their properties. Doing this would not affect the companies' income tax because the surplus appraisal is an unrealized gain. But the developers are reluctant to provide surplus appraisals, arguing that appraisals can differ widely. One possible solution is a "rainbow" range of appraisals.

Real estate development companies are traditionally capital intensive and management lean. Olympia & York, with $3.5 billion in assets, has only about 250 employees. Manufacturers and retailers would have at least ten times as many workers. Bell Canada, for example, has 57,000 workers.

But while their wage costs are low compared with other industries, real estate developers are just as vulnerable to inflation as manufacturers and retailers when it comes to paying interest. "Inflation helps developers, but interest rates hurt them," says Stephen Moore of Burns Fry Ltd.

As an antidote, developers have built up piggy banks of cash reserves and short-term investments in securities as a rainy day fund. In some cases, the fund is equivalent to 10 percent of assets. The money is not only used as a buffer when business is down but also to snap up bargains.

Daon, for example, dipped into its cash fund late in 1980 to pay $47 million for a 50 percent interest in the Place Victoria stock exchange tower in Montreal and another $23 million for a joint interest in the Omni International hotel, office, and retail complex in Atlanta.

High interest rates are also causing developers to devise what they term either innovative or creative financing. The type getting the most attention is the limited partnership given to the public in office buildings or shopping centers. The pioneer in this has been Daon, which financed its head office and three Alberta shopping centers this way.

Just how good a deal this is for investors is debatable. "The consumer investor will become more educated and realize that for his share of the risk, he deserves a bigger piece of the pie," says Harry Rannala, real estate analyst at Walwyn Stodgell Cochran Murray Ltd., a Toronto investment dealer.

High interest rates are only one problem facing the developers. Another problem stems from their ability to build tremendous projects. Unless the vacancy rate is tremendous, one or two of these huge projects soak up immediate demand.

Lurking in the background is still another worry. Will U.S. politicians, bowing to growing concern over foreign acquisitions of companies and real estate, put a freeze on such investment?

Several U.S. congressmen, furious at recent Canadian acquisitions of, and takeover bids for, many of the largest U.S. companies, have threatened retaliatory legislation. The suggested measures have included a moratorium on the acquisition of more than 5 percent of a U.S. mineral resources company.

One of the stiffest anti-Canadian investment attacks was launched by Cities Service Co. of Oklahoma after Nu-West bought 7.2 percent of its stock this year. Although Nu-West maintained the purchase was made only as an investment, Cities Service believed Nu-West really wanted to force a swap of its Canada Cities Service Ltd. stock for Nu-West's shares in the U.S. parent. Such swaps have become common practise by Canadian firms since the Canadian Government's October 1980 National Energy Program called for greater Canadian ownership of Canadian energy resources.

The Americans are also threatening a crackdown on the use of borrowed money by foreigners in their acquisition of U.S. firms.

Foreigners would have to make a 50 percent down payment just as U.S. firms must. So far, this rule has not applied to foreigners using foreign credit.

Canadian developers have rarely acquired U.S. firms and so would not be seriously hurt by such a blow. Moreover, the developers have been invited to submit bids to redevelop major U.S. cities and have frequently been awarded such projects. U.S. developers so far have not complained about a Canadian invasion. But there is some concern that the Canadians' eagerness to build may contribute to a glut of office space and possibly even a hammerlock on rent levels.

For example, in Dallas alone, Cadillac Fairview and Bramalea account for three million square feet of the 4.65 million square feet announced or under construction. Olympia & York is redeveloping 25 acres in downtown San Francisco, and Cadillac Fairview is rebuilding huge sections of New York, Houston, and Los Angeles.

An ominous note was sounded for the industry in the fall of 1979 when Oklahoma Attorney General John Cartwright ordered Hillcrest Investments Ltd. of Calgary to sell its $150 million worth of real estate investments in the state. However, Cartwright lost the case and similar action did not occur elsewhere.

Michael Galway of CIPREC says that Canadian investment of $6 billion in the U.S. is less than one percent of the total $10 trillion estimated value of U.S. real estate.

But while a visit to any major U.S. city shows the vast opportunities for redeveloping blocks and blocks of rundown areas, some of the Canadian developers are no longer content to rely on real estate alone. These men of property are becoming oilmen, too, as they branch into natural resources in order to break their vulnerability to the cyclical nature of the real estate industry.

"Real estate will always be cyclical because, like every other industry, it over-reacts to demand and supply and nothing will change this," says Harry Rannala of Walwyn Stodgell.

Housing in particular is subject to population and income trends and, as a result, demand bounces up and down. During the coming decade, a combination of a decline in the number of new households and a rise in housing prices is expected to result in a leveling off in new housing construction.

The leaders in the recent diversification trend have been Nu-West, which has moved into oil and gas, and Olympia & York, which has interests in oil and gas, newsprint, and financial services. But they are 30 years behind Genstar, which has always been a diversified company with interests in transportation, cement, construction, and financial services, as well as real estate.

This diversification is expected to accelerate, perhaps to the point where some real estate companies will have as large as, or even larger, investment in areas other than in real estate. Real estate will just be one arm of the business.

"There are limited opportunities in the income property (shopping center and office buildings) area and the substantial size of the developers necessitates more and more work to keep them busy," Rannala says. "The cash flow from the income properties also has to be re-invested and diversification provides an avenue."

While diversification should bring in more money, it could also cause management problems because the developers are venturing into unfamiliar territory. "Although the developers will leave in place the management of acquired companies, they can't understand every one of the operations," Rannala says.

"They may rely too much on existing management at those firms and that management may not have the same incentive as in the past, since they are no longer their own boss.

"Not all the diversification will work out. Some investments may have to be sold off. The sheer success of these companies in growing big will breed mistakes as they enter new fields."

Although the future holds challenges to the industry from the increased participation of insurance companies and pension funds in real estate development (see Chapter 12), it is unlikely that the developers will face competition from many newcomers.

"Joining the league of the largest developers isn't open to newcomers because of the size of the existing developers and their extremely close connections with the banks," Rannala says. "Why should the banks risk dealing with the little guy when they have established clients who have a proven record of success?"

And so the chances are more and more that the house you live in, the office you work in, the shopping center you shop in, whether in Canada, the U.S., or, increasingly, overseas, will be owned by one of Canada's top ten developers.

Chapter Two

OLYMPIA & YORK DEVELOPMENTS LIMITED

"The important thing is to study and organize and discipline your thinking."

ALBERT REICHMANN
PRESIDENT
OLYMPIA & YORK

OLYMPIA & YORK DEVELOPMENTS LTD.

President:	Albert Reichmann	
Executive Vice-President:	Paul Reichmann	
Operating Executive Vice-Presidents:	Gordon Hendry	
	Keith Roberts	*(Construction)*
	Gilbert Newman	*(Finance)*

OFFICES

Canada
Toronto (*Head Office*), Ottawa, Calgary
United States
New York (*U.S. Corporate Office*), Los Angeles,
San Francisco, Dallas, Hartford

Millions of dollars of business are transacted every day in four skyscrapers—one black, one gray, one granite, and one white marble—located on each corner of the windswept intersection of King and Bay Streets in downtown Toronto's financial district. On the northwest corner, in the 72-floor white marble tower, called No. 1 First Canadian Place, are the little known (to the general public) brothers Albert and Paul Reichmann, the president and executive vice-president of Olympia & York Developments Ltd., the world's largest developer. It is the only Canadian developer with overseas real estate investments.

In 1976 the Reichmanns attracted worldwide attention when they bought eight New York City buildings at a time when the Manhattan real estate market was in its worst slump since 1929 and the ensuing Depression. Those buildings, now leasing at three to five times their 1976 rents, include the ITT, Harper and Row, and Chemical Bank headquarters. The Reichmanns also own such other landmarks as First Canadian Place in Toronto, Doulton House in London, England, and La Boursidière in Paris.

From their 32nd floor offices, furnished expensively but not ostentatiously, the Reichmanns oversee a real estate empire that already stretches across Canada and is now spreading throughout the United States and into England and France.

In fewer than 30 years, typical of the rush by Canadian developers to massive size and wealth, Albert's and Paul's company has amassed an estimated $3.5 billion in real estate assets. That estimate is probably on the low side. Just how big the assets actually are is a mystery because Olympia & York is privately owned by Albert, 51 years old, Paul, 50, their mother, their younger brother, Ralph, 48, and the wives of the three brothers.

The Reichmanns are the only immigrants among Canada's top developers, except for Cadillac Fairview's chairman, John Daniels. They were born in Hungary and later moved to Tangiers and then to Canada.

The Reichmanns are also the only developers in Canada's top ten, besides Robert Campeau, who did not attend university. But Albert Reichmann says that "When you learn the Talmud, you learn everything." (The Talmud is the body of Jewish civil and religious law and related commentaries and discussion.)

"Many people study one thing and end up doing another," Albert Reichmann continues. "The important thing is to study and organize and discipline your thinking."

One way of appreciating Olympia & York's magnitude is to com-

Albert Reichmann, president, Olympia & York (Photo: The Globe and Mail, *Toronto)*

Paul Reichmann, executive vice-president, Olympia & York (Photo: The Globe and Mail, *Toronto)*

pare it with other large corporations. Olympia & York's assets are larger than those of General Motors of Canada ($2.2 billion) and of Ford Motor Co. of Canada ($2.3 billion). It is on a par in assets with such U.S. corporate giants as McDonnell Douglas ($3.4 billion U.S.), Coca Cola ($2.9 billion U.S.), Pepsi Co. ($2.8 billion U.S.), and Colgate-Palmolive ($2.4 billion U.S.) All comparisons are in 1979 figures.

Olympia & York's accomplishments are even more impressive in that they have come entirely through internal growth. By contrast, the size of the number two developer, Cadillac Fairview, is the result of a merger.

Olympia & York's reach, however, extends far beyond being the world's largest developer, substantial as that achievement is. It is also well on its way to being a huge holding company in which real estate will be only one investment, albeit the largest. This diversification is a pace-setter among Canadian developers, many of whom see it as a buffer to the cyclical nature of real estate.

Its tentacles stretch into nearly every aspect of Canada's economy. Olympia & York's portfolio of investments contains some of Canada's biggest natural resource producers, its largest trust firm, and two other real estate companies and is worth about another $1.25 billion on top of its $3.5 billion real estate holdings.

The outside investments include:

- 3.9 million shares of Royal Trustco Ltd. (value around $78 million)
- 88 percent of Abitibi-Price Inc. ($502 million). Abitibi-Price is the world's largest newsprint producer.
- 50.1 percent of Brinco Ltd. ($78 million). Brinco is active in asbestos, as well as in oil and gas exploration in Canada and the U.S.
- 1.05 million shares of Bow Valley Industries Ltd. ($24 million), one of Canada's hottest oil and gas companies. Investment analysts say Olympia & York may buy more.
- 1.065 million convertible preferred shares of Noranda Mines Ltd. ($106 million). Noranda is Canada's leading copper producer.
- 2.13 million shares of MacMillan Bloedel Ltd. ($90 million). MacMillan Bloedel is Canada's largest forest products company.
- 12.6 million shares of Trizec Corp. ($378 million), one of the big ten Canadian real estate developers.
- Control of Block Brothers, a major British Columbia real estate broker. Because Block's is privately owned, the value of Olympia & York's holdings is not known.

"Olympia & York is the real estate arm, which is still the most important part of our business, but under that is a so-called holding company," says Albert Reichmann. The holding company is called Olympia & York Investments Ltd. Reichmann says that the diversification will continue "as opportunities arise" both within and outside Canada.

"We really started five years ago when we got involved in New York City and later in 1978 we bought Block Brothers. We came to the conclusion we shouldn't have all our eggs in one basket.

"It's not essential for a real estate company to diversify, but we had got to a size where expansion was very difficult without buying into companies and there are few opportunities to buy real estate companies, because most smaller ones have been bought."

In 1979, the Reichmanns bought into one of Canada's other large developers, Trizec (assets: $2.1 billion), of which it owns 49.99 percent. (Peter and Edward Bronfman own 50.01 percent through their holding company, Edper Investments Ltd.) Olympia & York obtained its 49.99 percent by purchasing 100 percent of the previous holder, English Property Corp. of London, England, for $156 million.

Real estate investment analysts say that such unrelated diversification by many developers will continue because it is cheaper than buying quality real estate. "Most share prices, outside the oil industry, are cheap relative to the asset value of the company," says Ira Gluskin, real estate analyst at Brown, Baldwin & Nisker Ltd., a Toronto investment dealer. "It's a lot easier to buy Abitibi-Price than to buy quality real estate, which is very pricey."

While its multi-million dollar acquisitions may be a comparative bargain, how is Olympia & York footing the bill, especially when it is simultaneously spending hundreds of millions of dollars on new real estate projects in Toronto, Calgary, New York, Portland, San Francisco, Dallas, and Boston?

That is something Albert Reichmann politely says he "would like to leave out. We work with banks and financial institutions and use leverage."

Real estate analyst Stephen Moore of Burns Fry Ltd., a Toronto investment dealer who frequently acts for Olympia & York in its acquisitions, further explains how the company can do so much at once. "The banks will lend them the difference between the cost of the building and its current value. Also, Olympia & York's long-term debt could, if it wanted, be as high as 95 percent of equity because as an office developer it has rents coming in every month which provide the money for the interest payments on its debt."

The purchases also have tax advantages. The expenditure reduces overall income and, thus, defers taxes.

Olympia & York's banks are the Bank of Montreal, Canada's third largest and the prime tenant in First Canadian Place, and the Canadian Imperial Bank of Commerce, Canada's second largest bank.

Olympia & York has achieved its dominance strictly through office building development. But now it is about to give Cadillac Fairview, the second largest developer, a run for the money in competing for redevelopment projects. Such projects have become identified with Cadillac, which is developing Houston Center, California Center in Los Angeles, and River Walk in New York, and which developed Toronto's Eaton Centre and Vancouver's Pacific Centre.

However, in 1980 Olympia & York beat out Cadillac and 11 other firms to redevelop 25 acres in downtown San Francisco at a cost of $500 million. The project will include a hotel and condominiums. Although the rate of return on most housing is usually less than on office buildings, Albert Reichmann says that multi-use projects can be "more interesting than straightforward office buildings and if the market is good, residential can do well."

On a smaller scale, Olympia & York is turning an eight-story former warehouse on Toronto's waterfront into a complex of shops, restaurants, offices, and condominiums. It is one of the largest renovations ever in Canada.

There is, nonetheless, one drawback to Olympia & York's expansion. It focuses more attention on the company, and the Reichmanns

No. 1 First Canadian Place, Toronto

prefer a very, very low profile. Still, since they intend to sit on the Boards of the companies they are purchasing, they cannot avoid being in the public eye more. "We don't like this, but we can't do it any other way," Albert Reichmann says.

While their wealth would easily make them part of Canada's close-knit business establishment, the Reichmanns prefer to remain apart. They do not belong to any business or golf clubs; they do not own football, hockey, or baseball teams like other Canadian moguls such as the Bronfmans; they do not head up charity drives (although they are generous private donors); they are not on civic committees; and business and personal life are kept strictly separate. Business and family life are the two paramount interests of the Reichmanns.

Although thousands of people work, shop, and eat in Olympia & York buildings in Toronto, New York, London, and other major cities, the average person would not know the Reichmanns, especially as they have not allowed newspaper pictures to be taken of them since 1965. (A limited number of unauthorized photos have been obtained at annual meetings of companies on whose Boards the Reichmanns are.)

As a result, a fascination for and awe of the Reichmanns has developed in the business world. But while they eschew publicity, the Reichmanns apparently closely follow what is said about them. When *The New York Times* wrote an editorial in July 1980 criticizing Olympia & York for evicting the Whitney Museum's downtown branch at 55 Water Street in Manhattan for not paying $90,000 in rent, Olympia & York executives were riled.

The Whitney branch had paid $1 a year to its previous landlord when the New York real estate market was depressed. Although the editorial was relatively mild, saying that Olympia & York should have "taken the lead in exploring ways to raise new contributions or helping find another location," Olympia & York executives said the $90,000 was a token rent.

Actually, the $90,000 charge was not that much of a bargain. Since rents in the Water Street area were $20 to $25 a square foot and the museum occupied 5,000 square feet, the $90,000 rent was in fact a deduction of only about $30,000 from the going rate. When its lease expired in September 1980, the Whitney branch moved to rent-subsidized quarters.

Usually, the Reichmanns do not get embroiled in controversy. But the Whitney museum flap was one of two unpleasant high profile disagreements in which Olympia & York got involved in 1980. The other occurred when Olympia & York lost its anchor tenant in the second phase of its flagship building in downtown Toronto, First Canadian Place. The tenant was Sun Life Assurance Co., Canada's largest life insurer, which is moving many of its executives and employees to Toronto from its former head office in Montreal, due, the company

American Brands, 245 Park Avenue, New York

said, to the election of a separatist government in Quebec. Sun Life opted to build its head office a block away after a dispute with the City of Toronto (over various building requirements) delayed construction for close to a year.

The construction delay cost Olympia & York $7 million as well as the loss of Sun Life, which would have occupied 400,000 square feet of the one million square foot tower. But Olympia & York was unconcerned about Sun Life's pullout because Toronto has a shortage of prime downtown office space. Also, it quickly signed up another prime tenant — the Toronto Stock Exchange, which will occupy several floors.

Such publicity is rare for the Reichmanns who have become legendary not only because of their astute deals, but also because they are an enigma. In the real estate world, there are the Reichmanns and then there is everybody else.

Competitors smilingly and ruefully admire their deal-making skill. Associates will say another developer is the best at making deals "except for the Reichmanns," the most private "except for the Reichmanns," one of the fastest growing and best managed "except for the Reichmanns."

They are the deans of the real estate development world, unparalleled chess players in making deals, possessed of infinite patience and down-to-earth common sense and practicality.

Perhaps because they come from Europe, there is an old world merchant prince aura about the Reichmanns. Appropriately, Reichmann, a name of German origin, means "rich man," denoting both wealth and experience. The brothers speak softly with impassive poker faces, but a pleasant smile constantly plays on Albert's face, while Paul's eyes show inner amusement. They are terse and to the point, but their wealth and eminence have not eroded their courtesy.

While Cadillac Fairview's chairman John Daniels stalled for months and had a public relations spokesman arrange and cancel interviews for this book, Albert Reichmann had his secretary call and apologize for changing appointments during a peak period for the company. And while the Reichmanns rarely give interviews, when they do, they answer directly with no public relations person sitting in, unlike at Cadillac where public relations spokesman Bert Petlock attends interviews with Daniels, often tape-recording them.

The Reichmanns took a circuitous route to Canada. The family originated in Hungary where Albert's and Paul's father Samuel was involved in the distribution and exporting of eggs. During the apprehensiveness in the 1920s about a possible Soviet invasion of Hungary after the Russian Revolution, the family fled to Austria.

In Austria, Samuel bought an ailing glass factory and turned it around. But with Hitler's ascent to power in the 1930s, Samuel realized that Austria was unsafe for his Jewish family and moved to Tangiers, where he established a major banking house. In the 1950s, when Algeria split from France, Samuel again thought it wise to move, this time to Canada where the purchase of a floundering Montreal plastic tile business introduced the Reichmanns to the construction industry.

They came across the business by chance through a for sale ad in the *Wall Street Journal*. The business, now known as Olympia Floor & Wall Tile Co., is one of the largest in Canada with sales of around $50 million. Today, it is run by the third brother, Ralph. (Two other brothers, Louis and Edward, live in the U.S. and are not connected with Olympia & York.)

Albert and Paul gradually moved into real estate development, starting with industrial buildings along Highways 400 and 401, the commuter roads leading into Toronto. Their first building was a warehouse for the tile business.

Then, in 1962, they branched into office tower development, choosing as their first location the then outer limits of Toronto — a northeast suburb of Don Mills. They bought the land at bargain prices from U.S. real estate entrepreneur William Zeckendorf who was suffering financial reverses. (Zeckendorf played a major role in the development of Place Ville Marie in Montreal and the formation of Trizec Corp.)

What was regarded as near idiocy in 1962 is today hailed as tremendous foresight because the buildings are in the heart of a huge modern plant and apartment district. The project, called Olympia Square, also provided the first half of the company name. The other part is named after the county of York in which Toronto is located.

Business colleagues have high praise for the Reichmanns. "They are totally reliable," says George Hamann of Bregman & Hamann, Canada's largest commercial architectural firm, which has designed about one-fourth of Olympia & York's Canadian projects over a 17-year association. It started when Paul Reichmann arrived, without an appointment, at Bregman & Hamann to say that he liked one of their buildings in Toronto and had found out they designed it.

"Their word is their bond. They demand service and expect results, but also set one of the highest standards among Canadian developers," Hamann continues.

Real estate agents also have high praise for Olympia & York. "Although they rarely speak to the press, they're very approachable to the real estate brokers community, particularly if they know you're not going to waste their time," says William Moore, senior vice-president, office leasing, at A.E. LePage Ltd., Canada's largest real estate firm.

"They also are very creative in their deals. They don't just quote a price, but give a good deal that makes both sides happy. If Olympia & York were a public company, it would be more concerned with a minimum return on investment because it would have a responsibility

55 Water Street, New York

to its shareholders. But since it's a private company, it can take a deal with a lower return than other companies would find acceptable, if it likes the long-term aspects."

Olympia & York is one of four of Canada's top ten developers headed by Jews. (The others are Cadillac Fairview, Bramalea, and Trizec). The Reichmanns make their respect for their religion very much a part of their business life.

The Reichmanns are Orthodox Jews, the branch of Judaism which adheres most to observance of Jewish tradition. They wear yarmulkes (skullcaps) at the office. Mezuzahs (excerpts from the Old Testament attached to doorposts for good luck) are affixed to the walls alongside each elevator. Olympia & York contracts also carry clauses stating that no subcontractor may work on the Jewish Sabbath or sacred days. Head office also closes on Jewish holidays. The time off is made up by double pay time. Also, Sunday is often a work day for one or both Reichmanns, their secretary, and some top company executives.

Albert is about 5'8", clean-shaven, with thick brown hair, virtually untouched by gray. He is a non-smoker. Paul, over six feet tall with pitch black hair and a beard, chain smokes Lark cigarettes. They dress very conservatively in black or gray suits with white shirts and dark ties.

Both brothers have a dry sense of humor. When Albert is asked why Olympia & York, alone among the developers, has former (Toronto) city planning officials on its staff, he quips: "We don't discriminate." And Paul, when queried why the company is on the 32nd of the 72-floor First Canadian Place, ripostes: "Middle is more comfortable."

Whereas some of the developers play golf or ski, Albert and Paul, according to Albert, "just work. We are either with our families or at work."

Since Albert, Paul, and younger brother, Ralph, all have large families, it is likely that Olympia & York will remain a family run business. The chances are that it will also remain owned by the Reichmanns. "We will probably not go public," says Albert, by which he means that barring the unforeseen, the company will stay privately owned.

Albert has four children, ranging in age from 7½ to 23. The 23-year-old Phillip is the only second generation Reichmann old enough to be in the business. He is making the rounds of each department and is now in the leasing division. Paul and Ralph each have five children.

Olympia & York's headquarters are spacious and tastefully, quietly, and expensively furnished. The corridors are lined with pictures or architectural renderings of company projects interspersed with the occasional piece of modern art.

Albert has a corner office, but it is not the largest Olympia & York executive suite. Unlike Daon president Jack Poole's office suite, which has a dining and living room, Albert's is purely an office without the extras. Done in browns and beiges, it has a cube-shaped perlato (caramel colored with black specks) marble sidepiece, a mahogany chest of drawers with a mirror, a huge cactus in a glazed blue and white planter, and more pictures of Olympia & York projects, but none of family.

Board meetings are held down the hall in a large boardroom dominated by a big round table and containing beige suede furniture and more tall cacti. Wall alcoves contain models of current projects and there is a movie projector for screening information about buildings.

Although Albert is president and Paul executive vice-president, they are, Albert says, "more or less interchangeable." Albert handles most out of town projects, traveling about six days a month but often more. Paul, however, has responsibility for New York City stemming from his handling of Olympia & York's coup in buying the eight blue ribbon office buildings there in 1976.

The legend is that Albert and Paul handle even the smallest deal, which they frequently do. But they are also backed up by a strong management team.

Like most developers, Olympia & York is heavy in its need for capital but is lean in management. Head office has only 250 people. Executive compensation is supplemented by a mixture of profit sharing for some with bonuses and merit pay for others. Turnover, consequently, has been very low.

Key functions, such as development, design, and construction, are supervised by a five-man team, including William Hay, who was president of Trizec in the early 1970s, and Ronald Soskolene, formerly chief city planner for Toronto. Hay is senior vice-president at Olympia & York and Soskolene is vice-president of planning and development. Activities in the U.S. are directed by a 100-person office in New York City. The executive vice-president there is Michael Dennis, previously housing commissioner for Toronto.

Regional offices in Los Angeles and Dallas will be opened as more projects are developed. European operations are supervised by London-based English Property.

Albert Reichmann says that the company likes to hire former city planners because it is "important to know how they think on the other side of the (negotiating) table, especially in multi-use projects. They are used to working with different interest groups which is very important in multi-use projects."

Management of Olympia & York properties is run according to a strict formula based on 100 three-ring operations manuals developed by head office. Put on computer five years ago, the system is based on more than 200 control forms covering 280 subjects ranging from building maintenance and damage repairs to bilingual and bicultural considerations in the province of Quebec.

Property managers are given six binders of memoranda covering administration. There is also an in-house management training course backed by frequent staff meetings and seminars. Property administrator Jack Gringorten has also developed a set of hundreds of form letters for property managers covering everything from preparing office space for tenants to security and building management.

The company turns to outside architects for designs but usually does its own construction, both in Canada and New York. Joint ventures are rare. One such project is the 25 acre San Francisco project, which Olympia & York is developing with Marriott Corp., the hotel chain, and Rouse Co., a U.S. retail developer and builder.

Although it is diversifying into natural resources and financial services, Olympia & York is concentrating on its basic business of real estate development, especially in the United States. The company already has 25 percent of its assets in the U.S., with the bulk of it—12 million square feet—in New York City.

Olympia & York's development plans call for office towers to be completed over the next two years in Hartford, Los Angeles, Dallas, Boston, San Francisco, and New York City.

The New York project is, at $1 billion, the costliest, involving the construction of six million square feet of commercial space in Battery Park. The design by Yale University Dean of Architecture Cesar Pelli of the four office towers, with granite at the bottom phasing into glass at the top, has received high praise. *New York Times'* architecture critic Paul Goldberger has described it as "the finest group of skyscrapers since Rockefeller Center."

The U.S. will be the major source of Olympia & York's growth both because its market size is ten times that of Canada's and because the Canadian developers have a financial edge. They are helped by their close ties to Canada's 11 national banks.

The crucial role of the Canadian banks in the expansion of developers like Olympia & York cannot be over-estimated. The Canadian banks—especially the Big Five—are world-scale operations both in size and their global networks.

Wherever a Canadian business wants to expand, a branch of the cash-rich Big Five—Royal Bank, Canadian Imperial Bank of Commerce, Bank of Montreal, Bank of Nova Scotia, and Toronto Dominion Bank—is there, eager to provide the money. And because the developers are so large, they have plenty of leverage when it comes time to borrow for the next multi-million dollar deal.

To appreciate the size of the Canadian banks, some number crunching is necessary. The Big Five rank among the world's top 75 banks in terms of assets. The Royal is 34th; CIBC 41st; BMO, 54th;

BNS, 62nd, and TD, 74th. With assets of $62.8 billion, the Royal is about half the size of either Bank of America or Citicorp, the closely ranked top banks in the U.S., which rank second and third in size in the world.

But these comparisons to Bank of America and Citicorp can be misleading. Because the U.S. banks are localized, with Bank of America in San Francisco and Citicorp in New York, their clientele also tends to be more localized. Potential customers in other cities would have to travel to or phone either bank.

By contrast, because the Canadian banks have branches throughout Canada, with corporate financing departments in major cities, businesses do not have far to go for help. And with several of the banks setting up U.S. divisions based in New York and European offices based in London, Canadian businessmen are never far from a friendly banker.

Much of Olympia & York's growing fame and success is based on its buying a large piece of downtown Manhattan five years ago at a time when others were fleeing the wormy real estate scene in the Big Apple. As its Don Mills, Ontario, purchase in 1962 showed, Olympia & York has a penchant for buying projects with an unhappy history but intrinsically good value, which others overlook because of that poor record.

In 1976, Olympia & York bought eight office buildings in New York City from National Kinney Co., including the executive offices of International Telephone & Telegraph and American Brands Inc., for a bargain basement price of $350 million.

The purchase threw U.S. real estate developers into a tizzy because it went counter to their strategy of avoiding the severely depressed New York market. Also, the deal was the largest single move, up to that time, by a Canadian real estate firm into the United States. Most Americans hadn't the slightest conception of the size of Canadian developers.

While the purchase seemed like a gamble at the time, it has paid off handsomely. The eight buildings alone are now estimated to have tripled in value to $1 billion. That escalation — on paper — gave the Reichmanns the increased borrowing power they needed for their diversification into other businesses.

Average rents in 1976 to 1977 ranged from $7 to $13 per square foot, depending on the building's location. Today, the rents range from $18 to $45 per square foot. Moreover, the high vacancy rates which plagued New York in 1976 and 1977 have been replaced by a tight market.

The deal was brought to the Reichmanns by Ficor Inc., a New York real estate consultant firm which had been working for some years in both Canada and the U.S. sniffing out deals for the Reichmanns. "I knew they had a strong desire to expand their U.S. operations and New

York is geographically near Toronto," recalls president Edward Minskoff. "I also knew Kinney needed the money and it was an opportunity for Olympia to acquire a major package at a very good price."

Kinney had purchased the buildings in 1973 when the New York real estate market was very strong. But a year later the economy and the city went into a tailspin. The negotiations, conducted by Paul Reichmann, started in September 1976 and reached the handshake and agreement in principle stage by November 1976. Then the lawyers took over and final agreement was reached in September 1977. The contract itself ran to at least 100 pages and was backed up, Minskoff says, by "thousands and thousands of pages of documents."

Olympia & York's winning argument in obtaining projects such as Battery Park in New York and the 25 acre Market Street redevelopment in San Francisco is its promise to complete construction in half the time others say it would take.

"Techniques are a part of it, but it is more a matter of the number of stages into which a project is divided," Albert Reichmann says. "If it is done in three to five stages, it takes longer than two stages. Our San Francisco project is being done in two stages. The first stage will include the retail, office (one million square feet), hotel (1,500 rooms), and part of the residential. The second stage will complete the residential (1,000 condominium units).

"There are enough people available for construction. As for the cost, the different components just happen to be in the same area."

Olympia & York has also developed many high speed, cost efficient techniques. These were pioneered on the five-year-old First Canadian Place, estimated to have cost $160 million. At 1,650,000 square feet, the building accounted for about 25 percent of all new office construction in Toronto in 1975.

The building had the most of everything in a Canadian office tower: the most marble (16 miles), the most windows (9,300), the most wiring (284 miles), and the most fire sprinklers (15,000). But while no expense was spared in making the building a landmark, every attention was paid to how to keep construction costs under control.

The normal rate of progress is one floor of structural steel a week. First Canadian Place's schedule called for three floors of structural steel a week so that the 72-floor building could be finished in a record 16 months. (By contrast, it took close to two and a half years, from 1964 to April 1966, to build the 57-floor Toronto Dominion Tower.)

Olympia & York was able to achieve this rapid pace by using conveyor belts for concrete, a sophisticated electronic system for plotting and tracking operations, and elevators that were large enough to carry trucks up to floors under construction. The materials' moving system cost about $2 million but reduced construction time by 1.3 million manhours.

The bank building, which at 935 feet replaced the Chase Manhattan Bank in New York as the world's tallest bank tower, also had Canada's first two tier elevators, capable of serving two floors at once, and the first automatic window cleaning system. The electrically powered unit, operated by one man pushing buttons, can clean the whole building in an hour. It would take two men a month to do the same job manually.

In the last two years, though, the Reichmanns have attracted far more attention for their acquisitions than for their equally spectacular development projects. The kickoff was the Reichmanns' gaining 49.99 percent of Trizec in March 1979 (see Chapter 3). The other 50.01 percent is held by Edper Investments Ltd., the holding company for Peter and Edward Bronfman. Edper is a contraction of their first names.

Trizec has leaped from near bankruptcy in 1976 to robust financial health and is breathing close on Olympia & York's number one spot among Canadian developers in terms of assets. If Trizec obtains New York's World Trade Center (a decision to be made by the New York port authority which owns the Center), its assets will top $3 billion and be close to Olympia & York's estimated $3.5 billion. Like Olympia & York, Trizec is primarily a developer of large office projects, although, unlike Olympia & York, it also has a substantial shopping center division.

"Management of a company of Olympia & York's size is in a position to know the true value of someone else's company, as opposed to the stock market value, and thus they knew Trizec was undervalued," says Harry Rannala, real estate analyst at Walwyn Stodgell Cochran Murray Ltd., a Toronto investment dealer.

The Trizec deal gives a good look at how the Reichmanns operate. Trevor Eyton, now president of Brascan Ltd. but then a lawyer at the Toronto firm of Tory, Tory and Deslauriers, who was representing Edper, recalls:

"Edper was about to make a counter bid for Trizec. Harold Milavsky, the president of Trizec, and I accidentally ran into Paul Reichmann in London, England (the headquarters of English Property), as he was getting out of a taxi to go into his hotel. He said it was wrong for us to be fighting each other.

"We then met in Montreal a few days later for six to seven hours with my acting as the go-between. We reached an agreement that Edper would retain control of Trizec and drew up a letter of intent. Paul and Albert did not have a lawyer. They were a delight to deal with because they stated their decisions clearly and were prepared to accept some of Edper's submissions. They were sympathetic about the Bronfmans doing a lot to build up Trizec and their wanting to retain a major role.

"The discussions were concluded at Olympia & York. They were held in Albert's office because he is neat and tidy, whereas Paul's office is piled with papers. Whenever we reached a difficult point, Paul and Albert would excuse themselves, step outside the door for a minute, but return just after 30 seconds, with a little smile saying they had had a Board meeting and here was their answer."

The relationship between the Bronfmans and the Reichmanns, which started out edgily, has worked out well. Taking advantage of Trizec's shopping center experience, Olympia & York has referred some proposals to Trizec because it gets a payback as a large shareholder. One such example is Trizec's recent $270 million (U.S.) purchase of Ernest W. Hahn Inc., a California-based shopping center development firm. Although the deal had been pitched to Olympia & York first, the Reichmanns reasoned that Trizec was more experienced in shopping center development.

Real estate analysts say that eventually Olympia & York will probably sell its interest in Trizec—at a tremendous profit—to Edper. "Regardless of what both sides say, there have to be conflicts of interest," Rannala says. "There will likely be a compromise along the way and Olympia & York will cash in its shares. But the Reichmanns won't let Edper off easily, because Trizec continues to grow in value."

In August 1980 the Reichmanns signaled their intentions of diversifying into natural resources when they acquired 50.1 percent of Brinco Ltd., a firm with interests in asbestos and a small, but growing, interest in oil and gas. Brinco plans to spend $80 million to $100 million by 1985 in oil and gas exploration. It is also searching for oil and gas in the U.S. This year its total U.S. budget was $2.5 million compared with $450,000 in 1980.

In March 1981 the Reichmanns increased their stake in natural resources when they paid $502 million for Abitibi-Price Inc., the world's largest newsprint producer. Olympia & York had originally bid for 45 percent of Abitibi-Price. It upped its offer when a coalition of Thomson Newspapers Ltd. and Nu-West Group, also one of Canada's top developers, made a counter bid.

It was the first time Thomson, which has taken over Hudson's Bay Co., Canada's largest department store chain, and the large FP group of newspapers, including Toronto's *The Globe and Mail*, had lost a takeover battle.

Nu-West, which already owned 200,000 Abitibi-Price shares, emerged from the fight with an $800,000 profit after Olympia & York purchased the newsprint company. Nu-West's vice-president, development, Stephen McConnell, took the defeat good-naturedly. "Olympia & York is one of the most prestigious and well-endowed family companies in North America," he says. "We knew if Olympia & York wanted it, they could bid for it."

Less than a week after it bought Abitibi-Price, Olympia & York was in the news again when it enlarged its interest in Royal Trustco Ltd., Canada's largest trust firm, from 15 percent to 23.3 percent. It bought the eight percent from Campeau Corp., which had sought unsuccessfully to take over Royal Trustco in August 1980. During the takeover fight, Olympia & York briefly considered buying up to 50 percent of Royal Trustco.

While Royal Trustco bitterly fought Campeau, it has never objected to the Reichmanns' purchases of shares. Because Olympia & York owns more than 20 percent of Royal Trustco, it will be able to include, on an equity accounting basis, its portion of the trust firm's profits in its own balance sheet. Last year, Royal Trustco had a profit of $37.5 million.

The Reichmanns' acquisitions have all been into companies with good management and they plan to leave daily operations to existing executives. Board membership will give them a say in major policy decisions.

The 1980s should be good to Olympia & York. "Business will be very strong in office development because white collar workers are increasing faster than blue collar," says Albert Reichmann.

He smilingly dismisses the notion of Olympia & York's being in a competition to stay number one among the world's developers. "We're just going at our own nice pace," he says.

Since that "nice pace" has led to Olympia & York's owning a large chunk of Canadian, American, and British real estate, as well as meaty portions of some of Canada's leading industrial and financial companies, it is a safe bet that the Reichmanns have a strong head start on all their rivals.

Chapter Three

TRIZEC CORPORATION

"If the asset base is there, it's worth taking a chance if you can get the people who can turn the company around."

PETER BRONFMAN
CHAIRMAN AND MAJOR SHAREHOLDER
TRIZEC

TRIZEC CORPORATION
SENIOR MANAGEMENT
(Except where noted, located at head office in Calgary)

Chairman:	Peter Bronfman
President:	Harold Milavsky
Executive Vice-President:	Edmund Sardachuk *(Development and Construction)*
Senior Vice-Presidents:	Kenner Ames *(Shopping Centers)* (Based in Toronto)
	Machiel Cornelissen *(Finance and Administration)*
	Edward Elford *(Development)*
	Jack Rabinovitch *(Eastern planning)* (Based in Montreal)
	James Sherbut *(Operations)*
Vice-Presidents:	Thomas Gilmour *(Development)*
	Mitchell Grossman *(Development and Retail Leasing)*
	Arne Hansen ⎫ *(Design and Construction)* David Lewington ⎭
	Stephan Kuzoff *(Retail Leasing)*
	Tom Stephenson *(Operations)*

CANADA

Trizec Equities Ltd.
Calgary
General Manager: William Elliott
Halifax
General Manager: Michael Griffith
Montreal
General Manager: Rolland Baribeau
Toronto
General Manager: William Seli

Place Quebec Inc. (Quebec City)
Vice-President: Jacques Plante

Central Park Lodges (Toronto)
Executive Vice-President: Allan Duncan

UNITED STATES

Ernest W. Hahn Inc. (El Segundo, Calif.)
(Shopping Centers)
Chairman: Ernest W. Hahn
President: Ronald Hahn

Hahn Property Management Corp.
(La Jolla, Calif.)
Senior Vice-President: Gary Doyle

Hahn Devcorp (El Segundo, Calif.)
President: Stanley Gribble

Trizec Western Inc. (Los Angeles, Detroit)
Vice-President: William Liebowitz

Mobile Home Communities Inc.
(Englewood, Colorado)
President: James Hankins

Not only cats can have many lives. Trizec Corporation is living proof that a real estate development company can also be reborn.

Trizec is the only major Canadian real estate developer formed to finish a venture (Montreal's Place Ville Marie) that was in trouble and in danger of otherwise not being completed. It is the only one that has had, at various times, British, American, and Canadian owners. It is the only company controlled by two of Canada's wealthiest — and most invisible — families: Peter and Edward Bronfman, owners of Edper Investments Ltd., and Albert and Paul Reichmann, owners of Olympia & York Developments Ltd.

The Bronfmans bought their share of Trizec when it was on its deathbed. Since then, it has bounced back to become a $2 billion in assets company, placing it in a near tie with Nu-West and Daon. If it acquires the $900 million World Trade Center in New York City, its assets will balloon overnight to $3 billion. That would place it just behind Olympia & York and in a dead heat with Cadillac Fairview ($3 billion).

And if all this does not make Trizec unusual, it also is the only developer to move its headquarters across the country, from Montreal to Calgary, to its president Harold Milavsky because he did not want to move. Finally, it is the only one that builds retirement and nursing homes and mobile parks. Its main businesses, however, are office buildings and shopping centers, the two most profitable areas today in real estate development because inflation raises their market value and the rents that can be charged.

In November 1980, Trizec's assets were nearly doubled, from $1.3 billion to $2.1 billion, when it acquired a major U.S. shopping center developer, Ernest W. Hahn Inc., for $270 million (U.S.). Hahn has 28 centers in operation, eight under construction and 20 in the planning stage. About 60 percent are in California. Many are over one million square feet and have five or six department stores. When the undeveloped centers are completed, the Hahn acquisition is expected to add $2 billion in assets to Trizec.

It is also well on its way toward acquiring 20 percent of the Rouse Co., a major eastern U.S. shopping center developer of more than 50 malls. The 20 percent interest will allow Trizec to share in Rouse's profits on an equity accounting basis.

Trizec has had the bumpiest history of the Canadian developers, experiencing the roughest tumbles and now undergoing a remarkable resurrection from virtual bankruptcy just five years ago. "It has become a nice, clean company," says Stephen Moore of Burns, Fry Ltd.

Trizec's problems were never due to doing shoddy, cut-the-corners work but due to its having caviar dreams on a hamburger budget in its early years. Trizec has always built top quality, landmark buildings, such as Place Ville Marie in Montreal and Calgary Place, home of Mobil Oil (Canada) and Canadian Superior Oil.

What went wrong was that management and financial controls were not given the same loving attention as the buildings. Formed in 1960, Trizec had become North America's largest publicly owned real estate developer by 1972. Four years later, the victim of bickering, weak management, inflation, high interest rates, and wobbly financial systems, Trizec was on the threshold of bankruptcy.

The architect of Trizec's recovery is thin, balding, quiet spoken, watchful but humorous Harold Milavsky, who was handpicked by Peter and Edward Bronfman to head the company after they gained control in 1976. Milavsky, an accountant, had worked for the Bronfmans since 1969, at an earlier real estate venture. Previously, he had worked at the Mannix Co., a leading Calgary construction firm, which has been a training ground for many leading Albertans including Premier Peter Lougheed, once a lawyer at Mannix.

Milavsky, who in January 1981 turned what he calls "the big FIVE 0" (50 years old), may be the only chief executive who had the mountain come to Mohammed when the Bronfmans, in their zest for lassoing him as president, set up an executive office in Calgary where Milavsky lived. He is also the largest individual shareholder in Trizec, with 351,928 shares (1980 high-low on the Toronto Stock Exchange, $54-$26½).

Born in Limerick, Saskatchewan (1976 census population: 112), Milavsky had spent his working career in Calgary and did not want to move. So, for four years, Trizec had its executive office in Calgary and its head office in Montreal. In 1980 everything was consolidated in Calgary and, as it turned out, Trizec's location gave it a head start as Calgary became a boom town.

Confident, but not boastful, Milavsky has a very fast wit. He jokes that his son, Gregory, an engineering student at the University of Toronto, would like "to be the head of General Motors because his initials are G.M." Asked how he achieved the first-ever development in Canada in which two banks (Royal Bank and the Canadian Imperial Bank of Commerce) are only yards apart in the same plaza (Bankers Hall in Calgary), Milavsky quips: "They don't call me King Solomon for nothing." And it was Milavsky who came up with the cute publicity gimmick for opening Trizec's new tower, the Calgary office of Texaco, at Fifth Avenue and Fifth Street: he gave out 300 records of Beethoven's Fifth Symphony played by the Calgary Philharmonic, a tenant in the building.

Milavsky is known among friends for his boundless energy. He plays tennis at 10:00 p.m. week nights at Calgary's Glenmore Racquet

Harold Milavsky, president, Trizec (Photo: Susan Goldenberg)

Club where he says he ranks as a "strong B" in the club's four levels of playing skill. He is also an enthusiastic skier who goes to Sunshine Ski Village in Banff, Alberta, every year. "He is tireless," says Trevor Eyton, president of Brascan Ltd. (also controlled by Peter and Edward Bronfman), a member of Trizec's board of Directors and a skiing buddy of Milavsky. "He's always the first up the hill at Sunshine and the last down. The lift starts at 8:00 a.m. and Harold is up by 7:00 a.m. so he can have breakfast and be first in line for the lift. By contrast, I would be happy starting at 10:00 a.m.

"For two days one year, Harold was up at 7:00 a.m. and would bang on my door to get me up. On the third day, I decided I had had enough. So I got up at 6:55 a.m., banged on his door, and went back to bed. He assumed, when he didn't see me in the dining room, that I'd already eaten and gone to the lift and he went out to join me." Eyton accompanied him later in the day — after a good rest.

Milavsky also sets aside a week each year to take one of his five children, on a rotation basis, on a skiing trip alone with him to Colorado. The family also dressed up in colonial clothes for a photograph to blend with the Quebec habitant period furniture in Trizec's sitting room.

Canada's major real estate developers tend to be low-key, their gambling instinct tempered by caution. This is in stark contrast to William Zeckendorf, Trizec's founder. There probably has never been anybody as colorful, as daring, as outrageous, as innovative, or as controversial on the North American real estate scene as the high-living, hard-driving Zeckendorf. At his peak, he was said to have the world's largest real estate empire. His projects, which he liked to open on Friday the 13th, include Place Ville Marie in Montreal, Canada's first major downtown redevelopment project, Century City in Los Angeles, and assembling the land for the United Nations Plaza in New York. Place Ville Marie is still one of Canada's most successful developments with more than 36 million visitors a year (compared with 52 million at Toronto's Eaton Centre).

Born in 1905 in Paris, Illinois, the son of a hardware merchant, Zeckendorf dropped out of university to work for his uncle who was in the real estate business. In 1933 he joined a large, 15-year-old New York commercial real estate firm, Webb and Knapp. Seward Webb, related on his mother's side to the wealthy Vanderbilt family, and Knapp, formerly president of another New York firm, Douglas Elliman and Co., had got their start by handling New York Central railroad leases. Zeckendorf's job was to handle magnate Vincent Astor's real estate holdings.

A master showman who courted publicity and attention, Zeckendorf lived in grand style, conducting business from a huge circular office on Madison Avenue, in his big black Cadillac limousine, or in his richly appointed DC-3 plane. He was said to have been the only person who, during a discussion with President Dwight Eisenhower, was called to the telephone for a business call. His trademarks were a Homburg hat and a constant cigar. He was liked and respected by his business colleagues and by the financial media for his creativity, even while Webb and Knapp was collapsing. By then he was company chairman and his son, William, was president.

In 1957, Zeckendorf had a brainwave which led to the rehabilitation of downtown Montreal and, simultaneously, to Zeckendorf's downfall. Place Ville Marie, still the crown jewel of Montreal, was the first major building proposed for Montreal in more than 50 years. As Zeckendorf later recalled in his autobiography *Zeckendorf*, his idea met with a frosty reception and no major company would sign up to be a tenant. Without a major tenant, Zeckendorf could not get mortgage financing from insurance companies or bank loans to finance construction. "Essentially our trouble was nobody believed we would ever put up a project as big as we said we would," Zeckendorf recalled in his memoirs.

The ice was broken, however, when Zeckendorf forced the then head of the Royal Bank, James Muir, to move into a new tower, which would be named after the bank, in Place Ville Marie. This was not an easy task since Muir, according to Zeckendorf, disliked Zeckendorf because he was American and Jewish and had hired an architect of Chinese origin, I. M. Pei (who later designed the John F. Kennedy Library). (Zeckendorf convinced Muir by saying Muir would be "king of the hill" because the new Royal Bank building would tower over the rest of Montreal.)

There is no question that Zeckendorf was a genius whose creativity and imagination reshaped Montreal, New York, and Los Angeles. But his creativity landed him in trouble since it was impossible to finance all his grandiose schemes at one time. In a classic case of the domino effect, when one part of his empire began to topple, the rest of it crumbled, too.

Zeckendorf epitomized the entrepreneurial, risk-taking nature of real estate that has made many tycoons. But he also epitomized the dangers of leverage—the main springboard for real estate deals in which projects are financed through using other property as the leverage for borrowing.

Zeckendorf believed firmly that inflation was here to stay and was a reliable cushion because property values would constantly soar. What he failed to take into account was that real estate is one of the highest risk fields, and while huge profits can be made in inflationary times, crushing losses can be suffered when interest rates soar and when the market slumps.

Zeckendorf enjoyed the complexities of deal-making. He never bargained over prices and did not care if costs escalated as long as a project turned out as he had envisaged. He did not worry about how much something would cost; what mattered was if he could borrow the money for it. After all, borrowing had enabled him to build Webb and Knapp up from a net worth of minus $127,000 (U.S.) in 1942 to $75 million in 1954 and assets of $300 million in 1958, when Place Ville Marie got started. Place Ville Marie was under the supervision of Webb and Knapp (Canada) Ltd., formed in 1955 by Zeckendorf.

Place Ville Marie was one of Zeckendorf's favorite projects and also the one that started the downfall of his empire. Construction costs soared by $25 million due to problems in design, materials, and construction. At the same time, Webb and Knapp was bleeding from entering the New York City hotel business just before it went into a long-term slump. By 1958 Webb and Knapp had slid into debt.

Over the next seven years, Zeckendorf sold off properties and pledged $5 million of his shares as collateral in a vain effort to reduce his high-cost debt. Then in May 1965, shortly after it was delisted on the American Stock Exchange, Webb and Knapp was put into uncontested bankruptcy by one of its smallest creditors, Marine Midland Trust Co. of New York to which Webb and Knapp had $4.3 million (U.S.) outstanding in payments.

Western Canadian Place, Calgary

At the time, Webb and Knapp had debts of $31.8 million, including $2.49 million (U.S.) to the Bank of Nova Scotia and $3.83 million to U.S. Steel Corp. Marine Midland placed Webb and Knapp in bankruptcy because it was afraid that unsecured creditors would otherwise be left on a limb. Zeckendorf formed a new real estate business with his son, William. (Zeckendorf died in 1976 at the age of 71.)

As Zeckendorf sank into debt in the U.S. and Canada, he turned to a large English insurance company, Eagle Star Insurance, to bail him out. Eagle Star's chairman, Sir Brian Mountain, was willing to pitch in because he wanted his then 56-year-old firm, which already had extensive real estate holdings in the United Kingdom, to expand into North America.

Trizec was born in October 1960 out of Sir Brian's ambition and Zeckendorf's desperation. *Tri* stands for three (Zeckendorf, Eagle Star, and one of Eagle Star's real estate subsidiaries, Second Covent Garden), and *Zec* for Zeckendorf, Eagle Star, and Covent Garden. As part of the deal, Eagle Star and Second Covent Garden bought $16.3 million worth of debentures toward the funding of Place Ville Marie.

Throughout the 1960s, Webb and Knapp Canada, like its U.S. parent, overextended and piled up debts. Consequently, it had to sell projects it had either developed or was building. One significant sale was parts of Flemingdon Park, a $100 million development in northeast Toronto. They were sold, at distress prices, to Olympia & York, providing a launching pad for that company to move from building warehouses to office towers.

Webb and Knapp Canada remains in business today as a very small developer, based in British Columbia. With 1980 revenue of $2 million and net income of only $170,000, it has no connection with Trizec.

The collapse of Webb and Knapp in the U.S. and the weak condition of Webb and Knapp in Canada allowed customers to get extraordinarily good deals. One such case is Yorkdale Shopping Centre in north Toronto, which was under construction during this period.

The T. Eaton Co., which owned the land and had initiated the project, insisted on a $1 million good faith deposit by Webb and Knapp that it would complete Yorkdale. In addition, Eaton's got a bargain rent of under $1.50 per square foot for the first 30 years of the standard 100 years a shopping center contract runs. After the first 30 years, by 1992, the rent will drop to one-third, or only 50 cents a square foot. By contrast, today's rents in Yorkdale average $21 a square foot. (The project was called Yorkdale after the road that leads to it which was paid for by Eaton's. Toronto does not allow streets leading off highways to be named after commercial enterprises and Yorkdale Road is an exit from Highway 401. Eaton's said it would pay any road costs exceeding $800,000 — a miscalculation on its part, since the road cost close to $3 million.)

Furthermore, Eaton's got Webb and Knapp to agree to another concession. Part of the compensation Webb and Knapp paid Eaton's for its land was related to the success of the Centre in its first three years. Thus, if the Centre turned out to be a success — as it did — Eaton's would get a piece of the action. This is something that developers are reluctant to do because they are, in effect, giving away some of their profits.

Department store chains always have negotiating clout since they are needed as anchor tenants in order for developers to attract other tenants. Hence, developers are willing to forego getting their money back on the department stores in rent and to let them serve as loss leaders for securing rents from other tenants. Moreover, what the developers do not get in rent, they make in other ways. (They get a sliding percentage of sales with stores having a higher volume paying a lower percentage of two to three percent and stores with a low volume paying up to seven percent.)

TRIZEC'S CHRONOLOGY

1960/Started by American William Zeckendorf, president of Webb & Knapp of the United States, and Eagle Star Insurance of England and its real estate subsidiaries Second Covent Garden and English Property.

1965/Webb & Knapp goes bankrupt in U.S. Webb and Knapp Canada's major properties, including Place Ville Marie in Montreal and Yorkdale Shopping Centre in Toronto, are taken over by Trizec. Webb & Knapp Canada goes off on its own to concentrate on British Columbia real estate.

1971/Trizec acquires Great West International Equities Ltd., a real estate investment firm controlled by Peter and Edward Bronfman through their holding company, Edper Investments. Edper gets 10 per cent of Trizec.

December 1975/Trizec, in financial trouble, sells $96 million worth of assets, primarily shopping centres, to Bramalea Ltd. of Toronto, another company backed at one time by Eagle Star Insurance. Trizec receives $25 million in cash and a $25 million note and Bramalea assumes $46 million worth of mortgages.

March 1976/Trizec, near bankruptcy, cannot meet payroll.

June 1976/English Property, in financial difficulty because of the weak English real estate market, sells control of Trizec to Peter and Edward Bronfman for cash and a half interest in a newly formed holding company.

Before Sale

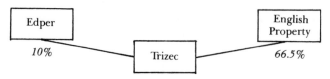

After Sale

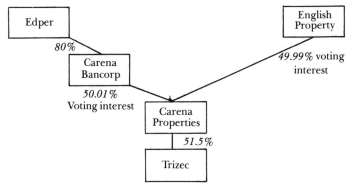

Note:
Edper and Bank of Nova Scotia acquired Canadian Arena Company, owner of the Montreal Forum, in December 1971, and subsequently changed the name to Carena Bancorp.

1977-79/Carena Properties' interest in Trizec increased to 58 percent. In March 1979 Olympia & York Developments acquires control of English Property.

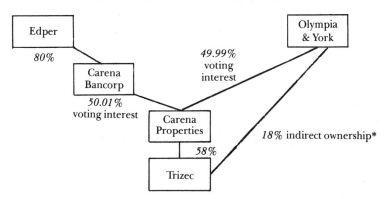

*Carena Bancorp gets option to buy half of Olympia & York's 18 percent indirect ownership. Option exercised fall 1980 and finalized January 1981.

January 1981

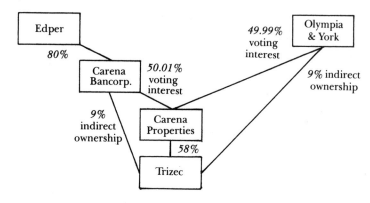

Trizec's early history was marked by bitter personality clashes and financial disorder as tangled and troubled as that of Zeckendorf.

In 1961, its first year in business, Trizec had revenue of only $131,000 and a loss of $154,000. It was not until 1967 that Trizec moved out of the red when it recorded a slim profit of $257,000. In 1968, with assets of $240 million (versus $178.6 million in 1967), revenue of $27.9 million, and net income of $1.1 million, Trizec went public at $1.80 (in 1980 it traded between $26½ and $54).

In quick succession Trizec acquired two large western development companies — family-controlled Cummings Properties Ltd. (assets $115 million) and Great West International Equities Ltd. (assets $77 million) controlled by Peter and Edward Bronfman. On the plus side, the acquisitions gave Trizec a strong western presence and assets of $500 million, making it one of North America's largest publicly owned real estate companies.

On the negative side, Trizec executives had bit off more than the company could swallow since it lacked adequate financial controls and management skills for its doubled-in-size business. Unfortunately for Trizec, the negative aspect far outweighed the positive features of the acquisitions.

Before going on with what happened — the eventual takeover of the company by the Bronfmans — it is important to understand how they got involved in real estate in the first place.

Peter and Edward are nephews of Samuel Bronfman, founder of Seagram Co. Although their father Allan was Samuel's right-hand man, Samuel wanted his liquor business to remain directly in his family (it is now run by his sons Edgar and Charles). In 1960 Samuel bought out Peter's and Edward's 600,000 shares at $26 each, $2 less than their market value. He threatened to throw their father out of the company if they did not sell.

It was, in retrospect, probably the best thing that could have happened to Edward and Peter, since it resulted in their building up their own empire. Edward, then 33, and Peter, then 31, took the $15.6 million proceeds and set up a holding company called Edper (a contraction of their two names) Investments Ltd. In the 1960s they participated in 30 real estate projects across Canada, including Calgary Place (home of Mobil Oil Canada and Canadian Superior Oil), the IBM building in Edmonton, and the $13 million Lougheed Mall in Vancouver.

Many of these projects were done with a Calgary developer, Samuel Hashman, and in 1969 the Bronfmans decided to institutionalize their holdings under Hashman's management in a firm called Great West International Equities Ltd. The Bronfmans owned 50 percent, Hashman 25 percent, and the public the rest. Harold Milavsky was hired as executive vice-president.

Great West's first big venture was to form Hyatt International Ltd., a joint enterprise with Hyatt International Corp., and to build the 600 room, 33-floor Vancouver Hyatt House and the 540 room, 35-story Toronto Hyatt House (now the Four Seasons Hotel).

In 1971, Great West acquired a 10 percent interest in Trizec and Peter Bronfman and Hashman joined the Board of Directors. For the next five years the Bronfmans took a passive role in Trizec, but beneath the surface tensions were boiling. The troubles were twofold: management and financial problems.

There was competitive friction between Trizec executives and the incoming Bronfman team. Hashman and Milavsky, in the opinion of the Bronfman camp, were "isolated" through the creation of Tristar Western Ltd. to handle business in western Canada. Hashman and Milavsky were sold one-third of the new company and, in return, Hashman was asked to resign from Trizec's Board of Directors. At the same time, there were difficulties in merging the management and systems of Cummings Properties.

On top of all that, Trizec's management was constantly feuding with executives at English Property which controlled 66 percent of Trizec. "They would spend their day answering telexes from England and had no autonomy," an insider at that time recalls.

While the executive war was raging, Trizec's financial situation was becoming disastrous. The 210 unit cooperative Park Regis apartments on New York's upper east side, in which Trizec had a 40 percent interest, cost double the projected amount. Business at its Detroit office buildings was being drained away by the new Renaissance Center. The firm had become embroiled in a battle with Winnipeg city officials over its $180 million Winnipeg Square project. Interest rates were soaring;

joint ventures had become derailed; hotel revenues were down; and not enough of its buildings were completed to bring in sufficient rent to cover all the company's expenses. On top of this catastrophic state of affairs, the parent company, English Property, was in a financial bind due to slumping real estate demand in the United Kingdom.

By the end of 1975 the situation was so grave that Trizec opted to sell its interest in the Hyatt Hotels, the IBM building in Edmonton, and its seven shopping centers in Manitoba, Saskatchewan, and Alberta, as well as its 50 percent interest in two Vancouver malls to Bramalea Ltd., for $96.1 million. The deal, the largest exchange of real estate assets in Canada, put Bramalea, then a small firm, in the big league.

Two features of the deal show just how badly off Trizec was. Bramalea got a bargain because the properties were then worth about $150 million at market value and now are worth about $250 million. In addition, Trizec ended up with a profit of only $5 million because it had to complete one of the malls—the 236,000 square foot Marlborough Shoppers Mall in Calgary—and pay taxes.

Thus, while the sale was meant to pay off the $66 million debt Trizec had to repay in 1976, it ended up putting almost no dent in Trizec's mountain of bills. In March 1976, three months after the sale to Bramalea, Trizec had the mortification of being so short of cash that it could not meet its payroll.

Gasping for funds, floundering English Property asked the Bronfmans, in June 1976, to assist in refinancing Trizec and restoring management stability by replacing English Property as the leading shareholder. The complicated transaction was done through creating a new holding company, Carena Properties Ltd., in which the Bronfmans held 50.01 percent voting control and English Property 49.99 percent.

The new company was an outgrowth of Carena-Bancorp Inc., formed in 1972 by the Bronfmans, which had 60 percent originally (later 80 percent), and the Bank of Nova Scotia, which had a minority interest. Carena-Bancorp Inc.'s main business was ownership of the Montreal Canadiens hockey team and operating the Montreal Forum. The Bank also provided an indirect conduit between the Bronfmans and English Property because Sir Brian Mountain, who was chairman of English Property, was also a director of the Bank.

Here's how the complex deal worked. In return for transferring 2.9 million of its original 5.1 million common shares of Trizec to Carena Properties, English Property was paid $52 million by the Bronfmans and got a 49.99 percent interest in Carena Properties. At the same time, Edper Investments, the Bronfman's holding company, sold 1.1 million shares of Trizec to Carena-Bancorp for $16.6 million. In return for this transfer, Carena-Bancorp received $1.8 million plus a 50.01 percent interest in Carena Properties.

The result of this complicated maneuver was to establish Carena Properties as a holding company with four million, or 51.54 percent, of the common shares of Trizec. The rest was publicly held. Through later purchases of shares, Carena Properties increased its interest in Trizec to 58 percent.

Much of the credit for structuring the shrewd deal goes to Jack Cockwell, a South African-born financial whiz whom the Bronfmans hired in 1968 as their chief of staff when Cockwell was a 27-year-old accountant at Touche Ross & Co. in Canada. Today, the unassuming Cockwell is executive vice-president and chief operating officer of Edper Investments, the umbrella for the Bronfman Holdings, and executive vice-president at Brascan Ltd., which the Bronfmans acquired in 1979.

The beauty of the deal Cockwell designed was that for relatively little money the Bronfmans now controlled a company with $896 million in assets. "If the asset base is there, then it's worth taking a chance if you can get the people who can turn the company around," Peter Bronfman says about why Edper upped its investment in the floundering company.

The Bronfmans financed their acquisition of the controlling interest in Trizec largely through the sale, in 1978, of their interest in the Montreal Canadiens at a $20 million profit and through leasing the Montreal Forum for a gain of another $20 million. At the time of the deal, much was made of the fact that the British controlled firm had been Canadianized and that this would remove restrictions on its growth prospects to which it had been subject when it was foreign-owned. The newly created Foreign Investment Review Agency was cracking down on acquisitions of Canadian firms by foreign companies and the Ontario government had introduced a 20 percent land transfer tax on non-residents buying land. It was true that Trizec could have been hurt by these regulations, but its troubles had nothing to do with these government rules. The real reason for the deal was that English Property was in dire need of a cash transfusion.

When they gained control of Trizec, the Bronfmans went through the usual polite ritual of saying that management would not be replaced. But it was obvious, in view of Trizec's dismal performance, that management would be replaced eventually. A clue to how numbered their days were was that Trizec chairman James Soden and president William Hay were kept ignorant of negotiations.

Under the surface of business as usual, the Bronfmans launched a three month in-depth study of Trizec by Cockwell, Milavsky, and newly recruited Machiel Cornelissen, senior vice-president, finance and administration. By the end of the study in August 1976, Soden, Hay, and most of the previous Trizec staff had departed. (Hay is now senior vice-president at Olympia & York.) Milavsky became president and

Cornelissen senior vice-president, finance and administration. Cockwell was lent to Trizec for a year to help clean up the financial side.

The Trizec deal had significant ramifications for Peter and Edward Bronfman. It put them on the real estate scene in a big way. No longer were they overshadowed by cousins Charles and Edgar, who already owned a substantial interest in Cadillac Fairview. And it triggered their investment in a wide cross-section of Canada's biggest companies, including Brascan Ltd., John Labatt Ltd. (food and beer), Continental Bank of Canada, London Life Assurance Co., Ranger Oil, Canadian Cablesystems (sold in 1979), and Astral Bellevue Pathé (film distribution).

Since the early 1970s, Edper Investments has earned more than $500 million, representing an average compound rate of return on equity of more than 30 percent. In addition, the assets it controls have increased to more than $10 billion.

Because Edper's strategy is to diversify and make acquisitions via Brascan, Peter Bronfman says that Trizec will remain strictly a real estate company and not shift into other fields as Olympia & York (oil and gas, mineral resources, and newsprint) and Nu-West (oil and gas) have done. But Milavsky told Trizec's April 1981 annual meeting that the company might diversify into other businesses.

There was also a hidden ramification to the Bronfmans' bail-out of Trizec. It came back to haunt them in 1979 and led to the powerful Reichmann family, owners of Olympia & York, gaining a big stake in Trizec in the spring of 1979. According to a letter sent to English Property shareholders at the time of their agreement with the Bronfmans, there was a prohibition against either disposing of its shares in Carena Properties before July 1, 1979. After that date, either English Property or Edper could sell its shares in Trizec, with the other one having the right of first refusal on those shares.

Since English Property gave no indication of wanting to increase its holdings of Trizec, Edper would have had a clear field in acquiring more of the company after July 1, 1979. While this clause escaped general notice in 1976, it was known to the real estate industry and whetted the interest of the Reichmanns. In February 1979, a healthy five months before the July 1 open season date, the Reichmanns pounced and bought control of English Property for $156 million.

The purchase severely annoyed the Bronfmans. As they saw it, they had poured over two years into turning around Trizec. Moreover, they felt the 1976 agreement, giving them a head start in acquiring more of Trizec, was in jeopardy especially as Olympia & York would not promise to honor the terms.

Between February and March the two legendary, privacy-loving families were locked into the unwelcome glare of publicity as they shuttled back and forth to England. Employees at both companies dubbed the fight "the battle of Britain."

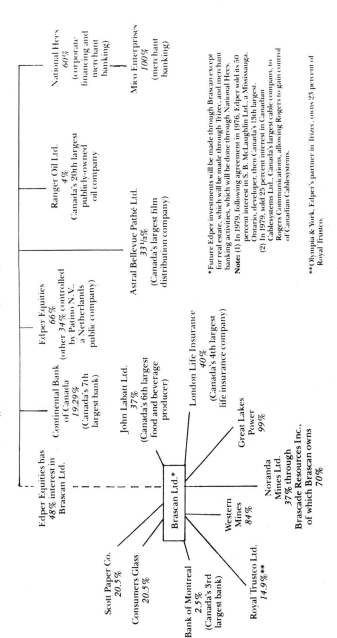

EDPER GROUP

Other Investments In Addition To Trizec
(Rank given if one of Canada's largest companies)

By March 1979, the Bronfmans, anxious to protect their position in Trizec, were ready to make a counter-bid. But a compromise was worked out by Bronfman lawyers John Tory and Trevor Eyton, then senior partners at Tory Tory Deslauriers and Binnington, a leading Toronto law firm.

"The Reichmanns must have been more afraid of John Tory, Jack Cockwell, and me than they were of Kenneth Thomson and Ralph Scurfield," says Trevor Eyton in a reference to Olympia & York's tough battle with Thomson (head of the Thomson newspaper chain and owner of Hudson's Bay Co.) and Scurfield (president of Nu-West) for Abitibi-Price Inc. in early 1981. Ironically, John Tory is now deputy-chairman of Thomson Newspapers Ltd.

The peace treaty gave operational control of Trizec to the Bronfmans, while leaving the Reichmanns with their fat piece of the financial action. The arrangement called for the Bronfmans to appoint 14 of the 18 directors and the three top executive officers. In addition, any conflicts of interest between Olympia & York and Trizec are to be resolved in Trizec's favor and Edper got an option to buy half of the 18 percent of Trizec that Olympia & York acquired indirectly. This agreement was completed in early 1981.

Albert and Paul Reichmann joined Trizec's Board of Directors. The shotgun wedding of Edper and Olympia & York seems to be working out amicably, even though they have opposite styles due to their differing nature and history.

Olympia & York does not own half of Trizec's assets. Ownership of assets stems only from owning all of a company. But because it owns more than 20 percent of Trizec, Olympia & York can participate in its profits on an equity accounting basis.

However, real estate analysts predict that eventually Edper will buy out Olympia & York's interest, with Olympia & York making a big profit on the deal. "It's a case of one real estate giant barging into another's territory because Edper fell asleep over the significance of the July 1979 clause in its 1976 agreement to buy control of Trizec from English Property," says Harry Rannala of Walwyn Stodgell.

"Edper can't have been too pleased about Olympia & York's buying in. The time will come when they will likely buy out Olympia & York, although Olympia & York won't let them off easily since Trizec keeps growing in value."

The Reichmanns handle much of Olympia & York's business personally and interchangeably, and so their company is not as formally organized as Trizec, which is run by professional managers on behalf of the Bronfmans. Also, with its track record of constant success, the Reichmanns are, according to Cockwell, "much more courageous."

"They believe that inflation will go on forever and are willing to buy at 20 percent interest, with a three percent return, figuring that it will work out in the end because inflation will drive up rents and property values." By contrast, Trizec, in light of its unstable past, is more conservative. "Consequently, Trizec can get its corporate financing on an unsecured basis, whereas Olympia & York has to pledge its buildings as security," Cockwell says.

Under president Harold Milavsky, Trizec has chucked its original free-spending image for a cautious approach. Trizec's head office in Calgary is modestly furnished. Its outstanding characteristic is its close observance of proper humidity. The temperature is kept warm in the small waiting room to protect the cacti there. It is kept cool in the company's cosy sitting room to preserve the Norfolk pine early Quebeçois furnishings, including a dining room table, rocking chair, buffet, and a hooked brown and orange rug.

The offices are on the 30th floor of the 40-story Scotia Centre in downtown Calgary, a square block office and retail shopping complex which is jointly owned by Trizec and the Bank of Nova Scotia. It is a source of pride to Milavsky. "The bank had owned the land for three years without doing anything with it and we offered to get it done and finished it in two years — on time and on budget," he says.

Milavsky has slowly doctored up Trizec, first whipping its finances into shape and installing a new management team between 1976 and 1978. However, that kept Trizec from participating to any appreciable extent in the real estate boom that began in 1976, and it was deprived of the precious momentum those years gave competitors. Now, with a solid financial and management foundation in place, it has embarked on an aggressive expansion program, primarily in the western U.S. and Canada.

Most of the senior staff was with Milavsky at Tristar Western. One innovation he introduced was the separation of the development and operations functions. The development division supervises the planning and execution of a project and then the development side looks after the completed properties. "Development and operations need different types of people," Milavsky says. "Development requires people with entrepreneurial flair, while operations needs detail oriented people." All Trizec operations, as of the spring of 1980, were consolidated in Calgary, except for shopping center planning which remains in Toronto because most large retailers have their headquarters there.

There are quarterly directors' meetings with Edper executives, but Trizec is autonomous on a daily basis. There is, however, a close knit relationship between the Edper companies with interlocking Boards of Directors aside from the Bronfmans. For example, Milavsky sits on Brascan's Board and Trevor Eyton and Jack Cockwell sit on Trizec's Board. Trizec's original owner, English Property, also has a member on the Trizec Board — Gerald Rothman, deputy chief executive of the British firm.

The team approach brings each company expertise from another part of the Edper network. "When Brascan (under its previous management) was battling for Woolworth's, Harold (Milavsky) helped us understand the retail business because Trizec builds shopping centers," Cockwell says. "And because we at Brascan deal on a daily basis with New York investment houses, we introduced Harold to people at Morgan Stanley when Trizec needed financing for its acquisition of Ernest W. Hahn shopping centers in the U.S. in 1980."

Trizec's rocky past has resulted in a cautious financing approach that has helped clean up the company's image in the eyes of the banking and investment community. Whereas other developers rely on interim financing at current and usually rising interest rates, Trizec prefunds its projects so that it will not be caught by climbing rates. Commitments for 85 percent of the debt are made before Trizec moves ahead with a project. In addition, it maintains $150 million in lines of credit to take immediate advantage of opportunities.

"Most other firms gamble that interest rates will fall, but Trizec ensures that it will not be subject to volatile interest cycles," Cockwell says. "For example, Cadillac Fairview got $700 million in floating interest rate money at a time when it was thought 12 percent interest rates would be high and now they're paying six percent more which wipes out their true cash flow. Trizec has escaped this because of its long-term fixed rate financing."

This has paid off on cash flow per common share. In the past four years, Trizec's cash flow per common share rose from $2.05 to $3.45 whereas Cadillac Fairview's dropped from $1.53 to $0.46.

Trizec originally dealt with the Bank of Nova Scotia, Toronto Dominion Bank, and Royal Bank and has widened that circle to include the Bank of Montreal and Canadian Imperial Bank of Commerce. Its brokers are Dominion Securities Ltd. and Greenshields Inc. Greenshields' president, Brian Drummond, is a Trizec director and Milavsky's university-age son, Gregory, has worked at Greenshields in the summers.

Unlike other developers, such as Daon, which rely heavily on leverage, Trizec prefers to issue preferred shares which it feels establishes it as very sound financially in the eyes of lenders.

Milavsky also keeps a tight rein on expenses. A monthly reporting system examines costs to date, estimated completion costs compared with the original budget, construction progress, leasing activity, financing arrangements (how much has been drawn down from lending sources), development agreements with the city, and contract terms with architects, builders, and any partners. In addition, photographs are taken monthly on the same day from the identical spot to track visually what is happening on every project.

With finances and management in good shape, Trizec has

embarked on an aggressive expansion program, including office towers in Calgary, Winnipeg, Toronto, Montreal, Detroit, Denver, and a 57 acre redevelopment of downtown Kansas City.

In 1980, in its first big acquisition since the new regime came into power, Trizec paid $270 million (U.S.) to acquire Ernest W. Hahn Inc., a major U.S. shopping center developer (assets U.S. $725 million). Hahn has 28 regional shopping centers in operation and 28 more under construction or development in California and the U.S. southwest, the hot growth areas in the U.S. The acquisition nearly doubled Trizec's assets from $1.03 billion to $2.1 billion and changed its ratio of Canadian to U.S. assets from 2:1 to an even split.

The deal is evidence of Milavsky's negotiating skill. He knew Hahn had been on the block for a long time but had not been bought by several firms, including Nu-West, because of its stiff terms. Hahn wanted to sell each part of its business — properties completed, under construction, to be developed — separately. Trizec wanted the whole package and got it because Hahn had been unable to find other buyers.

Trizec is the only major Canadian developer to build retirement lodges, nursing homes, and mobile parks, all of which are growth areas. All but one of the mobile parks (in Winnipeg) are in the U.S., but Trizec is now testing the U.S. market for retirement homes, with the conversion of an Orlando hotel into a retirement lodge.

A look at two Trizec projects — Winnipeg Square and Scarborough Town Centre in Toronto — provides a good example of the working relationship and haggling between the city, the developer, and the occupants of a project.

Winnipeg Square, a multi-phase joint venture of Trizec and the Bank of Nova Scotia, is located on the southwest corner of Winnipeg's famous Portage and Main intersection, the hub of Winnipeg's business and financial district. The first phase, a $35 million, 31-floor, 12-sided office tower, opened in July 1980 with the Winnipeg Commodity Exchange as the main tenant. The remaining phases include about 50 shops and a hotel. Trizec and the Bank had originally planned a small project, but the city wanted a magnum opus to encourage redevelopment of downtown Winnipeg.

Back in 1971, both candidates for mayor — Steve Juba, the incumbent, and Jack Willis, former chairman of the Metropolitan Corporation of Greater Winnipeg — urged Trizec to participate in a revitalization of the central core. Trizec agreed with the proviso that the city build a 1,000 car garage and an underground concourse linking the four corners of Portage and Main.

Such agreements between developers and cities are common as bait by cities to get the developer to build a multi-million dollar project. The developers can get the cities to build the sub-structure because they know how eager the cities are for redevelopment, which brings tax

Place Ville Marie, Montreal

dollars back downtown. In the case of Winnipeg, the city chipped in $18 million for expropriation charges, the parkade, and concourse.

Arguments by some members of the public that their taxes were going to subsidize a private development and environmentalists' concerns that the garage would cause congestion and pollution delayed the start of construction until April 1978. With two more years devoted to construction, it took a total of nine years from conception of the Square to its fruition.

That may have been part of the reason why the office tower had only 50 percent occupancy when it opened (it has since reached near full occupancy). Nevertheless, Milavsky says proudly that the project has indeed sparked redevelopment in downtown Winnipeg with both the Bank of Montreal and Cargill Co., the grain giant, planning buildings.

There is a popular belief that developers dictate and that tenants and city officials knuckle under. The Scarborough Town Centre in Toronto shows that developers, major tenants, and the government can be equally tough. The Scarborough Centre dates back to 1960 when the T. Eaton Co., which owned huge blocks of land on Toronto's outskirts, began to evaluate its expansion opportunities in the city and pinpointed the north central (Yorkdale), the west end (which became Sherway Gardens), and the northeast (Scarborough Town Centre).

In the early 1960s, Michael Spohn, vice-president in charge of negotiations for the T. Eaton Realty Co., bought 130 acres in Scarborough at the southwest corner of Markham Road and Ellesmere Road (about two miles from where the Centre ended up). That land was suitable for development, but lacked servicing (sewers and pipes). He got a terrific deal: for a down payment of a mere $100, Eaton's had a six month option to buy the land for $11,000 an acre. Today, it is worth $100,000 an acre.

Incredible as it seems, Eaton's head office executives did not seize the option. They were wrapped up in planning for the Pacific Centre in Vancouver and the Eaton Centre in Toronto and gave those projects priority. A few years later, however, the company got a second chance for the Scarborough area.

A housing development had been built on the first piece of property, but Spohn hired Joseph Barnicke, a Toronto developer, to act on Eaton's behalf without divulging that he was doing so. He scouted alternatives and found two farms on the northwest side of McCowan Road and Ellesmere.

"We only needed 60 acres, but because the farms were narrow strips, we had to buy the whole thing of 170 acres," Spohn says. The purchase price was $15,000 an acre, $4,000 more than the other land. But in retrospect, it was still a bargain because the land today is worth $300,000 an acre. "Inflation makes heroes of developers," Spohn says wryly.

Now the bargaining began with Scarborough officials. A road ran through the middle of the property, bisecting the planned development. Scarborough planners had intended the area to become a "golden mile of industry." A swap was finally arranged in which Scarborough got 30 acres free for municipal offices and Eaton's was allowed to re-orient the road to encircle the development.

The next problem was to get another major tenant. Eaton's prefers to be with another big department store, traditionally Simpsons, because it helps attract more shoppers. The problem was that Simpsons had a store two miles away at Markham Road and Lawrence Avenue in a Cadillac Fairview shopping center. Its contract with Cadillac said that Simpsons could not build a store within a two-mile radius.

Simpsons wanted to be in the Scarborough Centre. Eaton's wanted it there, too. Cadillac finally agreed. Spohn says Cadillac concurred because of good will, but a little arm twisting may have been involved, too. Cadillac was planning the Fairview Mall shopping center, also in northeast Toronto, and it wanted Simpsons as a tenant. Simpsons said yes to Fairview after Cadillac said yes to Simpsons' going into the Scarborough Centre.

Eaton's, as the land assembler and project initiator, also got a nice deal from Trizec. It pays a low rental of $4 a square foot for the first 30 years of the traditional 100 year lease and one-third of that for the remaining 70 years. It was given a 25 percent interest in the Centre which it later sold at a profit. Moreover, after 100 years, the land reverts to Eaton's.

But while it gave, Trizec also got. It was able to secure 100 percent financing for the Centre — always a Trizec goal — because it could say it had major and other tenants lined up and they ensured steady, long-term rents.

Moreover, Scarborough has turned out to be Trizec's most successful suburban shopping center with 9,400,000 visitors a year compared with 8,000,000 who go to Yorkdale Shopping Centre in north Toronto.

With Trizec back from the near dead to its current position of nipping on the heels of champion Olympia & York in terms of assets, Peter Bronfman says that there is no race to push past Olympia & York. "I would never call Harold Milavsky and say Trizec has to be bigger," he says. "I just hope that it will be amongst the best in bottom line performance and the future will take care of itself."

Chapter Four

NU-WEST GROUP LIMITED

"A company quits growing when it doesn't have the thrust from the bottom to do more things."

RALPH SCURFIELD
PRESIDENT
NU-WEST

71

NU-WEST GROUP LTD.

NU-WEST GROUP LTD.
President: Ralph Scurfield
Vice-President, Finance: Garnet Wells
Vice-President, Corporate Development:
Stephen McConnell
Vice-President, Secretary and General Counsel:
Douglas Watson
Head Office: Calgary

VOYAGER PETROLEUMS LTD.
President: H. Earl Joudrie
Head Office: Calgary

NU-WEST DEVELOPMENT CORP.
(Canadian Real Estate Operations)
Chairman: Ralph Scurfield
President: Rodney Gerla
Head Office: Calgary

Cairns Homes Ltd.
Head Office: Regina

Ashford Realty Ltd.
Nu-West Financial Services Corp.
Turner Lumber and Supplies Ltd.
Nu-West Structures (Calgary) Ltd.
T.N.W. Construction Ltd.
S.N.W. Construction Ltd.
Entek Engineering Ltd.

Head Office: Calgary

NU-WEST INC.
(U.S. Real Estate Operations)
Honorary Chairman: Ralph Scurfield
President: Kenneth Comyns
Head Office: Phoenix

NU-WEST FLORIDA, INC.
President: Robert Keenan
Head Office: Plantation, Florida

CARMA LTD. (48 percent interest)

In many ways, Ralph Scurfield, president of Nu-West Group Ltd., the largest homebuilder in Canada and the third largest in North America, epitomizes what is happening in the real estate development industry these days. Born into a fairly poor family in a small town. Worked long hours to build up a multi-*billion* dollar business in only 20 years. Expanded the Calgary-originated company geographically across most of Canada and into the United States. Moved the company from housing into shopping centers and office buildings so that it would not stultify. Diversified into oil and gas so that it would not be solely dependent on real estate. And, finally, devised an elaborate corporate management structure because he could no longer do everything himself.

However, Scurfield, now 53, has built up an empire that will be run in the future not by members of his family but by professional managers—a trend that is common in the real estate development industry. Although he has seven children, including a 25-year-old son who is a lawyer and has his own company and including three other children in university, Scurfield says they will not be working at Nu-West. "I feel they should find their own way," he says. "It's difficult to grow up in your father's shadow. Also, it's not good for the other staff."

Like other developers, Scurfield is nonplussed when asked how big he wants Nu-West to become. Since 1969, when the firm went public with $18.7 million in assets, it has grown to $1.9 billion in assets—a 100-fold jump.

"If we continue to grow by 40 percent a year, virtually doubling every two years, Nu-West would have assets of $8 billion by 1985, but it's unrealistic to expect to continue at that rate," he says. "However, we could reach $5 billion by 1985.

"We have a lot of management strength and my job now is to channel that energy. A company quits growing when it doesn't have the thrust from the bottom to do more things. When the excitement and drive aren't there, then you have to cut back. Fortunately, we have a management group with a lot of capacity, drive, and desire to grow."

That desire has resulted in Nu-West's expanding into the U.S., where it now has close to one-third of its assets, and buying Voyager Petroleums Ltd., one of Alberta's high-flying independent oil companies. Voyager's revenue soared 40-fold to $22.7 million between 1969 and 1978 when it was bought by Nu-West.

Early in 1981 Nu-West linked forces with Thomson Newspapers Ltd. in an unsuccessful bid to gain 23.1 percent each of Abitibi-Price Inc., the Canadian newsprint producer and the world's largest. Nu-West and Thomson were outbid and outmaneuvered by Canada's

Ralph Scurfield, president, Nu-West

largest developer, Olympia & York, which wound up taking over Abitibi-Price. Originally, Olympia & York had bid for only 45 percent of Abitibi but upped its offer when Thomson and Nu-West became involved.

"Greenshields Inc. (the investment house) came to us two and a half weeks before Olympia & York made its initial offer because Greenshields knew we are interested in resource company acquisition opportunities," says Stephen McConnell, vice-president, development, at Nu-West. "Greenshields later brought in Thomson."

Although Nu-West lost out, it did not lose face like Thomson which had won all its previous takeover battles for the FP newspaper chain (Toronto's *The Globe and Mail* is the best known of the papers) and Hudson's Bay Co., Canada's largest department store chain. Indeed, Nu-West even made some money on the deal.

"We owned 200,000 shares and when Olympia & York increased its offer from $28 for some of the other shares to $32 for them all, we made $800,000," McConnell says. "We were only interested in an equity accounting interest. To outbid Olympia & York, we would have had to invest more money than we would want to except for an oil company."

Like Jack Poole, the president of Daon, and Harold Milavsky, the president of Trizec, Ralph Thomas Scurfield was born in a small Saskatchewan town. Shortly after his birth on January 27, 1928, in Broadview, the Scurfield family moved to Ninga, a small farming community in south central Manitoba. It is so small that it is not even marked on the province's road maps. (Ninga Ltd. is now the name of the company owned by Scurfield's son, Ralph, Jr., which is a major partner in Village Lake Louise, an Alberta ski resort).

"Ninga had almost an even 100 inhabitants if you included some of the local pets and the odd family cow," Scurfield says. Although he grew up during the Depression years, Scurfield and his family, because they lived on a farm, never lacked for food. One of his chores was to take two gallon pails to buy milk from a neighbor for which he was paid 20 cents. In the fall, he worked for $1.50 a day harvesting grain.

Life in Ninga, according to Scurfield, was filled with hard-working people with the friendliness and staunch good neighborliness that small towns have always rosily been characterized as having. "Skating, curling, a hill to slide down, and a 'crick' to swim in. Gophers to be hunted, baseball in the summer, hockey in the winter. Every second Sunday there was a really big event — a trip to the big town of Boissevain (about 20 miles north of the U.S. border) to see a movie and to spend a whole 10¢ for a Coke and an ice cream," says Scurfield.

"We grew up dependent upon the people around us. We could trust our neighbors implicitly. We could always expect their help at any time and for any reason and everyone shared."

Growing up in a small town also affected the way he judged people. "A friend of mine in Toronto told me once that when hiring someone, one of his main tests was to check and see if the applicant's shoes were well-shined. To him it indicated industry and personal push. I sort of cringed and looked down at my shoes as he spoke, knowing I would seldom measure up and knowing that my reaction to an individual with polished shoes and manner was one of wariness and caution."

Rural life also gave Scurfield a feeling of confidence and strength. "Our gang knew that we were just as smart or better than any of those city kids and that we were twice as strong and twice as tough."

Today, Scurfield, with his reddish hair now fading to a sandy color and receding to baldness, his healthy pink skin, friendly smile, and careful deliberation before answering, gives a misleading initial impression of a folksy small farmer. But the outward appearance of openness conceals a computer-like brain that is able to plot and achieve long range strategy.

Although he is a multi-millionaire and part-owner of the Calgary Flames hockey team, Scurfield lives simply. He dresses casually and rarely takes long vacations, although the family has a cottage at Lake Windermere in British Columbia, a three hour drive from Calgary.

Nu-West's offices are similarly low-key. Located across from a Nu-West subdivision in Calgary's eastern outskirts, Nu-West's three-floor, $4 million, four-year-old building, spread in wings around a small inner atrium, was designed by 47-year-old Werner Mross, who started at Nu-West in 1961 as a carpenter and is now executive vice-president of the Canadian housing operations. "We wanted it as simple as possible," says Mross. "Instead of putting executives in the far corners of the building as is usually done, we put them in a rim around the corridor so all employees could walk by easily."

The lobby of the building has two massive abstract murals carved into the concrete walls. One represents the land development process of laying out lots, roads, and sewers, and the other symbolizes the city of Calgary.

Scurfield chose Mappa aspen wood, light in color with dark flecks and imported from the U.S., for the walls of his office and the furniture, which was made in Calgary for him. The chairs are covered in blue, a favorite color of Scurfield. There is a small dining room that can also be used as a board room off Scurfield's office. Scurfield is one of the few developers with family pictures in his office. A large portrait of his children hangs on the wall beside his desk.

Scurfield's route to housing development was circuitous. After receiving his science degree at the University of Manitoba, he taught in the province for two years. During the summers, he worked on construction jobs and in 1951 chucked his teaching career and drove in his old Austin car to Edmonton, lured then, as others are now, by stories of opportunity and wealth in Alberta.

Soon after his arrival, Scurfield got a job working for Cheseley McConnell, a small homebuilder who became one of Edmonton's biggest during the six years Scurfield, who was quickly promoted to construction manager, worked for him. In 1957, two of McConnell's partners, Clifford Lee and Gordon Clark, were saddled with a 12-year-old homebuilding company in Calgary — Nu-West Homes Ltd. It was rapidly sinking because nobody would buy its poorly constructed houses. Lee and Clark were looking for a manager to replace the one they had just fired.

Scurfield had wanted to become a partner in McConnell's business. Instead, it was decided that each would buy 25 percent of Nu-West's then $60,000 assets and Scurfield would move to Calgary to revive the company. To come up with his $15,000 stake, Scurfield, in a classic rags-to-riches saga, sold his house for $21,000, recovered the $9,000 equity, and used $1,500 as a down payment on another house. The remaining $7,500 provided half the money toward buying into Nu-West and the rest came from a bank loan. Today, Scurfield and his family own 26 percent of Nu-West, worth about $50 million. McConnell is the second largest shareholder with 21 percent.

Scurfield took Peter Vass, a Dutch immigrant who was 10 years older and who had worked as a construction crew leader for McConnell, to Calgary with him. They set about repairing the shoddy workmanship of Nu-West Homes and, hence, to polish up Nu-West's reputation. "There weren't educated customers then and people were just happy if they had a house," recalls Vass, who today is construction manager at Nu-West for southwest Calgary.

During the day, Scurfield and Vass would install towel bars and paint rooms that had been left unfinished. At night, Scurfield would do the estimating and bookkeeping and Vass would do draft designs for the 65 new houses they planned to build the first year. That first year, they used a flat table because they did not want to spend money on a slanted drafting table. To further clean up Nu-West's tarnished reputation, Scurfield offered owners of Nu-West homes a five year warranty, which he claims was the first of its type in Canada. In 1972, the warranty was expanded to a ten-year coverage.

Money — how to get it and keep it — was uppermost on Scurfield's mind and Vass recalls that Scurfield was so money-conscious that he would retrieve two by four pieces of lumber, then worth 30 cents, out of the mud for future use as a cost-saving measure. "Ralph likes to say he doesn't mind a $100,000 mistake, but he doesn't want $1,000 mistakes every day," Vass says.

The hard work paid off. Canada Mortgage & Housing, which had cracked down on Nu-West by chopping off $3,000 from any loan guarantee, removed the restriction. Nu-West's other major source of funds, Investors Syndicate Ltd., which had stopped providing mortgage money because of customer complaints, also restored Nu-West to its lending list. The firm's manager, Gardner English, also became a Nu-West director and remained on the Board until last year.

Scurfield slowly and methodically enlarged Nu-West, first through geographical expansion and later through a series of acquisitions starting in Canada and then in the U.S. sunbelt.

In just 12 years, since it went public in 1969, Nu-West has evolved from being a Calgary builder to one having operations in Canada in five provinces — Ontario, Manitoba, Saskatchewan, Alberta, and British Columbia — and in the United States in ten states — California, Nevada, Colorado, New Mexico, Arizona, Oklahoma, Texas, Georgia, Florida, and Hawaii. It is in such cities as Toronto, Thunder Bay, Winnipeg, Regina, Lloydminster, Calgary, Red Deer, Edmonton, Fort

McMurray, Vancouver, Seattle, Tri Cities, Las Vegas, Los Angeles, Phoenix, Albuquerque, Colorado Springs, Denver, Oklahoma City, Dallas, Atlanta, and Miami.

It plans to expand its operations in New Mexico and Texas and recently purchased a minority interest in two California homebuilders—Presley Cos. and Standard Pacific Corp.

In 1969, 12 years after Scurfield and McConnell bought into Nu-West, the company took a number of watershed steps. It was awarded the first contract—$3.7 million for 250 units—for married student residences at the University of Calgary. It redeployed its emphasis on duplexes and small apartment buildings into large scale apartments and townhouses, recognizing that these were the wave of the future in housing. And it went public, issuing 415,000 shares at $7 a share for a total of $2.9 million.

This money was used as a grubstake to enter the Edmonton market, where Nu-West built 54 homes and acquired 300 lots. In just 15 months, Nu-West had become the largest builder of single family homes in Edmonton, selling 231 in 1970, four times what it had sold there in 1969. Largely as a result, revenue climbed 34 percent to $18.5 million in 1970 from $13.8 million in 1969.

Expansion into Edmonton resulted in Scurfield's introducing the first of several corporate management structure plans which, like its successors, was based on decentralization or, as Nu-West calls it, "companies within a company." Four functional divisions—North Calgary, South Calgary, Edmonton, and contract work (for schools and the government)—and five operational divisions—land development, finance, legal, property management, and construction—were created. The functional departments reported to an executive vice-president of housing and the rest reported to Scurfield.

In 1973, when revenue had reached $69.4 million—nearly four times what it had been in 1969 ($18.1 million) when Nu-West went public—Scurfield made the company's first major acquisition—$2.9 million for Cairns Homes Ltd. of Saskatchewan. One of that province's largest homebuilders, Cairns had revenue in 1973 of $22 million. Just as important, it was active in Saskatchewan (Regina and Saskatoon) and Alberta (Red Deer and Calgary). The investment quickly paid off. By 1975, Cairns' revenue had doubled.

The Cairns' purchase marked the beginning of rapid geographic expansion by Nu-West. In 1974, Nu-West moved into the Ontario market by acquiring a 50 percent interest, at an undisclosed price, of Mayotte Ltd., a small Thunder Bay builder. The next year Nu-West moved into the British Columbia market, and in 1976 it made its first venture into the U.S. market when it established a Denver division. The company also got a toehold in the income properties (the term refers to shopping centers, apartments, and office buildings from which rent—steady income—is derived) field when it started three small neighborhood shopping centers in Toronto and California.

In 1977, Nu-West bought United Homes Ltd., a Seattle builder, for $5.5 million and had to establish three more housing divisions for central Ontario, Denver, and Seattle. Its one-year-old Denver venture was already going like wildfire with 200 homes built in 1977 compared with just 35 in 1976, and so Nu-West expanded into Arizona, acquiring 80 percent, at $15 million, of Hallcraft Homes Inc. of Phoenix, a 28-year-old firm that was one of the city's largest. During the next four years, Arizona became Nu-West's biggest market in the U.S.

In 1978, Nu-West continued to expand its U.S. operations, buying 5,800 acres in southern California that could accommodate homes for 25,000 people, acquiring another Washington state builder, American Pacific Corp., and buying shopping centers in Atlanta and Miami.

Although Nu-West's U.S. housing operations suffered during the general slump in 1980 due to high mortgage rates deterring purchases, they fared less poorly than the nationwide performance. For example, Nu-West's Phoenix sales dropped 17 percent and its Seattle market by 19 percent, whereas the average national decline was 26 percent. In Phoenix, its strongest market, Nu-West did better than its competitors who recorded an average decrease in sales of 32 percent, nearly double Nu-West's decline.

In 1980, through a share exchange, Nu-West acquired Headway Corp. of Thunder Bay, Ontario, which also had extensive holdings. In 1979 Headway had assets of $176.5 million in Quebec, Ontario, Saskatchewan, Alberta, and the U.S. sunbelt.

Former Headway president Robert Keenan is running Nu-West's rapidly expanding Florida operations. Over the next two years, he plans to develop ten shopping centers in the state.

Most of Nu-West's geographic expansion has gone smoothly, although some observers question whether it should have entered the Ontario market, especially as that province's housing market was in a severe slump. "Mayotte (in Thunder Bay) was a drop in the bucket, but a way of Nu-West's getting an eastern presence; however, they probably wish they hadn't," says a close observer of the company who is familiar with its inner workings. "Headway could be a wrong decision too, especially in melding its employees. There have been cases where less competent Headway executives have been brought in over Nu-West executives who subsequently left."

At the same time it has changed from being a one-city company, it has also changed from being a one-note company. In 1969, Nu-West was primarily a homebuilder. Today, it is also a land developer, commercial developer, property manager, and oil and gas producer as a result of its $196 million purchase in 1979 of Voyager. It has, in effect, become a diversified company whose main activity is in real estate and whose goal is also to increase its stake in the energy sector.

One way of judging the wisdom of this metamorphosis is to examine Nu-West's balance sheet. The impact has been enormous. Since 1969, assets have climbed a phenomenal 100-fold to $1.98 billion. Profit (net income) has gone from $1.1 million to $56.7 million.

Shareholders who had faith in Nu-West since its early days have also been rewarded handsomely. The stock price rose from $4.75 in 1969, when the firm went public, to a high-low range of $16.38-$6.63 in 1980 after a two for one split.

Over the years, Nu-West has changed both its name and management structure to reflect its expansion. It evolved from Nu-West Homes to Nu-West Development to its present incarnation as Nu-West Group. Nu-West Group is the holding company for Nu-West Inc. (U.S. real estate operations), Nu-West Development Corporation (Canadian real estate), Voyager Petroleums Ltd. (oil and gas in Canada and the U.S.), and its 48.7 percent interest in Carma Developers Ltd., a Calgary-based builders' cooperative (see Chapter 5). In 1980 Nu-West derived $22.9 million in net income from its Carma interest — or 39.4 percent of its total income.

Nu-West Inc., Nu-West Development, and Voyager each has its own Board, composed primarily of Nu-West executives. Scurfield is a member of all of them. Nu-West also has two members on Carma's 11-member Board (Scurfield and Nu-West Inc.'s vice-president Kenneth Comyns).

Like executives across the business spectrum today, Scurfield is a fervent believer in management by objectives. Executives, including Scurfield, attend Harvard University's 14-week advanced business management course. A team of five Harvard MBA students did a major reassessment of the company and its vulnerability to recession in 1977, and Scurfield used it as the bible for the company's rationale for going into oil and gas. One of the students, 28-year-old Stephen McConnell, became Nu-West's vice-president of corporate development in January of this year. Nu-West is also the only real estate developer that states in its annual report its corporate goals for business expansion, financial results, and diversification.

Scurfield laid out these aims for the first time in 1976. He has continued to do so and he has also achieved them. The goals include:
• A 15 percent annual increase in revenue, over and above inflation, and a 15 percent annual increase in profit. Although the 15 percent target was selected as a difficult goal to achieve, it has been exceeded every year since the corporate strategy was first outlined for shareholders in the 1976 annual report.
• To have a rainy day investment portfolio big enough to meet the company's cash needs in the event of a recession. It now totals $300 million.

- To be the dominant housebuilder in at least one market segment in each geographic area. With housing operations in 22 cities in Canada and the United States, Nu-West is the third largest homebuilder in North America, producing close to 6,000 in 1979. It is now Canada's largest homebuilder and after just six years in the U.S. is the 45th largest homebuilder there.
- To diversify in order to protect the company against cyclical operational and/or geographic downturns. By 1984, the goal is to have one-third of the real estate assets in Canada, one-third in the U.S., and one-third in energy resources. As of 1980, 24 percent of real estate assets were in the U.S., 16 percent in oil and gas, and the rest in real estate in Canada. If Nu-West had been successful in its second takeover bid for Transalta, Alberta's largest and fastest growing utility, it would have reached over night its target of one-third of its assets in the energy field.

Nu-West's purchase in the spring of 1981 of 7.2 percent of Cities Service Co. of Tulsa is further evidence of the interest in the energy field. Cities Service's Canadian subsidiary, Canada Cities Service Ltd., owns 17.6 percent of Syncrude Canada Ltd., which is developing the vast oil sands in northern Alberta. Nu-West has said that it may buy more shares of Cities Service, to which Cities Service is bitterly opposed. Both companies have sued one another over the purchase.

With operations across Canada and spreading through the U.S., Nu-West is run in a decentralized fashion, including financing for projects. Head office staff is very lean as a consequence. There are only six people in head office finance, and corporate development is a one-person department. The Boards of each division meet monthly and play a strong role in that division's strategic planning. While Nu-West gives considerable authority to young people (the Calgary manager is 30 years old and oversees $100 million in business), they are encouraged to draw considerably on the experience of the Board members.

The heads of the divisions confer quarterly and are encouraged to plan on a management by objectives basis. "The tendency is to travel a lot and so you can go a long time without talking to one another," says Garnet Wells, vice-president, finance. "Management by objectives forces us to sit down quarterly and discuss what we're doing and are going to do."

There also is an office of the chairman consisting of Scurfield, Wells, the vice-president of administration and corporate counsel (Douglas Watson), and the vice-president of corporate development (Stephen McConnell). The four work on expansion — and subsequent consolidation — strategies.

Besides Scurfield, the key executives, most of whom are in their 40s, at Nu-West are as follows:

- *Garnet Wells,* 40, is vice-president, finance. He joined Nu-West in 1969 after working at Winspear Higgins, which audited both Nu-West and Carma. (In 1980, Winspear Higgins was purchased by Deloitte, Haskins, and Sells.) Wells had worked on Carma's audit but not on Nu-West's. He is a tease who describes himself as "the slowest hockey player in recorded history" and quips "you should have" when Watson says he gave up golf.
- *Douglas Watson,* 39, handles a grab-bag of jobs: legal, public relations, and administration. Formerly at Texaco Exploration Co., the pleasant, soft-spoken Watson came to Nu-West in 1971.
- *Matthew Rodney Gerla,* 47, is president of Nu-West Development Corp. (the Canadian real estate division). Gerla, a chartered accountant, worked first as controller and later as manager at Cairns Homes Ltd. He started at Nu-West as vice-president, finance.
- *Kenneth Comyns,* 48, is president of Nu-West, Inc., the U.S. arm of the company. He moved the U.S. head office from Denver to Phoenix last year to reflect Nu-West's growing activities in Arizona where it has 54 percent of its U.S. operations ($200 million U.S.) compared with 13 percent (about $40 million U.S.) in Colorado. Comyns, however, is not in charge of Nu-West's Florida operations. They are handled by Robert Keenan, the founder and president of Headway, who wanted to stay in Florida.
- *Stephen McConnell,* 28, is the new (as of January 1981), Boston-born and Harvard Business School-educated vice-president of corporate development. He headed the Harvard study on Nu-West. "They diversified a year earlier than we recommended and did it ten times better," he jokes.

The youthful, lanky McConnell worked at Warburg Pincus, a venture capital firm in New York, for four years after graduating from Harvard. "I analyzed companies and transactions and did deal-oriented and strategic planning," he says.

McConnell says that he wants to see Nu-West play an increasing role in the energy field, "especially oil and gas, but perhaps also mining and coal." He also wants to enlarge Nu-West's position in the southwest U.S. "We're now number one in Phoenix and want to be the same in other markets," he says. A possible growth area is Texas where other Canadian homebuilders, including Carma, are already doing well. Nu-West is in Dallas only so far but not in Houston where most Canadian homebuilders went first in Texas.

McConnell says he also wants to expand Nu-West's activity in income properties (apartments, shopping centers, and office buildings) in which Nu-West became involved in 1974. So far, this policy has not been pursued aggressively.

Although it now has a staff of 3,700 people, Nu-West strives to maintain a team spirit through various incentive programs. Employees

The Nu-West head office building, completed in 1977

who buy a Nu-West home get a one percent discount after one year at
the firm, two percent after two to five years, and three percent after
five years. After every five years of service, employees are given shares
in the company, starting with ten shares after five years and reaching
100 shares after 25 years. Employee purchase of shares is also subsidized and company employees own about one million shares, or
about five percent of the company. Of that five percent, four percent is
owned by officers and directors.

There is a fitness facility and a pool table at head office for
employees. Executives who work on major public share issues are given
commemorative mementos. Past ones include a glass paperweight
containing a miniature prospectus and an inkstand embossed with a
reduced copy of the newspaper advertisement for the share issue.

Although Nu-West is very much a management by objectives company, Scurfield remains the daring entrepreneur who has been known

to write agreements on placemats and gamble on the outcome of a deal. "Ralph is an inveterate gambler and once bet whether Nu-West would pay $200,000 more than it wanted to for a land deal on the outcome of a golf match. He lost, but even at $200,000 extra, the deal was still a good price," says Allan Mar, who started and headed Nu-West's commercial division for six and a half years until August 1980. He now has his own firm, Patrician Developments Ltd. of Calgary. "But he will also bet on people, has an incredible sixth sense for opportunities, and is very perceptive," Mar continues.

The best way of illustrating Scurfield's creative, deliberate, cautious, and yet daring approach is to look at how Nu-West moved into the oil and gas business in 1978 when it bought Voyager. Voyager is a prime example of the fast growth of independent oil and gas businesses in Alberta in the 1970s, reflecting the boom in the oil-rich province after the Arab oil embargo. Voyager's revenue had soared from $577,000 in 1969 to $22.7 million in 1977, and its share price on the Toronto Stock Exchange had leaped from a high of $5.70 in 1969 to $23.75 in 1978.

At Christmas 1976, Scurfield took his first ever major holiday from the business and went with his family to the luxury Kona Village resort in Hawaii. There, while his family swam and suntanned, Scurfield charted the future for his company. His goal: to make the company recession-proof and stabilize earnings for shareholders by diversifying the company. His methods: build up the two-year-old U.S. real estate operations to one-third of company results and diversify into oil and gas.

As president and chief shareholder of the company, Scurfield could have imposed his plan instantly. Instead, Scurfield, whom employees describe as a "consummate politician," opted for getting a good business seal of approval on his idea. He went to Harvard, whose advanced business management course he had taken, and asked that Nu-West be used in the university's famous case history program as a study of how vulnerable a real estate firm could be to a recession. Coming on the heels of the 1974 recession in the U.S. that killed many real estate firms and at the threshold of fears of another recession, Scurfield's timing was impeccable. "He led them by the coat-tails," says one observer, and lo and behold, the students came up with the very conclusion Scurfield had reached: to be recession-proof, the company should diversify into oil and gas.

Always one to telegraph his intentions in advance to shareholders, Scurfield let them in on his plans in 1977, two years before Nu-West acquired Voyager in June 1979. "It is the company's intention to study opportunities for further diversification," Scurfield told shareholders in the annual report. "In particular, we will be seeking opportunities for major investments in less cyclical businesses such as the energy field to increase the portion of our income that is protected from the fluctuations that tend to affect residential construction."

The next step was for Nu-West to hire its first vice-president of corporate development. Scurfield had done advance planning on that, too. In 1977, Francis Maurice (Maury) Parsons, then 45 and a 16-year veteran of TRW Ltd. in charge of acquisitions, mergers, and diversification for the aerospace firm, joined Nu-West's Board. At the time, Parsons was an independent consultant. This accomplished two purposes for Scurfield. Parsons, an engineer and an economist, was an American, giving Nu-West, which wanted to expand its U.S. operations, an on-the-scene observer. Moreover, Parsons had plenty of experience in expanding a company through diversification and acquisitions, another Scurfield goal. A year later, Parsons, who had met Scurfield at Harvard's advanced management course, was appointed vice-president of corporate development at Nu-West. At the end of December 1980 he returned to being a consultant and self-described "deal maker" in Canada and the U.S. He continues, however, to be a consultant to Nu-West and Voyager and is on the Board of Nu-West Inc., Nu-West's U.S. subsidiary.

Parsons, a Scurfield-like combination of ingenuous friendliness and toughness, immediately developed a game plan. "Because Nu-West is Alberta-based and so are oil and gas, we would be going into an oil and gas business," Parsons says. "Moreover, the business practices of the oil and gas industry are very similar to those in real estate. One day you can be working with a company in a joint venture and the next you can be competing against them. But in both fields, land is the basis. In real estate, the profits are better from the land development than the building side, whereas in oil and gas, the greatest value is in determining that the land is oil- and gas-bearing."

Parsons laid out a careful three-part strategy for moving into oil and gas: acquire a small staff of experts to acquire land and exploration projects; joint ventures with established operations; and look for acquisitions in the $20 million to $30 million range. He spent six months laying the groundwork.

Then, chance and good fortune enabled the three-part, long-term strategy to be accomplished immediately. Sydney Kahanoff, the founder of Voyager Petroleums, was very ill (he died in the summer of 1980) and wanted to sell the business as no family members were involved in it to succeed him. Scurfield's wife, Sonia, and Kahanoff's wife had been college roommates and so Scurfield learned that Kahanoff wanted to sell.

Within a few weeks, Nu-West made a $196 million bid for Voyager without "the detailed analysis that would ordinarily be done," Parsons recalls. "We had to act fast because Voyager said it would sell to the first bidder to meet their asking price. If we hadn't been doing our homework for the past six months about oil and gas, we couldn't have moved so fast." The agreement to purchase was drawn up in 24 hours and ran only three pages, unlike the usual lengthy legal documents in such transactions.

"But we weren't worried because Kahanoff had an impeccable reputation for integrity and if he said an asset was there, it was and then some," Parsons said. "The company was conservatively and solidly managed. So we abandoned our three-part plan because we had achieved it immediately."

Of course, Nu-West's size, which made it easy for it to get a $148 million bank loan toward the purchase, once again shows how a big company can make instant acquisitions and become still bigger. After the sale, Kahanoff withdrew from the business and was replaced by Herbert Earl Joudrie, formerly senior vice-president of Ashland Oil Inc. in the U.S. and president of Ashland Oil Canada Ltd.

Although the federal government's national energy policy, introduced in October 1980, put a dampener on Voyager's activities in Alberta, it has stepped up its outside Canada operations where it has 84.7 percent of its acreage. It has 1.1 million gross acres in the midwest and western United States, 9.7 million acres in Australia, and small holdings in Guyana and offshore England. (Gross acres means the total number of acres in which Voyager has a full or partial interest). In 1980, Voyager had revenue of $34.5 million compared with $26 million in 1979.

The purchase of Voyager helped pump up Nu-West's share price from a high-low range of $3.75 to $7.25 in 1978 to a high of $17 in 1979. Someone who had bought 100 shares at $3.75 and sold at $17 would have made more than $1,300 within twelve months.

Although Nu-West's housing operations have spread throughout Canada and the U.S., its home base of Calgary and Cairns Homes' base of Regina remain the company's two strongest markets. In any single year, the market share in Calgary and Regina can range from 15 to 25 percent. In 1980, for example, Nu-West accounted for 14.4 percent (1,609 units) of housing starts in Calgary compared with 10 percent the previous year. Put into perspective, Calgary accounted for 40 percent of Nu-West's total of 4,918 housing sales in Canada last year.

Those figures give only part of the picture as to Nu-West's powerhouse strength in the Calgary market. Its 48.7 percent interest in Carma Ltd., which has a 35 percent market share in Calgary, must also be taken into account. This dominance has led to charges by competitors that Nu-West has a stranglehold on the Calgary market. Nu-West is very sensitive about this criticism and eager to defuse it.

"Only about 40 percent of the housing we build in Calgary is built on land we own and, on average, 20 to 25 percent of our housing is built on land we developed," says Rodney Gerla. "We have under 7.5 percent of the market in the six key cities in which we operate in Canada."

In 1972, Nu-West had only a one percent share of the Canadian market. It should be kept in mind, though, that the number of housing starts has declined so that Nu-West now has a bigger share of a smaller pie. In 1972 Canada had its third best year in the 1970s in housing starts with 206,954 built, compared with 125,013 in 1980, the lowest number in a decade.

Housing operations are localized so that "there are, in effect, a series of small builders who are expert in their areas," Gerla says. Each city is divided into territories (northwest, northeast, southwest, southeast) with a manager under whom there is a further divisional split into single family and multiple family divisions. Land banking is done to cover demand over ten years after research into how much demand is expected, if there will be a shortfall or excess, and how much product competitors have. Customer profiles are also developed to determine what type of housing will be required—single family, apartment, townhouse—often with twelve to thirteen different market segments, ranging from young families to couples to singles to the elderly being identified.

"Two to three years ago there was a big demand for multiple housing, but now the pendulum has swung back to single family," Gerla says. "The post-World War II baby boom generation has become second-time homebuyers and they want single family homes. However, there is a tug of war going on because of the higher costs of housing and energy. As long as we have comparatively lower energy costs in Canada, there will still be a demand for single family houses. But if Canadian oil prices go to world levels, the energy costs of running a home will be such that people will be switching to highrises."

The mark of a successful builder like Nu-West is to be flexible and know where and what to sell and what lures to offer potential homebuilders. Because the cost of mortgage money is making many people think twice about buying a home, Nu-West came up with a graduated payment mortgage and second mortgage plan to attract potential homebuyers. It claims its plans were among the first of their type in the housing industry.

The graduated mortgage reduces monthly payments in the first three to five years as well as the qualifying income for the mortgage. So far, it has been instrumental in about 17 percent of Nu-West sales, although it has been easier to get public acceptance than that of lenders used to high mortgage payments at the outset.

In addition, Nu-West has introduced second mortgages as a protection against rising real estate prices between the time the house is started and sold. The second mortgage offer is aimed at covering this gap.

Because its seven-member research department has found that people want to live closer to the city so that they can reduce their transportation costs when going to work, Nu-West is trying to acquire land nearer downtown. Other research discovered that homebuyers want more home and less front and back yard. As a result, Nu-West's small homes, which used to be 900 square feet sitting on a 5,000 square foot lot, are now 1,150 square foot houses on 3,000 square foot lots. "Homebuyers are taking the saving from land costs and applying it to the house," Gerla says.

Aware of the emphasis today on energy conservation, Nu-West incorporates such conservation features as more caulking, heavier insulation, and more airtight ceilings to reduce heat loss. These measures save homeowners about $150 a month in heating expenses, but the price for this cost saving is high: the energy controls add $4,000 to the purchase of the home.

Reducing its construction costs is also a high priority at Nu-West. It is using manmade lakes for storm water retention as one way of curbing expenses. The lakes serve a three-fold purpose. First, they are an excellent sales attraction because they provide recreation — skating in the winter and boating and fishing in the summer. Second, these activities make it possible to raise the price of homes because the area can be touted as a luxury development. And third, they can be more effective and less costly than conventional storm sewer systems.

The housing division has several lucrative auxiliary divisions in related supply and realtor services. Turner Lumber and Supplies Ltd., which sells building materials in Calgary and Edmonton, has sales of more than $30 million. Although Nu-West executives say Turner is independent and competes for sales to Nu-West, it obtains about 75 percent of its business from Nu-West. The other major subsidiary is Ashford Realty Ltd. It specializes in trade-ins and guarantees the purchase of a Nu-West home at a minimum price if the owner buys another Nu-West home. Ashford ranks among the top ten realty companies in Calgary, Edmonton, and Saskatoon and handles about 350 units annually, of which 150 are in Calgary. Other related activities include engineering services (Entek Engineering Ltd.) and the production of pre-fabricated homes by Cairns.

Nu-West has carried on Scurfield's tradition of fixing up dilapidated homes. It has a comprehensive customer service program aimed at building up a favorable word-of-mouth image, leading, it hopes, to new Nu-West homebuyers.

The program includes a pre-occupancy inspection of new homes as well as free follow-up visits within a week of occupancy and again three, nine, and twelve months later. A one-year blanket guarantee is also given, plus a ten-year warranty on structural items.

Five months after occupancy, Nu-West sends out a questionnaire on its performance to gauge how good the treatment has been by its sales staff and office personnel and the quality of construction. A tell-tale question is added at the end: Would you recommend Nu-West to your friends? Gerla says the rate of response to the questionnaire is 50 percent — a remarkable level since a one or two percent response to direct mail surveys is considered excellent. What pleases Gerla even more is that about 92 percent of those who answer say they would recommend Nu-West.

Since it is located in Alberta and active in British Columbia, where energy resource development is either underway or planned, Nu-West takes an aggressive role in building homes in resource towns. It has built more than $48 million worth of housing, for example, in Fort McMurray, site of the Syncrude oil sands project in northern Alberta.

It also had big plans to develop a 900 acre site near Imperial Oil's planned Cold Lake oil sands project in eastern Alberta until the federal government introduced its National Energy Policy in October 1980. The NEP resulted in Imperial's shelving its oil sands project and so Nu-West had to place its development on hold, too. The company will not say how much it had invested in land at Cold Lake, but during the boom surrounding the announcement of Imperial Oil's project, land was selling for as much as $200,000 an acre in the area. Nu-West recently sold half its interest to the Samson Indian band in Alberta.

In 1969 Nu-West went public by issuing 415,000 shares at $7 a share for a total of $2.9 million — "a big chunk of money then," says vice-president of finance, Garnet Wells. Its most recent issue was for 3,250,000 convertible (into common shares, if desired) preferred shares, at $20 each, for a total of $65 million.

"They have a voracious appetite for capital and a tremendous ability to sell," says Ira Gluskin, real estate analyst at Brown, Baldwin & Nisker Ltd. of Toronto. "It's one of the most popular real estate stocks among investors because it pays one of the highest price earnings ratio." (A P/E ratio is the multiple of the share price versus the earnings per share. Thus, if earnings per share are $1.00 and the stock is at $10, the P/E ratio is a multiple of 10.)

Nu-West has always dealt primarily with the Toronto Dominion Bank and secondarily with the Bank of Nova Scotia. The TD now provides 75 percent of Nu-West's line of credit and BNS the other 25 percent. Financing for individual projects and term loans comes from all of Canada's major banks. In the U.S., Nu-West borrows from the U.S. divisions of the Canadian banks, has a "large" line of credit with New York-based Citibank, and small lines with local banks. "They're so small, they can't support projects for very long," Wells says. As it is with most major real estate developers, Greenshields Inc. is Nu-West's lead investment dealer underwriter and Richardson Securities often supplements Greenshields. Montreal-headquartered Greenshields, unlike Winnipeg-headquartered Richardsons, has a corporate finance office in Calgary.

Like other Canadian developers, Nu-West, after the deadly effects on the real estate industry of the 1974 recession, decided to set up a rainy day fund of "liquid assets" — cash. It was started in 1976 with $15 million as its target and is now over $300 million and still growing.

Nu-West has a very tough policy about internal borrowing. "We borrow from the banks and lend it to the divisions at a little higher rate to ensure that we get a minimum return for our shareholders," Wells says.

After ten years of charging its divisions a 15 percent interest rate, head office raised the rate to 16.5 percent last year, reflecting the overall increase in interest rates by the banks. While the divisions, in view of today's high interest rates, are getting a pretty good deal, they weren't during the 1970s when interest rates were often half what Nu-West was charging.

"I'm being awfully kind-hearted now," Wells says. "I should be charging 35 percent. If the divisions weren't making enough money in the 1970s to pay 15 percent interest, then they shouldn't have been in business."

Maury Parsons likes to say that part of the reason developers have a poor image among some members of the public is that "they just know about our successes and not our problems."

Nu-West has had the occasional problem come to public attention. One such instance was Nu-West's pullout in 1979 from Eau Claire, a 40-acre residential and commercial project in downtown Calgary involving Nu-West, Oxford Development, and a group of Calgary businessmen. The root of the conflict appears to have been that Oxford, as a commercial developer, and Nu-West, as a residential developer, had nothing in common in development methods. (For more detail on Eau Claire, see Chapter 7 on Oxford.)

"There were too many cooks in the kitchen," Scurfield says. "Also, there was some difference of opinion regarding the timing and planning of the development. Moreover, the Eau Claire agreement precluded development of any other area in downtown Calgary."

Since the agreement had a clause allowing Oxford or Nu-West to buy out the other, Nu-West decided to sell. It came out a little under after taxes. It had purchased its interest in 1975 for $4.7 million and sold it for $5.1 million. After taxes of $1.2 million, it made $3.9 million on the sale, just under what it had paid for its share.

In October 1980, Nu-West also got involved in what turned out to be a stillborn bid for 48 percent of Calgary Power Ltd. (now known as Transalta Utilities Corp.). Calgary Power was Alberta's fastest growing utility with revenue of $326 million in 1979. When the deal fell through, some real estate investment analysts regarded it as a plus for Nu-West because Nu-West's $516 million offer was just a tiny bit less than the value of Nu-West. Nu-West was then trading around $30 on the Toronto Stock Exchange, making its 18,417,692 shares worth $552 million. In addition, analysts questioned the wisdom of acquiring a company whose utility rates were under government regulation.

Nu-West, however, regarded it as a good offer, because it would have increased its shareholder equity. It planned to raise 75 percent of the money through a $400 million line of credit at a floating prime rate plus one-quarter percent over a three year period from the Toronto Dominion Bank. The shareholders' equity would then have been enlarged since Nu-West stipulated that between 25 and 35 percent (or a maximum of $180 million) of the purchase price would be paid for through swapping that money for its preferred shares.

Nu-West became involved in what turned out to be a struggle of two Alberta giants for a third giant. Its bid followed one by Atco Ltd., an Alberta manufacturer of mobile homes, for 50.1 percent of Calgary Power. The utility bitterly contested that takeover proposal. Atco dropped out after Nu-West made its bid, which was greeted cooly by Calgary Power, but at least not with the same anger with which it had reacted to Atco's bid.

"Calgary Power is the cream of the crop in the utility business and had the deal gone through, it would have provided Nu-West with additional equity and continued growth in the energy sector," says Maury Parsons who developed the proposal for Nu-West. Indeed, in one swoop, Nu-West would have reached its 1984 goal of having one-third of its base in energy, compared with its then 25 percent of assets in oil and gas.

"Ralph Scurfield always thought there should be a third leg complementary to Nu-West's other areas of oil and gas," Parsons says. "We had been approached by an intermediary 18 months earlier, well before Atco's bid, about the possibility of investing in utilities, but no overt efforts were made. When Atco made its offer, we took a hard look at Calgary Power and thought we could make a more attractive offer." (Nu-West offered $24 a share, whereas Atco had offered $21.)

Then outside events came into play, and the final result was that Nu-West never made a formal offer. On October 28, the week after Nu-West made its interest in Calgary Power known, the federal government announced its national energy policy. Earl Joudrie, the head of Voyager, went to Ottawa to see Energy Minister Marc Lalonde and, in Parsons' words, "saw the near-term impact on Voyager and its cash flow and the derivative effect of the NEP on the Alberta economy, including real estate." So just 48 hours before Nu-West was to submit its formal offer, the company killed it and decided to wait for further acquisitions until economic conditions became clearer. About two months later, Parsons left Nu-West to start his own consulting business but he stresses that his departure had nothing to do with the collapse of the bid. "It was only six weeks out of four years of making acquisitions", he says.

Nu-West has not lost interest in this particular acquisition. It made a second offer in the spring of 1981, again for 48 percent. However, it got only 14.3 percent.

In the future, it can be expected that Nu-West, which started as a homebuilder in Canada, will put decreasing emphasis on this area and more on land development, shopping centers, office buildings, oil and gas, and real estate development in the U.S., all of which are more lucrative. The numbers all dictate this. Statistics Canada reports that housing starts of 150,999 in 1970 rose to a peak of 209,762 in 1976 and then declined to 125,013 in 1980. Clearly, homebuilding is not a growth industry in Canada.

Home building in the United States has been more stable because the population did not have the same post-World War II baby bulge and then as much of a falling off rate of population growth. Nevertheless, with competition intensifying in the sunbelt where Nu-West has set its sights, the company cannot expect as sharp growth there in the 1980s, especially the latter half, now that the migration from the northern and eastern states has slowed down. During the downturn in 1980 and this year, Nu-West was only building half of its planned housing in the U.S.

Moreover, housing construction is the least profitable area for Nu-West. In 1980 housing construction in Canada accounted for only 17 percent of Nu-West's profit, whereas land development provided 54 percent. In the U.S., Nu-West had an $11 million loss on its housing side in 1980, but a $26 million profit from land development.

None of these trends has escaped the attention of incisive and canny Ralph Scurfield. "We started as homebuilders, but now we're closer to being city builders," he says. "Our biggest diversification now will be in income properties and we will also strengthen our involvement in the energy field."

Chapter Five

CARMA LIMITED

"Knowing the economics of the market, where people want to live and what product they want is essential."

ROY WILSON
PRESIDENT
CARMA

CARMA LTD.

CARMA LTD.
Chairman: Howard Ross (1981)
(rotates annually)
Vice-Chairman and Chief Executive Officer: Joseph Combe
President and Chief Operating Officer: Roy Wilson
Head Office: Calgary

CARMA DEVELOPERS LTD. (Canadian real estate operations)
Chairman: Angus Scott Taylor
Chief Executive Officer: Joseph Combe
President: Rudolph Janzen
Offices: Calgary (*Head Office*)
Edmonton; Mississauga (near Toronto);
Surrey (suburb of Vancouver)

CARMA DEVELOPERS, INC. (U.S. real estate operations)
Chairman: Joseph Combe
President: Stanton Hooper
Offices: San Francisco (*Head Office*)
Aurora, Colorado; Houston; Phoenix;
Santa Barbara; Seattle

ALLARCO DEVELOPMENTS LTD. (financial services,
petrochemicals, insurance)

Chairman: Charles Allard, M.D.
Chief Executive Officer: Roy Wilson
Head Office: Edmonton

Carma Ltd. has become a big-time, $1 billion firm in just 23 years, but it has not lost the friendliness and warmth of a small town homebuilder.

Carma is unique among Canadian developers. It is the only one that is a cooperative of builders who banded together to buy land but who do construction independently. Last year, in a move that president Roy Wilson describes as a "mouse swallowing an elephant," Carma acquired Edmonton-based Allarco Developments Ltd. That changed Carma from primarily a land developer into the instant owner of a diversified empire of car dealerships, hotels and restaurants, a trust company, a printing company, farms, travel businesses, and a chemical company. Moreover, Carma leaped from the second tier of Canadian developers with assets of under $500 million to the upper ranks in the stratospheric $1 billion range. Between 1975 and 1980, Carma's assets had quadrupled to $398 million. The Allarco purchase enlarged those assets to $1.03 billion. Allarco accounted for 47 percent of that amount. Carma's real estate assets are still its largest sector, providing $871.3 million of its $1.03 billion total assets.

Although Carma is in the major leagues, management has retained the folksiness of a little league, seat-of-the-pants operation. At Carma's new $12 million head office in a remote area of Calgary that can be reached by bus only in the rush hours, executives make a point of introducing receptionists and secretaries and having them shake hands with visitors. Chief executive officer Joe Combe and president Roy Wilson exude the warmth of a small town business booster.

Despite this, some of the 135 builder-shareholders say Carma is like a family that has become so big that it has lost contact with some members. "It's like a family — or used to be," says John Neufeld, who has been a member since Carma's start. Neufeld, 53, has a small $6 million homebuilding business in Calgary with only three full-time employees.

"The other members give you extra pep. If things are down but everybody else is building houses, it gives you the ambition to go out and build. Also, other builders can help you with your problems, suggest good sub-trade firms, and good areas in which to build.

"But Carma has become a very large company and access to the staff isn't as easy as it used to be because they are always at meetings."

Wilson's and Combe's demeanor is genuine but deceptive, for underneath there is a sharp intellect that has built Carma up from a small Calgary-based outfit to a firm with operations also in Toronto, Edmonton, Vancouver, Seattle, San Francisco, Sacramento, Los Angeles, Houston, Denver, and Palm Beach. Many original Carma members who have chosen to move into these new areas have become millionaires.

Land held for development in Canada by Carma is double what it holds in the U.S. But it has development plans for such major U.S. locales as Los Angeles (where it holds 3,353 acres), Arizona (1,787 acres), Texas (1,483 acres), and Atlanta (750 acres).

Twenty-seven percent of its assets are now located in the U.S. That's not bad for a company that just entered the U.S. market in 1977, about three years after most other Canadian developers.

Carma was started in February 1958 by three Calgary homebuilders — Albert Bennett, Howard Ross (now president of Britannia Homes, a large Calgary and Edmonton builder), and Wilson. They decided to join forces because of concern over a shortage of serviced lots in Calgary. The city of Calgary, as the prime developer, was unable to bring serviced lots onto the market at a rate equal to the demands of the growing population. "People had to stand in line and sometimes even used sleeping bags to keep their place in order to get lots," Wilson recalls. "Consequently, the city encouraged us to form a land development company."

More concerned with building up their fledgling cooperative than with naming it, the three founders took an easy way out. Bennett had formed a company called Carma that was inactive and he, Ross, and Wilson decided to dust off the name for their new venture. "If we were choosing a name today, we probably wouldn't select one beginning with a 'C' because there are so many companies listed on the stock exchange that start with 'C'," Wilson says.

The goal was to get between 40 and 50 members, with 50 as the ceiling, because that was the maximum number of shareholders a private company could have. Carma started off with 45 members and assets of $250,000. Members could subscribe for a maximum of 20 percent, with the rules calling for them to buy a $100 debenture for every $1 share that was purchased. "A lot of people, though, subscribed for only one percent because they didn't know it would be a success," Wilson says wryly. New members were obtained in a pyramid fashion: the three founders selected a fourth, then the four agreed on a fifth, and so on.

Carma's biggest shareholder is Nu-West Group, Canada's largest homebuilder. It has $42.1 million invested in Carma and a 48.7 percent share that has been built up gradually over the years. Nu-West president Ralph Scurfield took over Nu-West a year before Carma was formed and Nu-West joined Carma about a year after it was formed.

Joining Carma ensured Nu-West of a steady supply of lots. In turn, Nu-West's investment provided Carma with a source of money at a time when some of the early shareholders pulled out. Today, 75 percent of the shares are owned by Carma members and the rest are publicly traded.

Wilson says that despite its clout, Nu-West has been a responsible shareholder and Scurfield "has never used a big club." Nu-West has only two representatives—Scurfield and Kenneth Comyns, president of Nu-West's U.S. division—on Carma's Board of Directors. Still, it would be naive to think that Nu-West, with just below 50 percent ownership, has not played a dominant role in Carma. Evidence of this is Scurfield's being chairman from 1972, when Carma went public, until 1979 when he stepped down. Wilson says Scurfield made this decision on his own, but an influencing factor may have been that some Carma members wanted a full-time chairman from their ranks. The chairmanship now rotates on an annual basis. The current chairman is Howard Ross, one of the three co-founders.

From 1958 to 1971, Albert Bennett served as Carma's president, chairing the monthly meetings. When he retired to Victoria, directors decided they wanted a full-time president and chose Roy Wilson.

Wilson, 49, a hearty man skilled both at answering and at deflecting questions, had had a family homebuilding business with his father and brother. They had built 12 houses in the year before Carma was started and 76 in Carma's first year. In 1969, the Wilsons sold their business to Engineered Homes Ltd., a division of Genstar. Two years later Wilson ran successfully for the Alberta legislature on the Social Credit ticket for the Calgary Bow district and was elected by 976 votes. That was quite an accomplishment because the long dominant Social Credit party was swamped that year by the Progressive Conservatives under Peter Lougheed. (Wilson was an M.L.A. until 1975.) From 1976 to 1980, he was a member of the Calgary Police Commission. With his brother, Wilson raises standard bred, harness race horses on a farm outside Calgary.

Wilson is a self-described "ardent free enterpriser." Carma's annual reports have frequently reflected these sentiments in outspoken comments against what it has viewed as government encroachment. The 1976 annual report had this comment: "For 1976, Carma paid $10.6 million in income tax, an amount exceeding the net income earned by the shareholders. Thus, in exchange for snarls of red tape, no investment and no assumption of risk, the government becomes the largest beneficiary of the company's operations." Last year, Carma had net income of $43.8 million after paying taxes of $28 million.

Wilson, however, emphasizes that while "Carma is very much a cooperative company, in the pecking order of contributions, Joe Combe is always the number one manager. Nobody is ever senior to him in management."

If office layout is an indicator of status, then Carma's layout bears Wilson out. Combe has a large corner office and his secretary also has an office, whereas Wilson's office is in the middle of executive row and his secretary sits outside, just as do all the other secretaries.

Combe, now 59, was the first executive hired by Carma in its formative days. It placed a newspaper advertisement that was answered by Combe, then district manager in Calgary for Texaco Canada Ltd. "Texaco wanted me to consider a promotion in eastern Canada, but I liked Calgary and my family liked Calgary, so the decision was made to join Carma," Combe recalls.

"My experience had been in finding new locations for service stations in Calgary and the surrounding area and having such sites zoned for service station use. This involved close contact with the planning department and the development of the sites regarding feasibility, engineering, off-site costs, and many of the things in which Carma would become involved. The challenge was intriguing and I liked the people."

Like many Western Canadian residents, Combe and his wife Marnie vacation in Hawaii where "we boat, swim, surf, golf, and plain relax." The Combes also have a cottage three hours from Calgary at Lake Windermere, B.C., where Nu-West's Ralph Scurfield has a cottage. Like Wilson, Combe is also a free enterpriser who scoffs at "politicians who believe continuing high interest rates help fight inflation."

Carma conducts its residential operations in Canada through builder-shareholder contracts. Builder-shareholders, who hold a marketing contract in the areas where Carma operates — Calgary, Edmonton, Vancouver, and Hamilton — may buy a proportionate percentage based on the number of shares they own.

Carma has 135 builder-shareholders in Canada (some builders belong to a marketing pool in more than one city, but they are counted only once). Lots are selected through a lucky draw and participation in each development is voluntary.

In 1977, Carma introduced two types of marketing contracts. The "A" contract covers all geographic areas. The "B" contract deals with joint ventures — between the builder and Carma — in Calgary and Edmonton.

To become a builder-shareholder, a candidate must already own some Carma common shares, have a good credit rating and reputation as a builder, and be approved by the existing members and common stock shareholders. There is, however, no yardstick for the amount of business a potential member does. Some may build only three or four houses annually.

This system is not used in the United States where Carma operates as a conventional homebuilder, acting as a corporate unit rather than using its Canadian cooperative style. The U.S. approach was the result of a painful lesson when Carma tried to transplant its system to Houston, probably the most fiercely competitive market in North America, and found it didn't automatically work. "You can't tell a Texan what to do," Wilson laughs.

Calgary Centre, $150 million twin office complex. A joint venture with Princeton Development Ltd. of Edmonton. (Artist's rendering)

The root of the problem is that while housing and subdivision styles are similar in Canada and the U.S., they are poles apart in development style. "In the State of Washington, for example, builders mostly do their own developing because of the small tracts of land available," Wilson says. "In Florida and Texas, though, developers sell lots to very large builders in big numbers—100 or more at a time."

Each division has its own advisory board, consisting of four to six builders, depending on the volume of activity in that area. The marketing pool for that city is divided into four to six groups with each having one representative on the board. The boards are appointed by Carma's Board of Directors for three-year terms and meet monthly. Members can be re-appointed a year after their term ends.

To illustrate how this whole process works, look through the eyes of its project manager, Greg Spearn, at the development of one Carma project: a 900 acre subdivision called Edgemont being planned for northwest Calgary and to be built over a ten year period. It will have about 5,600 housing units—mostly low density.

The process begins with Carma's developing an area structure plan, covering such items as type of housing (single family or high rise), servicing, streets, lot size, commercial space, parks, and schools. Carma's advisory board will have suggested lot sizes and housing density based on an informal survey of consumer tastes by its members. The site plan must also include an archaeological review because the Calgary area has a rich lore of historic Indian arrowheads and artifacts.

The plan is then broken down into pieces of 90 acres, sectioned to meet, but not glut, demand, and 62 copies are submitted to the various city departments and agencies, such as engineering, parks, and transportation. Sixty-two copies may seem excessive, but four, for instance, go to the engineering department alone, for the department head and the heads of the sewer, storm sewer, and water mains divisions. The city must respond within a month with any suggested changes.

Next stop is the Calgary Planning Commission, which reviews the street patterns and land use. This is followed by a public hearing, six to eight weeks later, before City Council. The whole approval system usually takes at least 18 months but more frequently runs two years.

With all the governmental levels hurdled, Carma then proceeds to divide each 90 acre section into three smaller parcels of 30 acres to start installing services. The reason for this further split is that the developer must sign a performance bond that it will maintain the services, repairing such things as cracks in the road, for two years.

Finally, the builder-shareholders get involved. Their advisory boards inform them that lots will be selected by a lucky draw on a certain date. All the members do not have to participate, but in a strong market like Calgary, the 44 members of the pool, ranging in size from a builder of two homes a year to Nu-West, which in 1980 built 2,056 in

Calgary alone, have turned out in full force during the past two years. Lucky draws, however, are held only for single family and duplex lots. Multiple family acreage is awarded on a tender basis because only one site is involved. Head office proposes a price that must be approved by the local advisory board.

An information brochure is sent to all the builders about ten days before the draw. The brochure contains a map of the subdivision, information on when the next phase will be available, a price list, and the terms of sale. The lot prices have to be approved by the advisory board in advance. The terms of sale usually call for a 15 percent cash deposit and for the lot to be purchased within a year. This provision is aimed at speeding up development. In the case of Edgemont, the board approves lot prices ranging from $36,000 to $47,000.

The lucky draw is held in a local hotel or motel, with large maps of the subdivision put on the walls. If builders are sick or on vacation, they can send a proxy. The draw, with names picked from a plastic ice-bucket, usually lasts half a day, but sometimes it takes a whole day.

Builders draw their lot numbers on an alphabetical basis. If a builder draws #1, he gets first choice on half the lots to which he is entitled. The number of lots he may have is based on the number of Carma shares he holds. All the numbers are then drawn with the last person getting all the lots he wants. Then the lot selection reverses itself, with the people who chose last in the first part of the draw selecting their numbers first in the second half. This ladder system was introduced five years ago after builders complained that Nu-West, with 40 percent of the Calgary Pool, was getting all the best lots.

Following the draw, builders have ten days in which to decide whether they want their lots. If they do, they must make a good faith deposit, usually $500 a lot. After another 20 days they must pay 15 percent of the purchase price and sign to pay the remainder within a year.

Carma provides financing at one point above the prime rate with quarterly adjustments to meet interest rate fluctuations. Small builders have to pay a higher interest rate. Large members, like Engineered Homes Ltd., which can get cheaper funds on their own, elect to pay cash.

If there are any lots left over after the draw, they are offered first to the member builders and then to the general public. The price is the same as for members, although if there are doubts about a buyer's financial status, Carma will either ask for cash in full or a down payment of up to 30 percent, twice the rate charged Carma members.

Like any other builder, Carma relies on home shows to market its houses. Ten to 15 lots are set aside on one street and builders are asked if they want to participate. Doing so is costly because the house cannot be sold for a year and the builder must shoulder the carrying costs

Woodlands housing development, Calgary

during that time. To attract small builders, Carma gives them the right to draw three to four more lots than they might otherwise get.

Carma will then pay for the landscaping around the show homes and matches the money the builders of these homes put into an advertising kitty (usually $50,000 from Carma and $50,000 from the builders). Besides media advertising, Carma will stage some sort of event. For example, the home show for its MacEwan Glen subdivision in Calgary featured Scottish bagpipe performers.

Because the subdivision is marketed under the Carma name and dozens of builders are involved, head office has devised strict guidelines to prevent a glaring mismatch of housing designs. Architectural plans must be submitted to Carma for approval. Luxury homes, for example, must not have aluminum siding or asphalt shingles. Builders must also pay a $500 to $1,000 damage deposit against such eventualities as breaking sidewalks when excavating basements. (Builders dislike this rule, arguing that they should not be responsible for damage caused by city utility trucks or cement haulers.) Houses are given a final inspection by Carma staff, who find broken sidewalks to be a common occurrence. Rebates of up to five percent of the lot price are given builders if they finish early.

A major component must be trees and Carma has strict rules regarding the number and type. At Edgemont, average size lots must have one tree on the front lawn. It must be six to eight feet high and 3½ inches in diameter. It can be an evergreen, birch, poplar, elm, or ash —

all of which have good survival rates. Larger lots must have three trees. Carma does its own curbside planting, too, with one tree for every 40 feet of frontage.

Getting trees is no problem because Carma has its own 30 acre tree farm in northwest Calgary. It grows ten varieties of trees with 4,600 planted this year. A second tree farm may soon be started near Edmonton.

Edgemont will also feature a pilot project for Carma. Carma will provide the land for a racquet club and pay $250 of the $400 membership fee for two members of a family. This will be an extension of Carma's penchant for sponsoring community activities to keep its name prominent and create good will. It likes to sponsor little league baseball and hockey teams and will often throw a clean-up party after construction is finished. The new homeowners are given a stampede breakfast of pancakes and bacon, as well as plenty of garbage bags for the debris to be picked up after the builders.

That's all very nice, but why does Carma not have the builders do their own cleanup? According to Spearn, the builders only have to pick up debris left on the property but not along the street. And somehow or other, most of the litter finds its way to the street.

Although Carma has spread into British Columbia, Toronto, and the southwest of the U.S., the home base of Calgary is still Carma's largest market. Its market share there has ranged from as low as 12 percent to 1980's high of 35 percent. Carma executives, however, bristle at the suggestion that the company has a near-monopoly in Calgary. "Builders don't have to belong exclusively to Carma, but can belong to other marketing pools, too," Wilson says.

According to a study by investment dealer Nesbitt Thomson Bongard Inc., Carma's Calgary and Edmonton operations have been the backbone of Carma's residential activities, producing about 90 percent of revenues and a higher percentage of net income. But, with the company's enlarging operations outside Alberta, Calgary's and Edmonton's contribution should decrease to 65 percent or 70 percent by next year, the study predicts. By 1981 about $19.5 million will come from Vancouver (compared with $13.5 million in 1979 and $16.5 million in 1980). But the biggest hike will come from its U.S. operations, which have taken off rapidly, and a probable move into eastern North American cities.

Carma was a late entrant among Canadian developers going into the U.S. It didn't penetrate that market until 1977, three years after many of the other firms had gone in. "We were more cautious and conservative and also smaller than a lot of the firms that preceded us into the U.S.," Wilson says. In 1973, Carma had net income of $3 million, up only $500,000 over 1972 despite a $3 million increase in revenue to $20.3 million.

Unlike other Canadian firms that have been battered by the highly competitive market in Houston, Carma has managed to survive there. Houston is so competitive because it has what developers have frequently said would be paradise — no zoning bylaws. "While in Calgary it can take three to ten years to get approvals, in Houston, it takes only three months," Wilson says. This has resulted in lots costing 25 percent of what they do in Canada.

In turn, it has led to the flourishing of another often-praised ideal — the unfettered free enterprise system. Lured by the population injection from the Atlantic states to the U.S. oil capital of Houston, developers raced to get in on the boom, building houses and acquiring land at a frantic pace. The result has been a glut of lots, with some firms stuck with 50 percent or more of their inventory. "There is the freedom to go broke," Wilson says dryly.

Carma also found Houston to be a nightmare at first, but it is now confident that it has solved its problem. "We ran it according to the formula of our Canadian operation and it was rocky at first," Wilson says. "Now, we've hired a Texan and everything is coming up roses because we have someone who knows the market and how to sell in it. Knowing the economics of the market, where people want to live, and what product they want is essential."

The Houston experience was a valuable lesson for Carma because it learned that the best approach in the U.S. is not to use the cooperative marketing pools that worked so well in Canada. Instead, it acts as a conventional developer.

So that it isn't bowed down with the carrying charges of a long-term land bank (land bought for future development), Carma buys only five years in advance and will sell land, even at a loss, if it has been lying idle for five years without reaching the development stage.

In addition, a hawk-like watch is maintained on the development to prevent cost overruns. "For example, we recently completed a $20 million, 392 home project in Orange County, California (the state's fastest growing area), located south of Los Angeles," Wilson says. "It was planned to the minutest detail before construction started. No storage space was allowed, forcing everything to be nailed up the date it arrived. Despite inflation, rising interest rates, and heavy rains, the project was finished on time and below budget. Indeed, there was only one unexpected extra — the municipality introduced a regulation calling for enclosures to be put around above-ground telephone installation boxes. But that only cost $16,000.

"If the project had been late, it would have cost us more interest, postponed when homebuilders could move in, and, hence, delayed when we would start getting revenue." And, Wilson adds, in a sentence that is both a cliché and a truism: "The tougher it gets, the more you have to know what you're doing."

In 1977, Carma and its largest shareholder, Nu-West, signed a joint venture agreement requiring whichever one acquired a tract of land in excess of 80 acres in the Calgary area to offer a 50 percent interest to the other. If the offer is accepted, the firm making the offer has the right to be the operator of the joint venture. The firm that purchases the land is paid a finder's fee of one percent of the purchase price and the operator is paid a fee of six percent of certain specified land development costs. Nu-West is entitled to 50 percent of the lots produced in addition to its normal proportion as a builder-shareholder of Carma.

"Land in Calgary comes in large tracts and if bought by just one company, all its money would be in one basket, whereas this way the risk is spread," Wilson says.

Just as its expansion policy is conservative and cautious, so is Carma's financing style. "We try to match long-term investments with long-term debts," Wilson says. "A lot of firms have gone broke in the past because they have financed long-term investments with short-term bank loans. At the height of the summer development season, we do get into short-term debt to pay for servicing costs, but we then issue public debentures and preferred share issues to balance the debt to equity ratio."

In 1978, along with its expansion into the U.S., Carma established regional operations for Calgary, Vancouver, Edmonton, Houston, and the U.S. west coast. Calgary, as its largest center, was further subdivided into south, northwest, and northeast sections. It must be kept in mind, though, that Carma is a cooperative and that the members do the tasks of running a business. Thus, the Calgary head office was always small (39 employees in 1975 and 150 now) and is only just instituting long-range planning, in which one employee says Carma has been "woefully weak," as well as in-house training programs.

The change would have happened anyway as Carma expanded, but it was accelerated by Carma's purchase last year of Edmonton-based Allarco Developments Ltd. for $130 million. Allarco had 1979 revenue of $119.9 million and net income of $19.8 million, compared with Carma's revenue of $142 million and net income of $29.8 million.

It was a brilliant move on several counts. First, Carma immediately became a diversified company with interests in chemicals, travel, hotels, restaurants, and car dealerships as well as real estate. Second, it had a dampening effect on the taxes Carma would otherwise have had to pay. And third, it forced Carma to re-evaluate its management structure because Allarco had more than ten times the number of employees at Carma (1,595 to 150). "We had to figure out how a bunch of carpenters would gear up for this," Wilson says.

The management restructuring was necessary also because Allarco was a one-man show, despite its size, by founder and president

Dr. Charles Allard. Now in his 60s, he has left Allarco to start a third career in radio ownership.

Wilson may sound "aw-shucks," but Carma took very au courant action. It had hired New York-based McKinsey & Co., one of the world's foremost management consultants, just before the Allarco purchase to restructure Carma to match its rapid growth. While McKinsey does not disclose its fee structure (which is by the project and not hourly), it does over $100 million in business for such blue chip clients as 24 of *Fortune* magazine's top 100 industrial companies, four of the top U.S. banks, three of the ten largest utilities, three of the ten biggest transportation companies, and governments in 16 countries. "Our style has always been to use minimal in-house staff and make maximum use of outside consultants," Wilson says.

McKinsey recommended that a holding company (Carma Ltd.) be established with three operating divisions, each with a president. They are Carma Developers Ltd. (Canadian real estate subsidiary), Carma Inc. (the U.S. subsidiary), and Allarco Developments Ltd. The umbrella holding company with separate operating divisions is a structure that is identical to that of Nu-West.

A three-day meeting of senior executives of Carma and Allarco was held, starting September 20, 1980, at the Banff Springs Hotel in Banff, Alberta, two months after the takeover bid was announced, to acquaint the two firms with each other. Between rounds of golf, steak dinners, the presentation of company ties, a gift to Charles Allard of a word portrait describing his business activities, and the breakdown of audiovisual equipment, the operational heads of each company outlined what the divisions did.

The acquisition of Allarco benefited Carma on the tax front as well. By applying what otherwise would have been taxable income to the purchase of Allarco, Carma was able to deduct the interest payments arising from the loan used to pay for Allarco from its income tax, thus wiping out the tax it would otherwise have had to pay in 1980. The debt could then be retired from Carma's cash flow from Allarco.

But most significantly for Carma, the acquisition of Allarco will make it less vulnerable to the traditional boom and bust cycles of the real estate industry. "The North American market is shrinking because of a slowdown in population growth, a change in demographics (fewer people in the homebuying age group), and the tighter market in the sunbelt states," Wilson says. "While we still intend to expand in land development, we don't want to put all our eggs in one basket.

"With Allarco, we now have financial services, natural resources, and retail businesses all in one company and can pick areas of investment that we think will be growth-oriented in the future."

Carma had bought a highly diversified company from Charles Allard. The Allarco network includes:

- North West Trust, Canada's 45th largest financial institution, with branches in the four western provinces. It also owns several shopping centers, apartment blocks, and land holdings throughout Alberta (1980 net income: $9.2 million).
- Seaboard Life Insurance (1980 net income: $2.5 million). Started in 1961 and based in Vancouver, it has operations in eight provinces and is moving into the U.S. market, starting with Washington and New Mexico. About 500,000 Canadians are insured by Seaboard.
- Privately-owned Alberta Gas Chemicals (40 percent by Allarco, 10 percent by Alberta Gas president John Lo Porto, and 50 percent by Nova, formerly called Alberta Gas Trunk Line). It has methanol plants in Alberta, New Zealand, and Minnesota. (Methanol is used to make anti-freeze for cars and lacquers, varnishes, and shellacs). Estimated 1980 sales were $88 million.
- Automotive dealerships. Crosstown Motors in Edmonton, a four-block complex, is one of Canada's largest Dodge and Chrysler dealerships, selling 4,000 new and used cars in 1979. Other dealerships based in Edmonton sell imported cars and vans.
- Several successful restaurants including Oliver's in Edmonton, one of the city's most popular dining spots.
- Redden Construction, which does industrial and commercial construction for Allarco (30 percent of its business) and other clients.
- Metropolitan Printing, one of Edmonton's longest-established printing firms.
- Fitness centers in California and Edmonton.
- Interests in a molybdenum mine in Idaho, uranium leases in Saskatchewan, oil and gas leases in Alberta, and an avocado farm in California.

In addition, Allarco has extensive land holdings in California and Alberta which it has never fully developed but acquired at low cost. In Palm Springs, California, the vacation mecca of wealthy Californians, Allarco has optioned 20,000 acres.

During the 1980s, Carma will continue to broaden from being solely a land developer and then a homebuilder (only in the U.S.), in the same mode as Canada's other developers. Its commercial and industrial division will come out of the shadows and the diversification, through Allarco, into natural resources will thrive. Already in New Zealand with Allarco's methanol plant there, Carma is looking at opportunities in South America and Europe.

"Continuing high interest rates will discourage major land banking and development on the scale we have known in the past," Combe says. "Carma will gradually revise its asset base, concentrating on the relative stability of leasing major commercial and industrial developments and considering other business ventures which will flatten out the peaks and valleys in the residential construction business."

Its commercial and industrial division, started in 1975 and now worth $40 million in assets, is expected to reach $700 million in assets by 1985. Much of the company's hopes are pinned on its 260 acre Deerfoot Business Centre in Calgary, where Carma's headquarters have been located since last December. The only office building, it has Carma's offices on the top floor of the three-story concrete building. The interior has a six-sided atrium with a fountain in the middle and plants flown in from Florida. The rest of the floors will be rented to outside tenants.

To date, not much else is at the Deerfoot Centre other than a bank and a small 30 acre light industrial plant. But Carma president Roy Wilson, while ruefully admitting it now "seems in the middle of nowhere," says Carma had "the courage of our convictions" in moving in first. High on Carma's priority list is a hotel which should do well because the site is near Calgary's airport.

A major shopping center was opened in August 1981 and a sports complex, professional building, and restaurant are planned. Completion of the center will take until 1989.

So far, Carma has taken its remarkable growth in stride, bubbling with the enthusiasm of a child with new toys. Whether the company's hallmark of folksiness, unique among Canadian developers, will continue as it gets even larger remains to be seen. But with its slogan of "involving you from the ground up," Carma seems committed to retaining its friendly informality.

Chapter Six

CADILLAC FAIRVIEW CORPORATION

"We are long-term people. We plant seeds for the future."

JOHN DANIELS
CHAIRMAN AND CHIEF EXECUTIVE OFFICER
CADILLAC FAIRVIEW

CADILLAC FAIRVIEW CORPORATION
Head Office: Toronto
OFFICE OF THE CHIEF EXECUTIVE OFFICER
Chairman and Chief Executive Officer: John Daniels
Vice-Chairman and President: (Plans to resign Fall 1981) Neil Wood
Vice-Chairman and Chief Financial Officer: Bernard Ghert

OPERATING DIVISIONS

Executive Vice-Presidents: James Bullock (*Shopping Centers*)
David Philpott (*Urban Development: mixed use complexes and office buildings*)
Michael Prentiss (*U.S. Southern Region*) (Based in Dallas)
Martin Seaton (*U.S. Western Region*) (Based in Los Angeles)
Gerald Sheff (*Land and Housing*)

OTHER SENIOR U.S. MANAGEMENT

Executive Vice-President, Cadillac Fairview Urban (Northeast) Inc.   Robert Blackman (Based in New York City) (Reports to President Neil Wood)

President, Cadillac Fairview Shopping Centers (U.S.) Ltd.   Peter Leibowits

COMMITTEES
(Cadillac also has two important committees)

Executive Committee: Chaired by A. E. Diamond (co-founder of company, retired from active operations), Daniels, Wood, Ghert, Leo Kolber (Vice-Chairman and Chairman of Investment Committee), and three members of Board of Directors—G. D. Shear (formerly with company), E. A. Goodman (company's Toronto-based lawyer), Richard Thomson (Chairman, Toronto Dominion Bank).

Investment Committee: Chaired by Leo Kolber (also President of Cemp Investments Ltd., the controlling shareholder in Cadillac Fairview), Daniels, Diamond, Ghert, Wood, Goodman, Shear, and Executive Vice-Presidents Gerald Sheff, Martin Seaton, and Michael Prentiss.

Some developers build only houses and apartments. Others build only office buildings and shopping centers. Still others construct new communities. A few specialize in major downtown developments.

Only Cadillac Fairview Corp. does everything, using each stage as a building block for the next, starting with housing and moving up the scale to development projects covering as many as 30 blocks. It is in the vanguard of Canadian developers moving into the U.S., where it expects to have nine-tenths of its activity within a few years.

It has been a pacesetter in multi-block, multi-use, megabuck downtown redevelopment projects like Toronto's three block long Eaton Centre, Los Angeles' 11 acre California Center, the 30 block Houston Center, and New York's 30 acre River Walk. Such ventures have become its trademark. Perhaps to a greater extent than any other firm, Cadillac Fairview has gambled that the far from first class districts, in which many of these projects are built, have excellent potential. So far it has been right.

Because of their magnitude, Cadillac Fairview will take in financial institutions as partners in joint ventures. This reflects the increasing trend among the developers to accomplish ambitious expansion programs.

The past year has been a bumpy one for Cadillac Fairview. It seems to have been undergoing considerable dissension in its executive suite. This has been manifested in the creation in December 1980 of a cumbersome three-man office of the chief executive, an abortive bid in May 1981 to merge with much smaller Bramalea Ltd., and the announcement in June 1981 by vice-chairman and president Neil Wood that he would resign in the fall of 1981. He is one of the three members of the office of the chief executive.

In addition, there appears to be a behind the scenes tug-of-war for control between management and the company's chief shareholders, the Montreal branch of the Bronfman family. The Bronfmans control Cadillac Fairview's pursestrings through their man-on-the-scene, Leo Kolber, head of Cadillac Fairview's investment committee. The committee decides when and where Cadillac Fairview will do projects.

Moreover, Cadillac Fairview suffered its worst year in its fiscal year ended February 28, 1981, since the merger of Cadillac and Fairview in 1974. The company's net income of $3.9 million was only slightly more than the $3.1 million Cadillac had on its own a decade ago in 1971. By contrast, the other publicly held large Canadian developers had record results last year.

Like most Canadian-based developers, Cadillac Fairview has become a North American firm, with 75 percent of its development

John H. Daniels, chairman and chief executive officer, Cadillac Fairview

program now in the United States. "In a few years, proportionately even more will be in the U.S.," says Cadillac chairman John Daniels. (In common usage, the firm is frequently called Cadillac.)

"Since Canada's population is only 10 percent that of the U.S., it follows that 90 percent of our effort should be in the U.S. We're not deserting Canada, but for our size company the opportunities are not as great as in the U.S."

Canada and the U.S. will remain Cadillac Fairview's two geographic areas of activity and the company will not move into South America or overseas in the "foreseeable future," Daniels says. "The opportunities are very substantial in the U.S. and to a more limited extent in Canada and we would be stretching our human resources if we were to go elsewhere."

A few years ago Cadillac did scout opportunities in Brazil, Hong Kong, and Europe but decided against going ahead because of the difficulties inherent in running a far-flung operation. It lacked sufficient personnel to send some abroad and it was reluctant to hire local people unfamiliar with Cadillac.

With $3 billion in assets, Cadillac Fairview is North America's largest publicly owned real estate developer and second in size to privately owned Olympia & York.

But it may not always remain publicly owned. The company is now controlled by Cemp Investments Ltd., the holding company for Charles, Edgar, Minda, and Phyllis Bronfman, whose first initials were used to form the name Cemp. Cadillac Fairview is Cemp's biggest investment outside Seagram Co., which was founded by Samuel Bronfman, the father of Charles, Edgar, Minda, and Phyllis.

Cemp does not disclose its financial results, but Cadillac accounts for somewhere between one-fourth and one-third of its holdings. Over the past year, Cemp has upped its investment in Cadillac Fairview from 35.7 percent to 40 percent of the stock.

"Privatizing has crossed our minds," says Leo Kolber, president of Cemp and watchdog of the Bronfman fortune. "It would provide more flexibility and Cemp would own more of a good thing."

Kolber says if and when Cadillac goes private would depend on the stock price. He says such action is not imminent but adds that its stock price high of around $50 ½ on the Toronto Stock Exchange this year was "cheap relative to the real estate value." Analysts say that Cadillac is undervalued and could be worth as much as $100.

Diversification operationally and geographically within its own industry means that Cadillac Fairview is not under the same pressure to diversify into other industries as one-note developers who can be knocked out by downturns in demand for office or residential space. Consequently, it has not moved into natural resources, as have Olympia & York, Carma, and Nu-West.

Neil R. Wood, vice-chairman and president, Cadillac Fairview

Bernard I. Ghert, vice-chairman and chief financial officer, Cadillac Fairview

"The cyclicality of real estate is not a sufficient reason for diversifying into other businesses," says Cadillac co-founder and current executive committee chairman, Allen Ephraim ("Eph") Diamond.

"Cadillac is not substantially involved in properties for sale, so it isn't as vulnerable to short-term cycles. We are more involved in the more stable area of rental property. Besides, it often takes the length of a downturn in the cycle to plan a project."

The beauty of being involved in rental properties like apartments, office buildings, and shopping centers is that inflation drives up their value and rents every year. A developer like Cadillac Fairview could decide to build nothing new one year and still see its asset base and cash flow increase 10 percent to 15 percent or more due to inflation.

"Our assets are now worth in excess of $3 billion at book value and rise by at least 10 percent a year because of inflation," Cadillac chairman John ("Jack") Daniels says. "If we were to stop doing any more projects, we would still have those assets. We can't be compared to homebuilders who, if they stop building or selling, are out of business.

"Unlike most businesses, developers in rental properties know on January 1 what their minimum cash flow will be because a certain proportion will be coming from leases and fixed rentals. Very few businesses have a similar stable and secure income."

Cadillac Fairview, however, is largely withdrawing from building single family housing both in Canada and the U.S., with the exception of Houston where it operates through an acquired company, General Homes Ltd., one of Texas' largest homebuilders. "Homebuilding is a very volatile business," Daniels says.

"It's better to use our human and financial resources in pursuing downtown mixed use developments, office buildings, shopping centers, land development, and high rise condominiums."

Coincident with its decision in August 1980 to de-emphasize its single family housing development, Cadillac Fairview took a write-down on $43 million of its land bank in Ontario. The $43 million represented less than 10 percent of the $455 million in land Cadillac held for development at that time.

Cadillac Fairview's problem was that it had small 70 acre to 150 acre subdivisions scattered around Toronto on which it was spending almost as much time as on bigger projects like the 8,000 acre Erin Mills new community west of the city. It came to the logical conclusion that it was more economical to devote staff and money to big projects rather than to small ones.

The problems in its land and housing operations caused Cadillac Fairview's net income, in its fiscal year ended February 28, 1981, to plunge to $3.9 million from $25.6 million a year earlier.

Comparatively speaking, Cadillac Fairview has not fared as well as some of its competitors in recent years. While Daon, the fastest growing public developer, recorded a seven-fold jump in net income from $7.7 million in 1976, Cadillac Fairview's net income has dropped from $15.2 million in its fiscal year ended February 28, 1977, to $3.9 million in its latest fiscal year.

Although these firms had the advantage of being headquartered in fast-growing western Canada, Cadillac had such heavy earners in its portfolio as Toronto's Eaton Centre and Vancouver's Pacific Centre.

"Cadillac Fairview waited too long, but unlike many companies, it admitted it had made a mistake and did something about it," says real estate analyst Harry Rannala. "I think highly of managements that are willing to admit their mistakes."

The $43 million write-down in the summer of 1980 was the first in a series of events that shook morale at Cadillac, already weakened by the departure of many of its senior staff in 1979 following the semi-retirement of co-founder and chairman Eph Diamond at the age of 58. In November 1980 the company reported a $2.4 million loss, a humiliation at a time when other developers were reporting significant profits.

While its main housing problems were in Canada, Cadillac Fairview was also having difficulties at its Indian Springs subdivision in Palm Beach due to slow production. These have now been ironed out under a new manager hired from U.S. Homes Inc., the largest U.S. homebuilder.

Then, in December 1980, there was a re-organization of the senior management. Chairman Jack Daniels, 53, was joined in a newly created office of the chief executive by president Neil Wood, 50, and executive vice-president and chief financial officer Bernard Ghert, 42. Wood and Ghert were also named vice-chairmen.

Daniels was given responsibility for U.S. operations, land, and housing and has ultimate accountability to the Board of Directors. Wood was given responsibility for shopping centers, urban development, and construction services. Ghert was put in charge of financial, administrative, and personnel functions.

It is not unusual for companies to split the chief executive responsibilities as they get larger and more complex. But Cadillac's action triggered a flurry of speculation on whether Daniels was on his way out. Chief among those making this prediction was real estate analyst Ira Gluskin, a long-time watcher of the industry and a much-quoted and listened-to voice of opinion.

Gluskin's comments caused an uproar. Cadillac Fairview's chief shareholder, Cemp, went so far as to deny publicly that Daniels was under the knife.

Several months later, with Daniels still at Cadillac Fairview, Gluskin said, "Perhaps I was a little hasty saying Daniels was on his way out." The first member of the triumvirate to leave is not Daniels but Wood, who will resign this Fall to go into business for himself. He will remain on Cadillac's Board.

Still, the question remains as to who is in charge at Cadillac Fairview. It would appear that Daniels still is, although Leo Kolber, the 51-year-old president of Cemp, is a powerful gray eminence.

It was he who suggested about two years ago that Cadillac Fairview establish an investment review committee, which he heads, when Cadillac's financial situation, due to its land operations problems, began to worsen. Kolber does not participate in day to day affairs at Cadillac, but insiders say he is a major policy-making force. "I keep in touch with the chief executive officer (Daniels), but he runs the company," Kolber says.

Kolber says that he spends a day and a half a week on Cadillac Fairview business and that the investment committee meets monthly. Its other members are Cadillac's senior officers and the company's executive vice-presidents.

"Real estate companies make investment decisions every day of the week and resources must be properly allocated between divisions and regions," Kolber says.

It was Kolber who moved Cemp into real estate in the first place. He became friendly with Charles Bronfman when they both attended McGill University and after graduating from law school was placed in charge of Cemp by Samuel Bronfman. That was in 1957 when Kolber was just 28 years old.

"I had specialized in real estate and it was my first love," Kolber recalls. "Therefore, I had a bias in that direction as well as an abiding respect for inflationary forces. It made sense to invest some of the Bronfman family's assets in real estate to weather the storm of inflation.

"It was logical to invest in real estate and especially in shopping centers because you get a percentage of the sales." (Shopping center rents are based both on square feet and sales volume.) In 1959, Cemp formed Fairview Corp. as its real estate arm.

"I remember telling Charles Bronfman that on every pair of 50 cent stockings sold, we would get six cents. It was simplistic, but a lot of good ideas are very simple."

Cadillac Fairview has no mandatory retirement age and Daniels is a dozen years younger than the usual retirement age. Still, some Cadillac observers wonder whether he will stay until he is 65. Daniels himself is somewhat noncommital. Over the past year, he has nearly doubled his share ownership in Cadillac Fairview from 7.7 percent to 14 percent. The shares would be worth more than $8 million, should Daniels decide to cash them in.

Daniels refuses to say whether he will stay at Cadillac Fairview until he is 65 but he does not seem in any hurry to leave either. "I plan to stay for the foreseeable future," he says. "It's a very demanding and taxing position as the company continues to grow, but it's also very exciting, challenging, and stimulating."

The office of the chief executive is not necessarily a permanent institution and whether it will be used by his successors will be up to them, Daniels says. "With the rapid growth of the company, it is humanly impossible for one individual to provide the leadership required of a chief executive officer," Daniels says.

"With our regions growing so fast, the re-organization permits me to provide the motivation, advice, assistance, stimulation, and exchange of ideas they need to function. But although my day to day activities and responsibilities have been removed and given to Bernie Ghert, I am still the chief executive officer and the final decisions are mine."

Daniels, Wood, and Ghert had no formal schedule for meetings. Connecting doors from Daniels' office to Wood's and Ghert's allowed constant informal conferences. "In this business decisions have to be made spontaneously," Daniels says. "There isn't the luxury of waiting for a formal meeting next week."

Daniels was born in Poland and emigrated to Canada with his family in 1939 just before the outbreak of World War II. An architect, he designed Erin Mills and Cadillac's former pink-hued headquarters with an atrium in north Toronto. Sporting a moustache (in his youth he wore a beard), Daniels is handsome in a riverboat gambler way. He lives in a Cadillac apartment complex in mid-Toronto. His 24-year-old son

Mark has just joined Cadillac Fairview, starting in the shopping center division.

"My first hobby is work and my second hobby is work," Daniels says. Adds Cadillac co-founder, Eph Diamond, with whom Daniels has a friendly bantering relationship: "And your third hobby is work." Daniels does play tennis and is active in Jewish community institutions.

He is described by associates and Cadillac directors as a tremendous entrepreneur. Says one director: "Daniels understands real estate transactions probably better than anybody on the continent except the Reichmanns of Olympia & York Developments Ltd. He has tremendous drive."

Colleagues like to joke that Daniels "would like to own the world and have an option on outer space." He is regarded as a person who loves to buy property and hates to sell weak projects because he feels a bad time does not last forever. This may be why Cadillac took so long to take the $43 million write-down on its Canadian land bank. A visionary, Daniels' aim has always been to broaden Cadillac's horizons and he was behind the company's push into the U.S.

More than any of the other nine major developers, Daniels is shielded from the press by his zealously protective public relations spokesman Bert Petlock, who has been with Cadillac for 20 years. Petlock sits in on interviews, often tape recording them and sometimes even answering for Daniels who tends to look out the window as he searches for replies. By contrast, Petlock did not sit in on interviews given by Cadillac president Neil Wood.

Although associates admire Daniels' entrepreneurial gifts, they say that he is not also a good administrator as was his predecessor, Eph Diamond. Diamond, according to Cadillac directors, believed in a consensus style of management.

The phrases commonly used to describe Diamond are "great administrator," "great negotiator," "very people oriented," "the type that didn't make enemies and everybody liked, no matter what happened at the bargaining table."

"He is conservative and yet venturesome and can project what will happen," says Joseph Berman, a co-founder with Diamond of Cadillac. Berman left Cadillac in 1976 to start his own business in energy conservation machinery.

Diamond is credited by executives from both Cadillac and Fairview, which merged in 1974, with smoothly pulling together the operations of the two different companies. (Fairview was primarily a commercial builder and Cadillac was a residential builder.)

"He had a lot of vision as to where the company was going and how it would get there," says Stanley Witkin, who went from Fairview to the new merged company to head its shopping center division. He left in 1979 to start his own shopping center consulting firm, Stan Witkin and

Associates, whose clients include Loblaws, Steinberg, and Cemp.

"The combination of Diamond's running the company and Daniels out looking for new opportunities was ideal," Witkin continues. "Diamond had the level-headedness and analytical ability to look beyond the glamor side of a deal and to see if it was in the best interest of the company."

Diamond, however, agreed to stay on for only five years as chairman of the new Cadillac Fairview and relinquished the position in 1979. He had had health problems and his family wanted him to slow down.

Besides remaining on Cadillac's Board and chairing its executive committee, Diamond is involved in private investments and community affairs. Unlike most of the developers, Diamond has always been a prominent leader in community activities. One former associate says that it was not unusual for Diamond to be out "seven nights a week." These days Diamond's interests include serving as vice-president of the Canadian Opera Company. He is a past president of the Toronto chapter of the Canadian Friends of Hebrew University in Israel.

Friends say Diamond is an inveterate raconteur, heavy cigar smoker, and self-admittedly bad golfer. One golfing companion says that Diamond, who like many golfers bets golf balls on the outcome of games, has "lost at least 1,000 golf balls in his lifetime." Jokes Daniels: "Eph plays golf like I play tennis."

Neil Wood came to the merged Cadillac Fairview from Fairview where he guided such major projects as the Toronto Dominion Centre, Vancouver's Pacific Centre, and Toronto's Eaton Centre. Wood is well over six feet tall and had to be given size 12 boots when touring the Eaton Centre while it was under construction. He was born in Winnipeg and holds an MBA from Harvard University. He owns 77,000 Cadillac Fairview shares — about one-fourth of what Daniels holds — and has an option on 75,000 more.

He first worked in the Toronto mortgage department of Great-West Life Assurance Co. While there, Wood worked on the financing for Cemp's first shopping center, Parkway Plaza in Toronto. Cemp had no staff then and Leo Kolber, who was executive vice-president, used outside architects, lawyers, and leasing agents.

Then, in December 1958, Cemp bought 18 properties — vacant land and shopping centers — from a troubled developer, Principal Investments Ltd., which later went out of business. Cemp formed a subsidiary, Fairview Corp., in 1959 to handle the real estate side.

Kolber realized that Cemp now needed its own staff. He turned to the then 27-year-old Wood, who had just accepted a job as assistant general manager at Don Mills Development Ltd. owned by tycoon E.P. Taylor. The firm had developed the Toronto suburb of Don Mills.

Wood decided "in the long run my future would be better at

Cemp," obtained a release from Don Mills Development, and became manager of Cemp Investments in Ontario and subsequently president of Fairview. In an ironic twist of fate, Fairview and Cadillac later jointly acquired Don Mills Development.

Wood golfs and wind surfs, water skis, snorkels, and scuba dives at the family cottage on Lake Muskoka, Ontario. A Cadillac Fairview director says Wood is "very knowledgeable, extremely thorough, and very detail oriented, although a little stubborn about his ideas."

He chooses his words carefully and is regarded as a first class administrator. "He can do letters, reports, and summaries better than anybody I've ever met," Witkin says.

Unlike Diamond, however, Wood is not an outgoing person and is little known even by many fellow executives. His critics say that he tends to choose solutions with the least possible risk and is too conservative.

Bernard Ghert, the third member of the office of the chief executive, is also an alumnus of Fairview, where he was vice-president, finance. He is described by insiders as "very brilliant with an incredible knowledge of financing and money markets." He holds degrees in mathematics, physics, and business administration. When Cadillac and Fairview merged in 1974, Ghert became executive vice-president and chief financial officer.

The creation of the office of the chief executive would appear to have drawn on the strengths of Daniels, Wood, and Ghert, with each one's weaknesses being balanced out by the others' abilities in those areas. Daniels' skill at ferreting out new opportunities is well suited to Cadillac's pursuit of growth in the U.S. Wood's experience in developing Toronto's Eaton Centre, Vancouver's Pacific Centre, and other shopping centers makes him a natural to head the company's shopping center and urban development group. And Ghert's skill in financing and administration makes him well suited to be in charge of financial, administrative, and personnel functions. Conversely, the differences in the three men's personalities may have led to a clash and sparked Wood's resignation.

The big question occupying the minds of possible heir apparents and industry observers is who will eventually succeed Daniels. Whether it will be an insider or an outsider is uncertain.

It would seem that Cadillac Fairview, originally two separate companies, remains divided between the Cadillac camp (Daniels and the semi-retired Diamond) and the Fairview side (Wood, Ghert, and Leo Kolber). Tilting the odds in favor of the Fairview team is its having been started by the Bronfman-owned Cemp Investments, which Kolber runs. Moreover, Leo Kolber controls Cadillac Fairview's purse-strings as head of its investment committee.

The apparent power struggle between the two groups surfaced in the spring of 1981 when Daniels, accompanied by Diamond, approached Bramalea Ltd. about a possible merger of the two firms. During the year before the negotiations, Daniels had doubled his shareholdings in Cadillac Fairview to 14 percent.

If the two Toronto-based developers had merged, they would have had combined assets of $4 billion to become the world's largest developer, surpassing privately owned Olympia & York.

After three weeks of negotiations, the talks fell through. The main stumbling block was over how the managements of the two companies would be integrated. Bramalea has very aggressive management and a clash with Cadillac Fairview executives would have been likely.

But it is clear that the new head of Cadillac will reflect its present move to a more institutionalized, financially oriented, return on investment approach than the entrepreneurial flair that built up the company. It is a natural evolution because Cadillac has built up a portfolio of some of the finest properties in North America and administering these holdings is equally important to selecting suitable new projects.

Cadillac Fairview is one of the oldest of Canada's top ten developers. It was started in 1953 by Montreal-born Diamond, a mechanical engineering graduate from Queen's University and the son of a shoemaker, Joseph Berman, an engineering and physics graduate from the University of Toronto, and Jack Kamin, owner of a Toronto lighting fixture distributor, Camesco Lighting.

Diamond and Berman met during World War II when both were posted in the Navy's radar division at St. John's, Newfoundland. After the war, Diamond joined Principal Investments Ltd. as a construction project manager. Formed in 1936, Principal was a pioneer developer of shopping centers in Canada.

Diamond bought lighting fixtures for Principal's shopping centers from Kamin, with whom Berman also had business connections. The three men decided to form a construction business and pooled $100,000, most of it borrowed from banks, to start their firm under the name of Cadillac Development Corp.

Choosing a name had been difficult. "We had dinner at the Town Tavern (a popular restaurant in downtown Toronto) and argued, without success, about a name," Berman says. "When we went outside, Eph (Diamond) got into his car — a Cadillac. We all decided that would be a good name.

"It got us into a fight, though, with General Motors, producer of the Cadillac car. We said the name was in the public domain because it had belonged to an Indian tribe. Subsequently, GM got a law passed, prohibiting the use by anybody else of the Cadillac name."

Cadillac, now headquartered in a 35-floor office tower at the Eaton Centre in downtown Toronto, started out in offices in the city's garment district at Spadina Avenue and Richmond Street. At first, there were only a secretary and a part-time bookkeeper. Later, the firm moved to bigger and bigger offices, located farther and farther north, winding up in five floor quarters in northeast Toronto until its move this year to the Eaton Centre.

The firm started out building houses, which Berman supervised, and apartments, which were Diamond's responsibility. Kamin was a silent partner.

Although the firm was based in Toronto, one of its first housing projects was 60 miles west in Guelph, Ontario, because no serviced lots were available in Toronto. Cadillac was one of the first developers to build high rise apartments. There was a big need for such housing in the 1950s in the wake of the post war baby boom. By the end of the 1960s, Cadillac had built 14,000 apartment units, all in Toronto, except for two buildings in Ottawa and one in Hamilton, Ontario.

Cadillac revolutionized the style of apartment buildings, providing innovative items that are now taken for granted, such as lobbies, carpeted corridors, health club facilities, individually controlled heating and air conditioning, underground parking, mechanical compaction of refuse to eliminate incinerators, and grounds landscaped with trees and fountains. Other innovations included fireplaces, two-level living rooms, two-car garages, and circular staircases in townhouses it built.

"Our philosophy is that whatever we do, we do for the long term," Diamond says. "We are very aware of the need for lasting, long-term values. It makes very good business sense, too. Because the buildings appreciate in value, we can charge higher rents and turnover is lower than average. As a result, we have sold no apartment buildings since 1964."

The company also got a substantial boost from the sale of a piece of property in north Toronto. That property became part of the site of the Yorkdale Shopping Centre. "We got an unsolicited offer from a mysterious buyer for the land at a much higher price than we had expected," Diamond's co-founder, Joseph Berman, recalls. "The buyer turned out to be the T. Eaton Co. and it gave us a $1 million cheque for the land."

In 1959 Jack Kamin pulled out of Cadillac and sold his interest to Jack Daniels. Daniels had been a co-developer on some apartment buildings with Cadillac and had done architectural work for the firm. At the same time, Gerald Shear, who worked at Cadillac's accounting firm, was given a participatory interest and joined Cadillac as its financial and administrative manager. Shear was executive vice-president until last year of Cadillac Fairview's corporate development group, which seeks out new opportunities, especially in the U.S.

Over the years Cadillac and Fairview Corp. occasionally came in touch when Cadillac built Fairview shopping centers. Between 1959 and 1961, Cemp had a one-third interest in Cadillac but later sold it back.

In 1968 they joined forces to purchase Canadian Equity and Development Co., a public company controlled by E. P. Taylor. Its largest holding was Don Mills Developments Ltd., which had developed Don Mills. It had also built a few shopping centers in Toronto and Hamilton. But its biggest attraction was its 8,000 acre Erin Mills land bank just west of Toronto.

Taylor wanted to sell the company because he was liquidating his Canadian holdings in preparation for moving to the Bahamas. Also, although the land had been acquired in 1954, Erin Mills was going nowhere because no municipal services had been installed. The project's master plan had not yet been approved by the Town of Mississauga, which had jurisdictional authority.

Nevertheless, Cadillac was interested in Erin Mills because it provided a huge area in which to build houses. Fairview was interested because the community would need shopping centers. "It was the opportunity of a lifetime, with a projected population of 170,000 and the need to provide schools, industry, parks, recreation, and churches," Diamond says.

However, as both Cadillac and Fairview began to expand their areas of operation, each began encroaching into the other's sphere of business. This began to create conflicts over the development of Erin Mills.

There were also problems of what to do when opportunities arose for Canadian Equity and Development Corp. "There were potential conflicts of interest over whether such opportunities should go to Cadillac or Fairview," Neil Wood recalls.

But, besides duplicating some areas, the companies also complemented each other's skills. "Merging allowed doing projects of a size that we could not do separately," Kolber says. (By contrast, Olympia & York has managed to enlarge on its own without mergers.)

In May 1974 Cadillac and Fairview resolved this problem by merging and folding Canadian Equity and Development into the amalgamated company. At the time, Fairview was 40 percent larger than Cadillac in terms of net worth and so got 1.4 shares for every one given Cadillac. Fairview wound up with 13 million shares in the new company and Cadillac got nine million.

A coin toss, flipped by Diamond and called by Wood, who lost the call, resulted in Cadillac preceding Fairview in the new company's name. The merged company had combined assets of $754.7 million (today, its assets are more than $3 billion).

There was never any question, however, over who would be chairman. The position went to Diamond. "He did an amazing job of tying all the facets together and brought a sense of order and knowledge of

Toronto-Dominion Centre, Toronto

reporting and financial procedures," says Stanley Witkin.

Diamond says that integrating the company took "many months," Kolber says "two years," and Daniels "many years." Making the task easier was the need of Bramalea Ltd. at that time for a mass infusion of senior executives. So while Bramalea (see Chapter 9) was thrilled at Diamond's generosity in letting Bramalea hire away key staff, their action reduced Diamond's problem of redundancy in top management at Cadillac Fairview.

The merger created a company that, alone among the developers, did everything—housing, offices, shopping centers, redevelopment, and new communities. But it also meant that the firm had to be rigidly structured to function. This did not appeal to Berman, who was then 54.

"The company was getting so large that it had to move into a managerial mode and I had to decide whether I wanted to stay on as a manager, with a formal structure and organization and committees, or remain an entrepreneur," Berman says. He decided to leave, although he still owns five percent of the company.

Berman formed Prime Energy Systems, which deals in systems for the recovery of heat and sewage treatment for school boards, hospitals, hotels, factories, and office buildings. "I selected energy conservation rather than exploration because I was more familiar with it and didn't want to spend big bucks on exploration," he says. Not that Berman is poorly off. He lives in one of Toronto's most exclusive districts and in addition to his energy conservation business, he has property interests in Arizona and Florida.

Over the years, Cadillac Fairview has changed from being a Toronto home and apartment builder to the developer most identified with reshaping huge sections of cities across North America. Cadillac Fairview now has regional offices in the U.S. in Los Angeles, Dallas, and New York. It is expanding activity in the mideast and southeast, where it will eventually open offices, too.

In 1975 Cadillac Fairview entered the U.S., during the worst days of the slump in the real estate market. Over-enthusiasm had created a serious over-supply and this, in turn, shoved many U.S. developers into bankruptcy.

While most businesses cut back in a slowdown, such times often are the busiest for healthy developers who can buy properties and land at bargain prices from less fortunate developers. "There are few fields of human endeavor that start without real estate and an interim period of slackness isn't significant in our business," Diamond says.

Adds Daniels: "Shelter is a basic human need like food. You can't let your long range planning be affected by short-term cycles."

Diamond and Daniels say that Cadillac Fairview has encountered no anti-Canadianism as it expands across the U.S. "When we announced plans a few years ago to build an office building (444 Market Street) in San Francisco, the Mayor declared a Cadillac Fairview day in our honor," Diamond recalls.

Daniels says this warm reception continues. "Canadians are highly regarded and the Americans are very cooperative and friendly."

The roots of this rebuilding of North America can be traced back to Toronto, Cadillac's home base in the 1960s. Little of what is now the financial center of the city at King and Bay Streets, which in turn is the investment capital of Canada, was there then. The intersection is known as the MINT for the four banks that have always been there — Bank of Montreal, Canadian Imperial Bank of Commerce, Bank of Nova Scotia, and the Toronto Dominion Bank. But most of the district was rundown small office buildings.

In the early 1960s Cemp, which had just established Fairview Corp. as its real estate arm, joined forces with the Toronto Dominion Bank with the goal of building a Toronto version of Montreal's newly opened Place Ville Marie office and retail complex.

The TD, Canada's fifth largest bank, was interested because it needed new head office space and wanted to establish a higher profile. The Bank was then relatively small, with only $2.3 billion in assets in 1962, the year the Centre was launched. It now has assets of $33.8 billion.

For its part, Cemp, newly entered into real estate, wanted major projects. "I called Eph Diamond and asked him what he thought would be the best location and he said King and Bay Streets, " Kolber recalls. "William Zeckendorf (developer of Place Ville Marie and co-founder of Trizec Corp.) had been in a month earlier to see Allen Lambert (then chairman of the Toronto Dominion Bank) but his idea, which covered much of downtown Toronto, was too grandiose to contemplate."

Cemp and the Bank came up with their own bold proposal — they would build Toronto's and Canada's largest office complex. The initial concept was to build a 600,000 square foot building, but it soon quintupled in size.

At 3.3 million square feet, the complex, called the Toronto Dominion Centre, is just slightly larger than the three million square foot Place Ville Marie. (After Cadillac and Fairview merged in 1974, the TD Centre came under the management of the amalgamated company.)

Although the project was an enormous gamble, it should be kept in mind that costs were much lower then. "Money was exceptionally cheap — some of the bonds were only at $4\frac{5}{8}$ percent interest," Kolber recalls. "The cost of the land was low, too — about $15 per square foot. Construction costs were reasonable, also, and the rate of inflation was only two or three percent."

The TD Centre was a trend setter in every way, pioneering what is today taken for granted in skyscrapers. It was not only Canada's largest office complex, but also four times bigger than any other Toronto office building. The largest of the complex's three towers — the TD Tower — was the tallest building in Canada at 55 floors. It touched off a battle between the major banks as to which would have the highest tower. That pinnacle is now held by the Bank of Montreal, Canada's third largest bank. Its First Canadian Place in Toronto, built by Olympia & York, has 72 floors. There were other firsts:

• The TD Centre spotlighted the close ties between the banks and developers and launched the joint venture agreements between the two that have characterized redevelopment across Canada.

• It was the first project with an underground shopping concourse. Over the years, this concourse has been tied, through underground walkways, to office towers in a five block stretch of Toronto running up to the City Hall.

- It was the first to be designed by an internationally renowned architect, Mies Van der Rohe, who brought the streamlined glass "box" tower to the American landscape. It was the first in Toronto to have tinted glass. The three towers have tinted black glass. By contrast, First Canadian Place, across the street to the north, is white marble, Commerce Court (head office of the Canadian Imperial Bank of Commerce) across the street to the east is silver-tinted, and the Royal Bank Plaza, across the street to the south, is tinted gold. The Centre bears a strong resemblance to the Seagram Building in New York, which Van der Rohe had previously designed for the Bronfmans.
- It was the first in Toronto to have high speed elevators.
- It was the first to have vast 25,000 to 30,000 square foot floors, two to three times bigger than in existing buildings. This enabled companies to locate on fewer floors.

Because of all these design firsts, the TD Centre also had another breathtaking first—the first office rents in Toronto to top $6 per square foot. The TD Centre asked for rents of up to $6.75 per gross square foot.

Since rents in the Centre are now $25 to $30 per gross square foot, tenants who signed the 20 year fixed rent leases, offered when the towers opened, got a bargain. (The fixed rent was on space alone; there were escalating clauses for taxes and operating costs.)

The Bronfmans and the TD took an enormous gamble in building the complex since they had no tenants lined up and the record high rents were not the greatest way to attract occupants.

"Of the two towers built first, the Toronto Dominion (finished in 1967) had 1³⁄₄ million square feet, of which the Bank was to take 200,000 square feet, and the rest had no pre-signed tenants." Says Gordon Gray, chairman of A.E. LePage Ltd., "It was a really gutsy move."

Back in 1964 when he was 35 years old, Gray was executive vice president of LePage and vice-president and director of Toronto Dominion Centre Ltd. His job was to assemble the six acres of land and lease the Centre.

It was not an easy task. There were 37 different pieces of property to be acquired. Code names were used to prevent speculators from guessing what was happening. Leo Kolber bought one building from its New York owner while he was in Manhattan on Seagram business for Cemp Investments.

Leasing was also difficult. There were nearly 1.5 million unoccupied square feet to lease in the TD Tower and no tenants had signed for the second tower, the one million square foot Royal Trust building (opened in 1969). A third tower, the Commercial Union, opened in 1974.

"It took five years to lease the Toronto Dominion and Royal Trust Towers," Gray recalls. "It was very difficult because the rents were the highest ever and it was an enormous amount of space. We had to take over a lot of leases and acquire a lot of properties of incoming tenants. The key element of success was that the then TD chairman, Allen Lambert, and Fairview president, Leo Kolber, had total authority and, therefore, could make very fast decisions."

The task became easier, though, since the first tenants signed up by Gray included such blue chip firms as Inco Ltd., Abitibi-Price Inc., McCarthy & McCarthy (one of Canada's leading law firms), IBM Canada Ltd., Royal Trust, Clarkson, Gordon (a leading chartered accountant firm), and Wood Gundy (a top management consultant).

The impact of the TD Centre on Toronto, Cadillac Fairview, and A.E. LePage was immense. For the city, it sparked the revitalization of downtown Toronto and boosted the tax base enormously. In quick succession, Canada's other major banks quickly erected monuments north, south, and east of the Centre. Because of its track record in renting the Centre, LePage became the agent for most of the other bank buildings and now is the dominant office rental agent in Toronto. And for Cadillac Fairview, the Centre was the kickoff for a whole new area of company business — downtown redevelopment, which is now its pre-eminent thrust.

It also marked the beginning of a partnership between Fairview, at first, and later the merged Cadillac Fairview, and the Toronto Dominion Bank. The Toronto Dominion is one of Cadillac's leading lenders and TD chairman Richard Thomson sits on Cadillac's Board of Directors. The only Cadillac-related representative on the Bank's Board is Cemp's president Leo Kolber.

The close tie between the Bank and Cemp was spotlighted recently when Cemp bought a five percent interest in Royal Trustco from the Bank. It had acquired the shares in the summer of 1980 during a battle for control of Royal Trustco by Campeau, another of Canada's large developers.

The three companies were also partners, along with the T. Eaton Co., Canada's largest privately owned department store, in two other landmark projects—Vancouver's Pacific Centre (opened in phases, starting in 1971) and Toronto's Eaton Centre (opened in phases, starting in 1977).

Both projects illustrate the length of time such undertakings take to get going. Each stretched out to nearly a quarter century of consideration and planning.

The Pacific Centre dates back to the 1940s, when Eaton's bought three square blocks in downtown Vancouver where the Pacific Centre, Eaton's store, and Robson Square, a government and court complex, are now located. At the time, the original Hotel Vancouver was a part of what is now the Pacific Centre.

The hotel had been closed during World War II and afterward

became the home of veterans' families. A new Hotel Vancouver was erected two blocks west.

Eaton's land purchases alarmed Spencer's, a long-established family-owned Vancouver department store firm, which feared that Eaton's would move into British Columbia and wipe Spencer's out. It decided to sell its downtown Vancouver store to Eaton's rather than face the competition.

The store was located, however, in a rundown section of Vancouver and, as a result, Eaton's fared poorly. "We weren't even third in market share and the poor image of the downtown store kept people from going to our suburban stores," says Michael Spohn, vice-president, T. Eaton Realty Co., in charge of negotiations.

During this time, Fairview (Cadillac and Fairview had not yet merged) approached Eaton's to redevelop the property it had held since the 1940s. The city was also anxious to redevelop the decaying area. Eaton's at first rejected Fairview's proposal because it disliked both the design and the financial terms. "The proposal offered too little money for the property and asked for too high a rent," Spohn says.

Another obstacle was presented by one of the occupants of the land that would be redeveloped. Originally, it was planned to be a three-way project between Eaton's, Fairview, and the Bank of Montreal, which was a major landholder in the area.

The Bank argued that the land sloped on the location proposed for its new office and this would affect the layout of its banking floor. Eventually, it agreed to withdraw if a replacement partner could be found and Fairview brought in the Toronto Dominion Bank. Eaton's, the TD, and the developer each own one-third.

The City of Vancouver assembled the land, saving the developers the cost and time of this procedure.

The Pacific Centre has turned out to be a major money-maker. "It changed our image from an old stodgy look to a modern, up-to-date fashion-oriented slant," says Fredrik Eaton, president of the department store company. "Also, it had a halo effect because that's what people thought of Eaton's, even if they went to our suburban stores."

It was a logical progression for the trio of Eaton's, Fairview, and the Toronto Dominion from the Pacific Centre to Toronto's Eaton Centre. This Centre has two office towers, one with Eaton's headquarters and the other housing Cadillac Fairview's, and three levels of shopping — three blocks long — in a galleria. A major new Eaton's department store is located at one end of the Centre, and an overhead walkway at the other leads into Simpsons' main Toronto store. (Simpsons is another major Canadian department store chain.)

The Eaton Centre has 301 stores, 62 restaurants, and 21 mini-cinemas. At a total of 2.6 million square feet, it is the world's largest retail-office complex. Its sales per square foot range from $300 to

$2,000, making it Canada's most successful shopping center.

About one million people (Metropolitan Toronto had a 1979 assessed population of 2,131,000) visit the Centre weekly and they spend $500 million annually there, causing one of its architects, Eberhard Zeidler of Zeidler Partnership of Toronto, to accurately tag it as a "giant cash register." About $2 million is collected monthly in rents, based on a percentage of sales sliding from five percent (for big volume) to 15 percent (on small volume).

Like the Toronto Dominion Centre and Pacific Centre, The Eaton Centre revitalized a rundown area of the city, bringing shoppers to a section of Toronto where few would venture before because of the crumbling buildings and wandering derelicts.

For Eaton's, which has its flagship store in the Centre, it has been a bonanza. The store was profitable in its first year, although it usually takes three years for a store to break even. Retail investment analysts calculate that this one store provides 10 percent of the estimated $1.5 billion annual sales of the national 111 store chain.

For Cadillac Fairview (merged while the Centre was under construction), it has provided a showpiece and selling point in its successful bids to redevelop the Houston Center, River Walk in New York, and the California Center in Los Angeles. With 1.5 million square retail feet, the Centre was nearly twice as large as Cadillac's previously largest shopping center.

The Eaton Centre had its share of controversy in its planning stages as protesters opposed original plans to get rid of such Toronto landmarks as the municipal courthouse, formerly the City Hall, and a church, Holy Trinity.

The concept of the Eaton Centre predated its May 1974 construction start by 20 years. From the 1950s on, Eaton's deliberated about what it should do with its downtown Queen Street store, which had been built in 1889.

Eaton's had hoped its showplace College Street store, located about a 20 minute walk north and opened in 1930 during the Depression, would shift shoppers' focus from the Queen Street store. These hopes never materialized. Although the College Street store was much more beautiful, with marble in much of the interior and a concert hall, shoppers persisted in going downtown. They were accustomed to dashing back and forth between Simpsons and Eaton's, which faced each other on Queen Street, as is done between the friendly rivals Macy's and Gimbels in New York City. The traffic was so heavy that a police officer had to handle the pedestrian and vehicle flow. Alan Burton, head of Simpsons at that time, used to call the crossway the "miracle of Queen Street."

In addition, when the Toronto subway opened in 1954, it brought more people downtown. And finally, there were more workers in office buildings around Eaton's Queen Street store than in the vicinity of the College Street store. Eaton's had hoped Simpsons would also move to College Street, but Simpsons stayed put on Queen Street.

During the early 1960s, Eaton's devised and then dropped several plans. It worked with Webb & Knapp Canada and the internationally famous architect, I.M. Pei, who had designed Place Ville Marie. Their plans included moving Eaton's several blocks south to King and Yonge Streets, nearer Toronto's financial hub.

Webb & Knapp and Eaton's, however, drifted apart as Webb & Knapp suffered financial problems in the 1960s (see Chapter 3). Next, Eaton's turned to Canadian Equity & Development Co., then owned by E.P. Taylor. Its plans did not satisfy Eaton's either.

In 1964 Eaton's hired David Owens, formerly president of Webb & Knapp Canada, and put him in charge of the Eaton Centre project. His plans called for Eaton's to expand west by buying and tearing down the old City Hall since the new City Hall had just opened. Because Eaton's wanted to continue operating during construction, his strategy was to tear down the old City Hall and build half of the new store there. When it was finished, Eaton's would move into it while the second phase was completed on the old site. The two halves would then be joined. But the plan to tear down the old City Hall met with stiff opposition from Torontonians and Eaton's withdrew its plan after a two year fight.

During this period, Eaton's, then under the leadership of John David Eaton, father of the present president, Fredrik, and of chairman John Craig Eaton, began yet another re-assessment of Eaton's future in downtown Toronto.

The study was completed in April 1969 and distributed to senior management in the "blue book," so-called because of its blue covers. The formal title was "Eaton's Future In Downtown Toronto." It listed land held in the city by the company, market conditions, and criteria for store location, such as being on the subway line.

Ten options were laid out, ranging from maintaining the status quo to renovating the existing Queen Street store or opening a new 750,000 square foot store downtown. The solution finally selected was alternate 6: relocate the downtown store to Yonge and Dundas Streets. It would be one million square feet and take three years to build.

The original target date was 1974, but approval delays resulted in its taking until 1977. Eaton's move to Dundas Street was crucial for the success of the Centre since it would act as a magnet at one end, with Simpsons, although still on Queen Street and not part of the Centre, acting as a magnet on the other end. Specialty shops located in a galleria between the two and a walkway between the Centre and Simpsons completed the attraction.

Eaton's had been approached by Olympia & York and also by Campeau but decided on Fairview (in the days before Cadillac and

The Eaton Centre, Toronto

Fairview merged) because they had worked together on the Pacific Centre. "Cadillac Fairview executives are very smart, hard-working, tough-minded negotiators and first class able businessmen," says Eaton's president, Fredrik Eaton. He adds with a sweet smile: "But we're tough, too."

Eaton's assessment is echoed by Donald Maclellan, now manager, company property management, at Eaton's. He was secretary of the eight-person committee Eaton's had supervising the project. "Cadillac Fairview people are very skilled and disciplined. Their word is their bond. If we agreed to something in 1974 and there was no documentation of it by 1976, they accepted what we said and didn't argue that we had bad memories."

Fairview brought the Toronto Dominion Bank in as a partner. It was always intended that the developer would be the major partner. It has 60 percent and Eaton's and the Bank each have 20 percent. It was named after Eaton's, however, because Eaton's originated the idea and is the main retailer in the development.

It was decided that the Centre should be ultra-modern in design, and so the elevator shafts, pipes, and ducts were all left exposed. Two innovative Toronto architects — Bregman & Hamann and Zeidler Partnership — were used. There was also considerable input from Phyllis Bronfman, an architect who had been the project manager on the family's Seagram Building in New York.

Bregman & Hamann are also the principal architects for Olympia & York. (They split the work. Sidney Bregman deals with Cadillac and George Hamann with Olympia & York.)

Their link with Cadillac dates back to the early 1950s when A.E. Diamond was the construction supervisor on the Lawrence Plaza in north Toronto. Bregman & Hamann designed one of the stores. The two architects and Diamond later worked in tandem on several other Toronto shopping centers and as Cadillac started on office buildings, Bregman & Hamann went along as the designer.

During the three-year construction period of the Centre, morale was maintained by mini-Olympics between the workers, a race to eat a 110 foot long sandwich, and a pre-season football toss between the Toronto Argonauts and the Hamilton Tiger Cats.

On a more serious note, adjustments and compromises were being made on the design. For example, originally heating and air conditioning equipment was to be lodged on the roof at the north end of the Centre on the rotunda outside the Eaton's store, but Eaton's agreed to have the system hidden in a corner of its store.

Another problem revolved around Holy Trinity Church. Eaton's initial plan was to tear it down, but like the old City Hall, the church became an emotional issue. Even E.L. ("Hank") Hankissen, Eaton's architect, then in his 50s, was scolded by his mother. "Your father and I were married there, so don't you dare tear down the church," she told her son. Mrs. Hankissen won out. Eaton's changed its mind and built its store in an L-shape around the church.

The planning and development of the Centre occurred under three different mayors and city councils. "The councils became increasingly more anti-development and if the project hadn't been done when it was, it would never have been approved," says Stan Witkin, who was in charge of Fairview's shopping center development.

"It was very difficult at the end. We had to make compromises about the height of buildings, the relationship of sunlight to the structure, pedestrian traffic, and the relationship between the Centre and the nearby old City Hall."

The delays in construction had a powerful impact on the rents charged tenants. "Our initial projections were that $12 per square foot, including the first year of taxes, would be needed, which was regarded as very high," Witkin says. "But the rent actually turned out to range from $15 to $70 per square foot, with an average of $25, and tenants had to pay taxes over and above."

For Cadillac Fairview the Eaton Centre has come to be a trump card in its bids to redevelop cities across the U.S. The company could say that it had experience in developing downtown projects which could handle large crowds at one time, that it knew what type of tenant mix would work (lots of restaurants and fashion stores), and that the Centre was a "people place," with entertainment facilities, in the heart of the city.

These arguments have won Cadillac contracts to redevelop River Walk, 30 acres along the East River in New York, 30 blocks in Houston, sections of downtown Cincinnati, Hartford, Philadelphia, and 11 acres in Los Angeles.

"Sometimes it is just as time consuming to do something small as it is to do something large," says Neil Wood. "A firm can grow more rapidly through getting involved in large projects. Also, large projects can be more prominent and attractive and, therefore, more valuable."

Although the districts in which Cadillac undertakes redevelopment projects are rundown, Wood says the company will go ahead if the community is showing growth and vigor. "The location doesn't have to be excellent now, but it should have the potential of being a superior area in a healthy and growing market."

The $1 billion Los Angeles project, called California Center, epitomizes the fierce competitiveness among Canadians, as well as Americans, for such U.S. projects, the concessions developers must make to win the deals, and the importance of joint ventures with local developers possessing on-the-scene knowledge.

The California Center will contain 900 housing units, a 400 room hotel, about 90 shops and restaurants, three office towers (two with 38 floors and one with 52 floors), and a 6.2 acre park running throughout the complex on three levels and containing pools, fountains, and streams. An area will be set aside for performing artists.

The project, covering five blocks, is the capstone of a 25 year, 30 block redevelopment of central Los Angeles. The area used to be a prestigious residential area, but like Toronto's Yorkville, it had degenerated into a shabby district of rooming houses. (Yorkville has been upgraded into a fashionable boutique shopping, restaurant, and residential area.)

In July 1980 Cadillac Fairview defeated four other proposals, including a joint one by Canadian rivals, Olympia & York and Trizec. It had to build a $16 million modern art museum, at its own cost, and give it to the city, which owned the land, as part of the terms of the deal. The project was also to be a "people place" with six acres of park land.

No developer would do all these things if it were not certain of making a profit from the other part of the project. Cadillac saw its profits coming from the office towers at California Center. At first it wanted four office towers, but agreed to three when the designers, Arthur Erickson Architects of Vancouver, said too much space would be used.

"John Daniels stressed that the office buildings were the economic basis for the project from which Cadillac would get the economic return to give the amenities to the City," says Bing Thom, Erickson's partner who headed the firm's design team.

"Daniels wanted to make sure that the office buildings would be simple, functional, and efficient. As a result, we are introducing a new system of daylighting which will save two million kilowatts of artificial lighting a year, special glass that will reduce the heating and air conditioning costs, and energy storage tanks. The tanks will store excess heat in the daytime and release it in the evening to warm the buildings. The various heat recovery systems should reduce fuel consumption by 400,000 gallons per year. Most of the housing faces southeast to make maximum use of solar energy." In total, energy consumption at California Center is anticipated to be 40 percent less than that allowed under California's energy code.

California Center also illustrates the battery of firms that join forces on projects of this magnitude. All had important local ties that probably also helped in their victory.

Cadillac Fairview is a 50 percent partner with two prominent California firms. Cadillac Fairview's already strong California presence probably helped, too. It owned four industrial parks, covering 413 acres, in Los Angeles, was building a prestige office building (444 Market Street) in San Francisco, and was a large homebuilder in the state.

Neither Olympia & York nor Trizec had similar roots in the state, although Trizec had just purchased a large California shopping center developer, Ernest W. Hahn Inc.

Cadillac's partners in the especially formed Bunker Hill Associates are Goldrich, Kest & Associates and Shapell Industries, who together were already building a $100 million condominium development in the area. The trio was backed up by a team of blue chip consultants in construction, market analysis, seismic evaluations of potential earthquake damage, energy conservation, traffic engineering, landscaping, and food retailing.

Fifty percent of the marks for the competition, being handled by the Los Angeles Community Redevelopment Agency, was based on design. The unprepossessing but incisive 40-year-old Thom, who looks like a university student, says that Erickson's goal was to design the project in themes "so it would have an identity. We wanted the museum, retail, housing, and office areas to be integrated," he says. "Therefore, the stores are art-related, to tie in with the museum, and the restaurants were placed in the park setting as outdoor cafés."

In February 1980, Cadillac and its competitors each made three hour presentations to the Community Redevelopment Agency. Then they had to wait a nail-biting five months until the Agency decided, giving Cadillac high praise: "It has a demonstrated record of taking risks, creating markets, and changing longstanding practices, all ultimately to the benefit of the firm and the city where it is developing.

"Only a developer with large resources could handle this type of equity commitment (paying for the museum and open air entertainment space) to set the tone, create the image and the market, and have the staying power to wait for development of subsequent, more profitable phases to reap the benefits of the initial investment. Bunker Hill Associates, with its known resources and from its past record of similar equity investments, is just such a rare developer."

Massive downtown redevelopment projects reflect Cadillac's penchant for doing things in a big way. It is also developing new communities in both Canada and the U.S.

Erin Mills, an 8,000 acre project near Toronto, dates back nearly 30 years to 1954. Smithville, a 2,000 acre site, has just begun construction. It is located near Atlantic City and the company hopes that it will be part of the boom surrounding the casino industry's entry into Atlantic City.

Erin Mills shows how a big developer can afford the long time it takes to complete a new community. The largest private land assembly of its kind in Canada, it is not expected to be completed until early in the next century and will eventually house 170,000 people. About 24,000 people now live there.

The project was started by E.P. Taylor's Don Mills Development Ltd. in 1954 as the firm neared completion of the Toronto suburb of Don Mills. Located just west of Toronto and named after the nearby community of Erindale and Don Mills, Erin Mills is five times as large as Don Mills.

The land was assembled at $1,000 an acre, three times the asking price of the time. Twenty years later, the owner of the first farm purchased, who had kept six acres, turned down an offer of $120,000 an acre for the land.

No development, however, was done between 1954 and 1971. The delay was due primarily to too few people living in the area at the time to justify municipal and provincial authorities' installing the water and sewer mains that are a must for any subdivision to proceed.

After 14 years of nothing happening, a lot of changes occurred in 1968. Cadillac and Fairview bought Don Mills Development. The province installed sewer and water trunk mains in the area because the population had quadrupled to 100,000. This also warranted the construction by municipal and county authorities of a parkway through the division. Previously, there had been only a gravel road, which made it impossible to drive in construction trucks.

With all this in place, Eph Diamond drew up a pro forma statement on a piece of foolscap on the costs and probable profits and gave the go-ahead. The project was supervised by Jack Daniels, as the project's architect, former Metropolitan Toronto planning commissioner Eli Comay, who served as a consultant on Erin Mills, former Don Mills Development manager James Murray, and a town planner experienced in the detailed layout of communities, John Bousfield.

"I have now worked with Cadillac on this project for 13 years and I have never had a contract or received written instructions," Bousfield says. "Cadillac executives have only said to do the best I can."

Erin Mills is being built from its southern limits north to meet another community, Meadowvale, being developed in a southerly direction by Markborough Properties Ltd., a subsidiary of Hudson's Bay Co., Canada's oldest and largest department store chain.

Ironically, the chief planner for Meadowvale is Mac Hancock, who planned Don Mills and assembled much of the land for Erin Mills while he worked for Don Mills Development. He now has his own firm, Project Planning Associates of Toronto.

Despite its size, Erin Mills is not a new town. New towns are built apart from other communities, whereas Erin Mills is basically an extension of Metropolitan Toronto. Still, there are some distinctions between Erin Mills and a typical subdivision.

"There is a larger proportion of open space, better landscaping, a more extensive walkway system of pedestrian underpasses," says Stephen Glogowski, manager of community planning in Cadillac Fairview's land and housing division. "We designed special light poles and glass bus shelters with curved roofs.

"With a large, continuous program, you can afford to design special street furniture and landscaping. If you set aside $10 per lot for 1,000 houses to provide extras, you can do more than if $10 were allocated for 100 homes."

Cadillac Fairview has built 20 percent of the housing in Erin Mills and the rest has been subcontracted. The community, after a slow start, has been doing well as housing sales picked up in the Toronto area. Recently, lots for 50 houses were sold in 90 minutes.

A two bedroom bungalow in Erin Mills ranges between $57,000

and $70,000. A larger 1,500 square foot house sells for $100,000 compared with $40,000 in the early 1970s. That comparison reveals only part of the escalation in prices because lot sizes have decreased from 50 feet by 120 feet originally to 30 feet by 120 feet now.

Unlike firms like Genstar and Oxford which grew through acquisitions, Cadillac Fairview has expanded primarily under its own steam. A major exception, though, which gave the company instant entry into the market, was its $24 million acquisition in 1978 of Houston-based General Homes Consolidated Companies, Texas' second largest homebuilder and the 75th largest in the U.S.

Leo Kolber says Cadillac Fairview will continue to grow internally because with acquisitions "the returns are so low. When you build something, you're like a wholesaler but when you buy something, it's like giving profit away to a middleman."

"We are not in a race to be the biggest," Daniels says. "Some of our projects are of a size that we never dreamt of or anticipated. Three or four years ago we never anticipated being involved in $1 billion projects. But Houston Center costs $4 billion to $5 billion in today's dollars and may increase to $7 billion due to inflation.

"We are long-term people. We plant seeds for the future. Our rewards come in the future."

How costly those dreams will be on Cadillac's balance sheet and management remains to be seen.

Chapter Seven

OXFORD DEVELOPMENT GROUP LIMITED

"We will not diversify but will concentrate on what we know best—real estate."

G. DONALD LOVE
PRESIDENT AND CHAIRMAN
OXFORD

OXFORD DEVELOPMENT GROUP LTD.

CORPORATE MANAGEMENT
(Located in Edmonton)

Chairman and President:	G. Donald Love
Executive Vice-Presidents:	D. A. Machum *(Corporate)*
	E. Alfred Picardi *(Design and Construction)*
	(Based in Denver)
	Kenneth Biggs *(Finance)*
Senior Vice-President:	David Thomson *(Corporate Development)*

GEOGRAPHIC DIVISIONS

Senior Vice-Presidents:

Canada

G. Vern Tatham (Based in Toronto)

United States

Western:	Robert Sanderman (Based in Denver)
Central:	Robert Hovelson (Based in Minneapolis)
Eastern:	Graham Brown (Based in Louisville)
West Coast:	Thomas Barrack, Jr. (Based in Los Angeles)

Oxford Development Group is the only one of Canada's top ten development companies to have grown smaller. It is also the only one to have moved from private to public and back to private ownership. The latest transition occurred at the end of 1979 when G. (Gordon) Donald Love, Oxford's energetic, highly regarded, and reclusive co-founder and owner bought the approximately 15 percent of publicly held shares. Another 40 percent is owned by the Toronto Dominion Bank, Canada's fifth largest.

The buyback, due not to choice but to necessity because Oxford's major backers were unhappy with its outlook, had a severe chain reaction. Part of Oxford had to be sold to finance the deal and this disenchanted several top executives who subsequently left the company.

In order to finance the buyback, Love sold the company's prized shopping center division in November 1980 to former Oxford employees and used the money to pay off the $260 million loan he had got from the TD to purchase the public shares.

In the view of many, the shopping center division had been Oxford's best feature, accounting for one-third of the company's $1 billion assets, one-third of its cash flow, and 70 percent of its profit. Since 1977, the division had doubled in size to become the second largest in Canada. By December 1980, it had 11 million square feet, compared with the 16 million of the leader, Cadillac Fairview.

In the short term, Oxford has been weakened by the loss of this profitable division and the resultant departure of top management. In the long term, however, Oxford will reap other rewards as its multimillion dollar redevelopment projects in Calgary, Louisville, Minneapolis, and Edmonton are completed and fully leased.

Oxford's transformation from a public to a private company was a somewhat curious affair. Its tightly held common shares were sold only through over-the-counter market transactions but never on the Toronto Stock Exchange. However, its preferred shares, issued in 1976, did trade on the TSE.

In 1979, Oxford announced on page seven of its annual report that it planned to "become a truly public company. Subject to market conditions, it is the intention of the company to change this by having in the near future an issue of the common stock, both through primary and secondary distribution."

The report, written by executive vice-president, administration, Donald (Sandy) Machum, was released on May 29, 1979. Only seven months later, on December 22, 1979, Oxford went private. Until then, 15 percent was publicly owned with the balance owned by Love, his two co-founders (John and George Poole of Edmonton), Great-West Life Assurance, Confederation Life Assurance, and Canada Trust. Love and his family purchased 60 percent, leaving 40 percent in the hands of the TD. The TD also has a five percent voting interest and the only two outside members on the Board of Directors (Ernest Mercier, vice-president and general manager, national accounts, and Ronald Ruest, general manager, international banking services).

What happened between May and December 1979 to cause such a reversal? At the time, the change of heart was attributed to Love's passion for privacy. The root cause more likely was a disagreement over strategy between Love and the financial institutions owning shares.

Love's commitment has always been to downtown redevelopment projects. As he says, "We like to go where an area needs redevelopment and the market can support it." It is something in which Oxford excels and, in fact, Oxford was one of the first major Canadian developers to enter the U.S. market.

Oxford has major projects underway in both Canada and the U.S., but all are being built simultaneously and many will not be finished until the end of the decade. They are also placing a heavy financial burden on the company. A conservative estimate of the current price tag is $1.5 billion, approximately equal to the existing $1.4 billion in assets.

During the mid-1970s, Oxford was expanding through new construction and major acquisitions despite skyrocketing interest rates. It was constantly money-hungry and ignored the pleas of the financial institutions to sell some of Oxford's property in order to finance the acquisitions. Love, like most developers, refused to believe that the day of the 20 percent interest rate would arrive.

As money got tighter, the tensions between Love and the other owners reached the breaking point, with the institutions going so far as to threaten a pullout. Love decided to act first by reclaiming the company.

Perhaps more than any other Canadian developer, Oxford is a one-man show. Co-founder, chairman, president, and principal shareholder G. Donald Love is described by business associates as an unparalleled salesman. "He is a fantastic enthusiast, an extraordinary entrepreneur, and a bubbly go-go promoter," says Clarence Elliott, in charge of real estate investments at Great-West Life at the time Great-West invested in Oxford.

Of average height, the boyish-looking, 54-year-old Love keeps fit by working out three times a week, pressing weights, and running on the spot. He jogs regularly, whether in Edmonton, headquarters for Oxford, or on business trips. He is a baseball, football, and the Big Bands fan.

Love is a rapid thinker who speaks in bursts of hearty enthusiasm. But this enthusiasm is restricted to business deals and colleagues. Otherwise, Love is extremely private and keeps a low profile. He almost never gives interviews and when he does, he gives the impression that he would rather have surgery. When interviewed, he sits in the shadows of his dimly lit 23rd floor office in the Edmonton Centre, Oxford's first major development project.

Opened in 1974, Edmonton Centre is located in what was then a rundown district and accomplished the enormous task of shifting Edmonton's business centre two blocks north of its previous location on Jasper Avenue. Originally, the Centre had three towers, a Four Seasons Hotel, and a Woodward's department store (western Canada's largest department store chain). Two more towers are being added. Its average of $350 sales per square foot in the 82 shops on three levels is among the highest in Canada.

Oxford is not a secretive company. Other executives talk readily about the firm. But Love cherishes his privacy. He does not like to reveal his first name (he uses only the initial G). He does not like to explain the origin of Oxford's name (it is derived from Oxford County near Waterloo, Ontario, where Love had his first job as a sales trainee for the Ford Motor Co.). He does not like to divulge why or how Oxford is doing something.

Love was born in Calgary in 1927. He studied engineering at McGill University in Montreal, then knocked around for a decade in several different businesses before going into real estate in 1960. His first job was as a sales trainee for Ford and subsequently as an oil scout for Phillips Petroleum in Calgary. Between 1952 and 1955, he sold cars in Windsor, Ontario. In 1955 he joined an investment house, Dominion Securities Ltd., in Toronto, and in 1956 he was transferred to Edmonton to open and manage the firm's new Alberta operations.

Love backed into real estate by chance when a local Dominion Securities client, Baker Medical Clinic, asked Love for help in expanding its building. The clinic wanted someone to buy its facilities, build an addition, and lease it back. Love could not find anybody, and so he got an option to do the job himself. For advice, he turned to another client, Ernest Poole, who had been in the construction business. Poole referred Love to his sons, John and George, who were then running Poole Construction Ltd. (They are not related to Jack Poole, president of Daon.) The trio then formed Polo Development Co., from *Po* for Poole and *lo* for Love, and handled the Baker deal.

Love regarded it as a one-shot effort and continued to work for Dominion Securities. He was transferred back to Toronto in the fall of 1959, but, with the success of the Baker Clinic deal in mind, he decided to return to Edmonton, where he formed Oxford in April 1960 with John and George Poole.

Because Love did not have any money to put into the business, the Pooles also invested nothing. Initially, Oxford did only small "build and sell" deals in which projects were sold immediately.

In 1964 the partners got a big break with a $2 million deal to construct a building for the Bank of Montreal in Edmonton. This was followed by a series of Royal Bank buildings in Edmonton, Halifax, Winnipeg, and London. They were done on ground leases with the banks, which did not require a lot of capital outlay by Oxford.

Love wanted Oxford to grow, but without greater sources of funds, its future was limited. So Love turned to Great-West Life, Canada's third largest life insurer (1980 assets, $5.1 billion). Great-West is 96 percent owned by Investors Group, Canada's largest mutual fund, which in turn is 96 percent owned by the vast Power Corp. of Montreal, one of Canada's largest holding companies. It also has interests in shipping (Canada Steamship Lines), newsprint (Consolidated Bathurst), finance (Montreal Trust), and transportation (Kingsway Transport and the Voyageur bus line).

Love's choice of Great-West was eminently logical because Great-West was a pioneer among Canada's life insurance companies in investing in real estate. As a result, its real estate assets, now $1.8 billion, rank it in size with Canada's top five real estate developers.

Great-West's involvement with Oxford was part of its long-term, deepening interest in real estate. After World War II, when many other lenders were leery of backing fledgling real estate entrepreneurs, Great-West took the bold plunge of granting mortgage financing in turn for bigger and bigger pieces of the action.

It started by requesting three to five percent of the gross income from the building, and it backed such well-known projects as the Inn on the Park in Toronto, O'Hare Inn in Chicago, Bayshore Inn in Vancouver, and National Trust head office in Toronto.

By the 1960s, however, Great-West decided it wanted a bigger slice, and it established three companies in which it had a 50 percent equity interest. First, in 1961, was Granite Holdings of Winnipeg, established with local developers. It built 12 nursing homes, with an average of 200 rooms, in Toronto, Ottawa, Winnipeg, Brandon, Regina, Saskatoon, and Moose Jaw. These were sold in 1968 to Trizec Corp. for $9.4 million, a substantial average annual compound rate of return of 25 percent.

"We had two objectives in building the lodges," says Clarence Elliott, then in charge of Great-West's mortgage operations and subsequently vice-president, investment, before his semi-retirement five years ago. "We wanted to make an acceptable return on our investment and upgrade the industry which was then mostly rundown 'Mom and Pop' homes."

The second joint project was the formation of Atlific Inns, which had the exclusive franchise for Canada, except in Ontario, for Holiday Inns. Great-West later sold its interest in Atlific and re-acquired 25 per cent. In 1968, Commonwealth Holiday Inns of Canada, which had been confined to Ontario and is now owned by Scott's Restaurants, gained the right to compete nationally against Atlific. (Scott's has the Kentucky Fried Chicken franchise for Toronto, Montreal, and Ottawa, where it is called Scott's Chicken Villas.)

The third venture, started in 1963, was with Dominion Construction Ltd. of Vancouver, a large west coast construction firm. Great-West (30 percent) and Dominion (70 percent) formed Bentall Properties Ltd., which built the four Bentall Towers in downtown Vancouver, a premier office address.

In 1963, attracted by Great-West's track record and needing more money for his expansion plans, Love approached Elliott about Great-West's acquiring an equity interest in Oxford. On December 23, 1963, Elliott gave Love a Christmas present — Great-West would buy 25 percent of Oxford. The terms were stiff: Great-West would have four years to pay the $1 million cost of its participation.

Why did Great-West gamble on Oxford, which in 1963 had fewer than ten employees and only a handful of properties? "Love and the Pooles made a good team," Elliott says. "Love was the promoter, while the Pooles were very conservative and methodical. The Pooles were incredibly successful general contractors who had introduced cost efficient methods, and they were to do all Oxford's construction."

Oxford also brought in the internationally famous architectural firm of Skidmore, Owings and Merrill to design its projects. Great-West regarded this continuity as very important, and as they continued to work together, each project was an improvement over the previous one.

"Between 1964 and 1967, Oxford grew very rapidly and its appetite for capital became so substantial that it could have consumed all of Great-West's mortgage financing and we felt it would be imprudent to put everything in one basket," Elliott continues.

"We searched around for more partners and brought in Canada Trust and Confederation Life." (Canada Trust is Canada's second largest trust company and Confederation Life is Canada's seventh largest life insurer.) The two new partners each got 10 percent of Oxford and provided 25 percent each of Oxford's debt capital, while Great-West provided 50 percent.

Canada Trust, which was not then a major lender, found it difficult to provide mortgage financing to Oxford. This role was taken over by Great-West, Confederation, and, for the first time, Oxford itself. Canada Trust did, however, continue to supply equity and junior debt (the difference between the mortgage financing and the amount of equity required).

G. Donald Love, chairman and president, Oxford

Great-West also had been in the U.S. lending market since 1904 and helped Love meet prominent U.S. businessmen when he decided to enter the U.S. market in 1973. That was just before the U.S. real estate market collapsed between 1974 and 1976.

The U.S. slump put a heavy demand on Oxford's need for capital at the same time that it was embarking on an ambitious acquisition program.

Between 1974 and 1979, Oxford made four major acquisitions: Cambridge Leaseholds Limited, most of the properties of a major Minneapolis firm, Y & R Properties Ltd., a major Toronto office builder, and Delta Hotels, a medium-priced chain based in Western Canada.

Cambridge, one of Canada's fastest growing and most aggressive shopping center developers, was purchased in 1975 for $47.6 million. In 1978, the last full fiscal year before Oxford sold it, Cambridge had revenue of $19.5 million, net income of $2.9 million, and assets of $166 million.

Cambridge was started in 1961 in Windsor, Ontario, by brothers and homebuilders Morris and Charles Tabachnik with Eastern Construction Ltd., which wanted to participate in the profits of centers it built. In its early days, Cambridge primarily built small centers with K-Mart as the main tenant. Later, it branched into large-scale regional centers containing two or more department stores.

In 1975 Eastern was experiencing financial difficulties as the real estate recession slashed the amount of construction. It was decided to sell Cambridge to Oxford which, at that time, wanted to diversify from its reliance on office buildings. Charles Tabachnik stayed on until 1978, but his desire for independence clashed with Oxford's desire for more control. In February 1978, Tabachnik and nearly all of Cambridge's senior management left to form their own firm, Chartwood Ltd. of Toronto.

Oxford parachuted in Lorne Braithwaite, formerly vice-president of development for Canada at Oxford, to head Cambridge. Braithwaite restored morale by promoting and hiring well-qualified people and Cambridge continued to thrive.

One area of particular pride to Braithwaite was and is Cambridge's reputation for the lowest common area maintenance costs in the industry. Through centralized purchasing of supplies and disciplined management of cleaning, Cambridge keeps its costs around $2 per square foot, about 25 percent lower than the industry norm.

The 1977 purchase of Investors Diversified Services (IDS) Inc. of Minneapolis stemmed from an Oxford plan to pursue redevelopment opportunities in that city. Their man on the spot, David Thomson, a development vice-president, learned that IDS wanted to unload most of its Minneapolis holdings, including seven office towers and a 230 room hotel.

Rather than have the headache of finding buyers for each piece of property, IDS sold everything to Oxford at a good price, considering the extent of the holdings, of $67.5 million (U.S.). That transaction made Oxford the largest single landlord in Minneapolis and gave it prominence when it negotiated to redevelop downtown Minneapolis and St. Paul in 1977 and 1978.

Starting in 1978 and ending in 1979, Oxford bought Y & R Properties Ltd. of Toronto for $60 million. Y & R (for Yolles and Rotenberg) was amalgamated in 1969 from a group of 50-year-old family businesses. It developed such Toronto landmarks as the Park Plaza Hotel, the Royal Bank Plaza, Continental Bank of Canada headquarters, and

Continental Bank of Canada, Toronto

the Richmond-Adelaide (Streets) Centre.

In 1977, the last year it reported its results separately, Y & R had assets of $116.1 million, revenue of $32.8 million, and profit of $1.9 million. Its president, George Vernon Tatham, remained as head of Oxford's new Y & R division.

Y & R was an ideal acquisition for Oxford. It gave Oxford, which then had only one building in Toronto, a substantial presence in Canada's financial capital. In addition, Y & R was a simple company because its operations were concentrated in one place, it owned its properties, and it was well managed.

It also was easy to acquire because ownership was vested in one person—chairman Rifet John Prusac. Prusac was regarded as the mystery man of the Canadian real estate scene because he operated quietly and never spoke to financial analysts or the media. President of a Toronto homebuilding firm, W.B. Sullivan Construction Ltd., Prusac became chairman of Y & R in 1971. In 1976, he purchased Y & R. Y & R president Kenneth Rotenberg, the R of Y & R, resigned one day before his contract was automatically to be renewed for another year.

"Oxford had had its eye on Y & R for quite a while and when we learned he wanted to sell, we did the negotiations in just a few hours," recalls Gordon Arnell, former executive vice-president, development, at Oxford.

(In an ironic twist, Great-West Life is a founding shareholder of Rostland Corp. of Toronto, which Kenneth Rotenberg started after leaving Y & R. Rostland is active in Dallas and Phoenix and also is the project manager for the new head office in Toronto of Sun Life Assurance.)

Oxford's fourth acquisition was Delta Hotels Ltd. in which it acquired 48.9 percent in 1974. Great-West already had 30 percent of Delta, and its two top executives on Oxford's board, Elliott and James Mitchinson, vice-president, real estate investments, stepped aside during the Oxford-Delta negotiations.

The timing of Oxford's purchase was unfortunate because a year later the hotel industry slumped. Oxford, accustomed to instant returns from its principal businesses of office towers and shopping centers, was not prepared to ride out the downturn. "Hotels are not our business," Love says.

In 1978, Oxford pulled out of Delta. It is now owned 30 percent by Great-West, 60 percent by Canlea Ltd. (a joint venture of the Canadian Imperial Bank of Commerce and A.E. LePage Ltd.), and 10 percent by its founder, William Pattison of British Columbia.

By 1978 Love was also under increasing pressure from Great-West, Confederation Life, and Canada Trust over what Clarence Elliott calls Oxford's "insatiable appetite" for capital because of its rapid-fire expansion and acquisitions. "Oxford was probably leveraged to the

Great West Plaza, Denver

greatest extent of any of the large Canadian real estate companies and this was of continuing concern," Elliott says.

The three financial institutions were also worried about Oxford's heavy reliance on short-term debt at floating interest rates at a time when interest rates were pushing toward 20 percent. Another concern was that Oxford might get caught in a credit crunch in which it would not be able to borrow at any price.

The firms repeatedly asked Love to sell some properties or an interest in them to raise money but these requests were ignored since Love, wrongly, as it turned out, thought 20 percent interest rates would never happen. Nor would Love slow down Oxford's rate of expansion. "We were at an impasse," Elliott says.

Great-West was also perturbed that it had received virtually no dividends in the 16 years it had put equity in Oxford. By 1979, it had $25 million invested in Oxford, making it Great-West's largest single real estate investment.

"The normal time we give for 'patient' capital (a long-term investment) is ten years, but we gave Oxford longer because of the underlying value of its real estate," Elliott says. Faced with the dissatisfaction of the three institutions and the probability of their withdrawal, Love offered cash to buy out them and the Poole brothers. The negotiations were conducted speedily but with little rancor.

"He told us in the middle of an afternoon and we had to answer 24 hours later, so we worked through the night," recalls James Mitchinson. Great-West did very well. It received $95 million in cash for a weighted average annual compound rate of return of 71.83 percent. "It was triple our normal yield of 25 percent," Mitchinson says. He adds, in an understatement, "It was a most profitable and successful investment."

Love also had to buy back the 15 percent of the shares that were publicly held and he did very well on this transaction.

Real estate stocks generally trade at a so-called "discount"—a price below the true value of the company's assets. This is not surprising because, with the exception of Daon, the companies give the book value of their properties and not the price they are worth today.

Oxford was trading at $15 when it went private. Love offered $26 a share to buy back the public shares. But if Love was willing to pay a premium of $11, obviously he knew the shares were actually worth far more. "It looked like a good price, but the current appraised value then would have been $42 a share," says Stephen Moore, real estate analyst at Burns, Fry Ltd.

Shareholders would have been justified in being upset, but at least they fared better than shareholders of Campeau did when founder and president Robert Campeau took its shares off the TSE in 1977. He paid $7 at a time when the real value was estimated at three times that amount. (What Love and Campeau did is not illegal since there is no law requiring real estate companies to disclose their true value.)

"I didn't really see the necessity of Oxford's being a public company," Love says. "We normally use long-term mortgages for financing, so we didn't need public share issues to raise capital. There is no advantage in being a public company, and there are far fewer restrictions in private companies."

Oxford's return to private ownership had an impact both on its operations and management. In November 1980, Love sold Cambridge Leaseholds Ltd. (then known as Oxford Shopping Centres) to Great-West Life (about 70 percent) and former Oxford Shopping Centre president Lorne Braithwaite and Oxford consultant Donald Priddle (30 percent). Braithwaite is now president of Cambridge, which reverted to its original name, and Priddle is executive vice-president in charge of finance and accounting.

Just how much Oxford received for Cambridge was not disclosed. Love asked for $300 million. Braithwaite says Love "didn't get anywhere near that." One tip-off is Oxford's director of communications James Nesbit's comment at the time that the transaction reduced Oxford's debt by about 61 percent. That works out to $198 million.

The end result, though, was that the Toronto Dominion Bank was no longer breathing down Oxford's neck for its $260 million loan for financing Oxford's move to private ownership. "There is no pressure on Oxford now about the loan," says Richard King, vice-president and controller at Oxford.

The Oxford share purchase and shopping center sale triggered a mass exodus of staff from a company that already had one of the biggest turnovers in an industry known for its high departure rate. Real estate is a business that requires entrepreneurial flair, a trait that leads to people wanting their independence. Moreover, while Love encourages initiative and decentralization, Oxford, in the final analysis, is still his fiefdom.

In December 1979, several top Oxford executives regarded the future as limited. There no longer were stock incentive plans, although merit bonuses were introduced, and the cost of the public share purchase would curtail expansion.

The most senior executive to leave was 46-year-old Gordon Arnell, Oxford's highly regarded executive vice-president in charge of development. Arnell used the $2.6 million he received for his 100,000 shares of Oxford to start his own company, Dover Park Development Corp. of Calgary, which does commercial development in Calgary, Regina, and Toronto.

One measure of the respect with which Arnell is viewed is that Confederation Life, which had withdrawn from Oxford, is backing him. In addition, his ten-member staff is composed of executives who were at Oxford either before or after Arnell joined in 1975. They include Douglas Pearson, western Canada development vice-president at Oxford, Vincent Thompson, construction manager in Toronto and St. Paul, and Gordon Bennett, executive vice-president at Oxford until 1974.

"I never stole anybody from Oxford," Arnell stresses. "They either had already left Oxford or were looking for jobs. I didn't leave Oxford because of negative feelings about it or Don Love. I don't want any ill will or to create rancor.

"I left Oxford for two reasons. First, I had the money to do something myself after my stock incentive schemes were cashed out when Oxford went private. Second, I foresaw the character of Oxford changing as it became a more closely held, private company, with a scaled-down level of activity.

"It was obvious that the shopping centers would have to be sold to finance the takeover. I regarded them as one of the best parts of the company, but Don Love did not agree. He is most comfortable with downtown mixed use commercial and retail office development.

"The change was not necessarily better for the professional managers (because there are no more stock options), although it was better from Love's viewpoint. Oxford had been one of the fastest growing developers in Canada, but now it will not be as visible a presence because of the need to scale down activity."

Following the departure of Arnell and others, Oxford underwent three re-organizations. It wound up by changing from a centralized organization, with all authority headquartered in Edmonton, to a decentralized organization. "Giving bottom line authority to the four divisional vice-presidents has resulted in speedier decisions and reduced the problem of the different time zones between operations," says John Knippel, vice-president, personnel.

Still, the strings remain tightly held in Edmonton by Love. Separate western and eastern Canada divisions were consolidated in the summer of 1981. The U.S. divisions are Los Angeles, Denver, Minneapolis, Louisville, and the U.S. west coast. All report frequently to Love, on a daily basis if necessary. Love flies to each division for monthly meetings, and quarterly conferences are held by all the divisional vice-presidents.

"Love is the most experienced guy in the company," says Knippel. "He believes putting people and capital together leads to fun. He allows people to expand their abilities. His criteria for hiring are honesty, integrity, aggressiveness, and selling ability. Experience is last as a qualification. For example, Dan McCaffery, the project manager for the expansion to Edmonton Centre, is a former schoolteacher."

Like such other office building developers as Olympia & York and Trizec, Oxford finances projects through long-term mortgages. During the construction stage, it obtains bank financing. When projects are completed, it obtains conventional mortgages from insurance companies and uses the proceeds to pay its bank debts.

Oxford's lenders are the Canadian Imperial Bank of Commerce (the lead banker) and Toronto Dominion with which Oxford has done projects in Edmonton (Edmonton Centre) and Calgary (Toronto Dominion Square). In the U.S., it uses local banks. Its long-term insurance company lenders are Confederation Life and Great-West Life, although neither are part owners any longer, as well as Equitable Life, Northwest Mutual Life, New York Life, Connecticut General, and Travelers Insurance.

Like the other developers, Oxford has a comprehensive cost control system. "It breaks down costs by land costs, architectural fees, engineer consulting fees, construction costs, leasing costs, and interim financing costs," says Richard King, vice-president and company controller. Oxford protects itself by provisional clauses against inflation in construction and leasehold costs. "We set a maximum price with the construction firm (Poole Construction Ltd. in Canada). If there is a cost overrun, they must absorb it. If the project comes in under budget, we split the saving."

A ceiling is also placed on leasehold costs paid by Oxford, such as partitions and carpeting. Once this allowance is locked in, the tenant must pay any extras if inflation drives up the bill.

A similarly tight-fisted policy is taken with renting space so that inflation and Oxford's rents keep pace. "If there is lack of space or a strong rental market, we hold off renting in early stages and rent toward the end," King says.

"With the exception of the lead tenant, we now review the rent on ten-year leases after five years, instead of waiting ten years as we used to do. This coincides with a five-year review on mortgage rates by our lenders. With the lead tenant, we still wait ten years to review rates. The frequent fluctuations in mortgage and interest rates will result in even shorter spaces of time between rental reviews."

Oxford has a three tier financial forecasting system. Each year, a one-year forecast of income and expenses is done as well as checking which leases are up for renewal and setting the new rents. Twice a year, a three-year game plan is done and every year a five-year crystal ball budget is worked out.

Oxford has four criteria for going ahead with a redevelopment project. First, Oxford must be able to own the land. Second, there must be enough people — at least 500,000 — to support such a major project. Third, Oxford will not build on speculation; it only proceeds if a major tenant is lined up. Fourth, the financing must be in position.

Getting a lead tenant depends on knocking on lots of doors, word of mouth, and a bit of luck. For example, Oxford snared Anaconda Co. (engaged in brass, aluminum, building materials, and copper mining)

Toronto Dominion Square, Calgary

as its main tenant in Denver Square after hearing via the grapevine that Anaconda was considering moving from New York and that Denver was on its list of possible new locations. As bait for lead tenants, Oxford and other developers name the building after them and may even assist them with their move or designing their quarters.

Love was also a pioneer among Canadian developers in moving into the U.S. market, starting with Denver in 1973. Today, Oxford has 55 percent of its assets in Canada (compared with 88 percent in 1977) and 45 percent of its assets in the U.S. (compared with 12 percent in 1977).

Love is sensitive about the interpretation that could be placed on this rapid turnabout. "Our business is providing office and retail space and there are ten times more people and markets in the U.S.," he says. "But we are not abandoning Canada, nor do we lack confidence in the Canadian market."

Oxford now has completed or is developing downtown sites in Louisville, Minneapolis, St. Paul, Phoenix, and Denver. The $100 million St. Paul Town Square illustrates the methodology and impact of these projects. The Town Square, like many other Oxford projects, is an integrated office, retail, and hotel complex. It covers two square blocks.

"The city of St. Paul did not select Oxford to develop Town Square; instead, Oxford bought the property on the open market about seven years ago," recalls St. Paul Mayor George Latimer.

"At that time, Oxford had no competition because no other developers wanted to do anything in downtown St. Paul. It was a period of stagnation for downtown property.

"One of the major impacts of the Town Square project was the revitalization of St. Paul's downtown. Property downtown is now more highly valued. Competition now exists for many development projects. There appears to be a continuation of investment in our city during a period of retrenchment and high money rates.

"In the next five years, 1,200 hotel rooms, 1,500 residential units, 500,000 square feet of office space, and 2,000 parking ramp spaces will be added downtown. Of the 3,000 jobs within the Town Square complex, it is conservatively estimated that 1,000 are new jobs in the downtown area. Within five years, when a number of new developments will occur as a result of Town Square, some 6,000 to 8,000 new jobs will be added to the downtown work force.

"In addition, as a focus for the second-story Skyway system (overhead pedestrian bridges between buildings) and a future pedestrian mall, the complex is a major force in tying the downtown together. Also, it helped spur a parking program for downtown, which concentrates short-term parking near the commercial/retail core with long-term parking shifted generally to the downtown periphery."

One of Oxford's most outstanding Canadian successes is the four-year-old square block $82 million Toronto Dominion Square, head-quarters of Dome Petroleum and Home Oil, in downtown Calgary. The project played a major role in the revitalization of downtown Calgary, but from the outside it is little different from any other glass and steel tower.

What is different is the 2½ acre park inside. The Devonian Gardens has 16,000 tropical plants, waterfalls, pools, and playful animal sculptures imported from England. Bird calls and carillon music are played. In the winter one of the pools is frozen for use as a skating rink. Nothing to match its scope had been done before.

The Gardens was the idea of the remarkable Devonian Foundation, created by legendary oilman Eric Harvie, who discovered the Leduc oil well in Alberta in 1946, which touched off the province's oil boom. Established in 1973 when Harvie died and administered by his son, Donald, the Devonian Foundation, unlike most philanthropies, was not meant to last indefinitely. Instead, its purpose was to spend on civic projects—primarily parks, but also scientific research and museums—immediately, before inflation eroded the number of things that could be done.

Since 1973, the Foundation has spent $68 million and has about $10 million left, of which most has already been earmarked to be spent over the next three or four years. The Harvie family did not want its name attached to the Foundation and chose "Devonian" after the Devonian geologic area from which came the oil that formed the base of the Harvie fortune.

In 1975 the Foundation selected as its priority downtown parks in Calgary and cast about for a central location. Oxford had just announced its multi-million dollar project, and so Horace Meech, president of the Foundation and a 40-year associate of Eric Harvie, went to see Donald Love. "He was all for it because it would attract attention and tenants," Meech recalls. "Love is quite forward-looking and excellent to deal with."

Originally, the plan was to make the gardens an open-air park on the roof of the three floor high retail area of the center. Later discussions led to the decision to enclose the park for year-round use.

"Then we went to the city since the idea was that it would own and run the gardens as a public park," Meech continues. "It wasn't easy. The then Mayor, Rod Sykes, fought it tooth and nail, objecting to the $9 million cost, of which the city would pay $1 million under the plan, Oxford $3 million, and the Foundation $5 million. It took 1½ years to get City Council's approval and another year to get it through the planning stages.

"Then we had to get the plants. Finally, we found a grower in Florida who sent us 17 vanloads of plants. The next step was to turn the flat concrete roof into an undulating garden. We were limited by the weight the building could take, so styrofoam was carved into different shapes and contours and put on top of the concrete, after which the grass and pools were installed," Meech says.

The Toronto Dominion Square also demonstrates how developers will spend millions of dollars with one hand and nickel and dime with the other. For example, Calgary city planners could not get Oxford to agree to provide an arcade or canopy to protect pedestrians from the wind or rain. Oxford also rejected a city request that it set back one corner of its building, at 8th Avenue and 3rd Street, to provide easy, non-congested access to the planned 3rd Street mall.

While Oxford and the city haggled over some features, the Square also illustrates how developers can benefit from cooperating with certain city regulations.

"In 1966 the city proposed a Plus 15 system in which pedestrians would be separated from traffic by overhead enclosed walkways, located 15 feet above the street, between buildings," says George Steber, Calgary's director of planning.

"The city didn't just want enclosed, climate-controlled bridges, but interesting communications links, and it came up with a system of bonuses as an incentive to developers. If a developer provides a public plaza at the Plus 15 level, he gets 15 square feet in increased density for every square foot of the plaza.

"If there is a public plaza also at the Plus 30 (30 feet above the ground or the third floor of a building), he gets an extra five feet for every square foot in the plaza. If there is a bridge across the street, the developer gets an extra 30 square feet for every square foot in the crossway."

Obviously, these bonuses are a pot of gold to developers who can rake in more rents from both office tenants on the resulting increase in floors and retailers in the plaza. As Steber wryly comments: "Their enthusiasm is relative to profit. The extent of the bonuses is unnecessary because the developers clearly understand the benefits and commercial return of providing plazas," he says. "In Minneapolis, which also has bridges, the private sector is footing the bill."

Until recently, Oxford had not been a residential builder, but it is now proceeding with a 40 acre commercial and residential project, called Eau Claire in downtown Calgary beside the Bow River, the biggest of its type in that city. It will have 1,500 luxury housing units — condominium apartments and townhouses — a 35-floor office tower, 325 room hotel, and a retail area. Construction started in early 1981 and is scheduled to be completed in 1988. The apartments will sell for $120,000 to $600,000.

Eau Claire is Oxford's biggest project as well as a test case that will determine whether Oxford will do other downtown commercial-

United Plaza, Phoenix

residential projects. "If we don't get a payback in five years, it will blow out our brains," says David Thomson, senior vice-president of corporate development in Canada for Oxford.

Redevelopment projects like Eau Claire tend to be endurance tests for the developer, interested citizens' groups, and government officials. Years are consumed in ironing out all the details. In the long run, the project is usually given the green light, but the passage of time and the ravages of inflation drive up the price tag. In the case of Eau Claire, the cost zipped from $150 million to $600 million during the four years of negotiations for city approval.

Like most large scale projects, Eau Claire dated back more than a decade before its actual proposal to the city. During the 1960s, a number of prominent Calgarians, eventually numbering 16 and including Jack Gallagher, chairman of Dome Petroleum, bought 28 acres in the rundown Eau Claire section of Calgary.

In 1976, this consortium linked up with Oxford and Nu-West Group. Gallagher and Oxford's David Thomson were acquaintances. Oxford brought in Nu-West because Oxford was unfamiliar with residential construction. But the marriage of Oxford and Nu-West did not last long.

Nu-West, primarily a residential firm, and Oxford, a commercial outfit, naturally had opposite business styles. "Residential firms are more traders in property and are used to finishing quickly, whereas, Oxford, as a commercial builder continues to own buildings after they are completed," Thomson says. "We are in for the long term and they want to sell assets quickly."

The Oxford/Nu-West arrangement had a clause allowing either to pull out, leaving the remaining partner responsible for buying the drop-out's share. That cost Oxford $5.1 million.

The problem with Nu-West was only one of a series of costly stumbling blocks encountered by Oxford. Another major expense occurred when the city planning commission rejected Oxford's first architectural conception as "insensitive and inappropriate." An inner city citizens' coalition group also objected to the design. "It was a series of high rise towers that would cast shadows onto the river bank and jeopardize the quality of the walkway," says Calgary planning director George Steber.

The rejection was a bitter lesson for Oxford. It scrapped $300,000 worth of architectural blueprints and started over again, this time consulting with the inner city coalition group. This conciliatory approach is being followed increasingly by developers, aware of the growing political power of citizens' groups to checkmate projects.

"Many developers now meet with city associations to get their views and support, so when they come to the planning commission and are asked about community reaction, they can say it is favorable," Steber says. The second time around, Oxford had this support and the project went through.

The new design replaced the glass exterior of the first plan with brown brick exterior walls to give a warmer look. (Brick is unusual in Calgary where housing is usually frame.) The townhouses and apartments will be built on graduated heights and will be clustered around courtyards.

Love says Oxford's future will be patterned after the present. "We will not diversify but will concentrate on what we know best — real estate," he says. "And we will continue to concentrate on downtown commercial real estate in Canada and the U.S."

That is the style with which Donald Love is comfortable and although Oxford has had its rough moments, it has given bold facelifts to much of western Canada and the U.S. This fits in with its philosophy, as stated in its last annual report: "It may be said of us that above all else we supply beginnings."

Chapter Eight

CAMPEAU CORPORATION

"If I believe in people I will help them. If not, I will fight them."

ROBERT CAMPEAU
CHAIRMAN
CAMPEAU

CAMPEAU CORPORATION

SENIOR MANAGEMENT TEAM

Chairman and Chief Executive Officer: Robert Campeau
Deputy Chairman: Jean Paradis
President: Ronald McCartney (*Residential development*)
Executive Vice-Presidents: David King (*Commercial*)
William ("Don") Carroll (*Finance*)
Senior Vice-Presidents: Pierre Benoit (*Housing and Land Development; U.S. Western Region*)
Clément Cadieux (*Special Projects—hotels, racetracks*)
Timothy Walker (*Treasurer*)

OPERATING DIVISIONS

Vice-Presidents: Bruno Chiricota (*Forestry*)
Kenneth Cooper (*Commercial Development, U.S. Southwest*)
Raymond Larocque (*Building Products*)
Donald McMaster (*Construction Management*)
Leonard McQuarrie (*Land Development, California*)
Grant Sedgwick (*Commercial Development, U.S. West*)
John Van Haastrecht (*Commercial Development, Eastern Canada*)

OFFICES

Canada
  Head Office: Ottawa
  Executive Office: Toronto
  Branches: Montreal, Calgary, Edmonton
United States
  Campeau Corporation Florida: West Palm Beach
  Campeau Corporation California: Newport Beach (*Head Office*)
  San Francisco, Santa Clara
  Campeau Corporation Texas: Dallas (*Head Office*)
  Houston

Hardy individuality and controversy stick to Robert Campeau like paper clings to glue. Urbanity is not his style. He has never hesitated to be pugnacious or combative (he has been known to jump up and down in protest at zoning hearings), such as during his losing battle for Royal Trustco Ltd., one of the fiercest takeover brawls in Canadian corporate history.

The 58-year-old Campeau is the only French Canadian among Canada's top ten real estate developers. His firm is also the only one of the select to be named after its founder. Campeau Corp. is the only developer to be headquartered in Ottawa, although most of the executives, including the president, Ronald McCartney, transferred recently to Toronto. Campeau himself remains in Ottawa.

While atypical in many ways, Campeau also is indicative of the metamorphosis the development industry is undergoing. Like other developers that started as homebuilders and land developers, Campeau Corp. has completely changed its thrust. It has withdrawn from building single family houses to concentrating on the more profitable area of income properties (office buildings, apartments, and shopping centers). It is also part of the drive to move into the United States, where 75 percent of its new projects are planned. And it reflects the trend among developers to diversify into energy resources as a hedge against the cyclical nature of the real estate market. Campeau has not yet moved into oil and gas but plans to do so, regarding such extension into other activities as a continuation of its geographical and operational diversification in real estate.

While the rest of the developers shun the limelight, Robert Campeau's name is frequently in the social columns, even though it is seldom seen in the business pages since he rarely gives interviews now that his company is well established.

Every Christmas, society columnists report how Campeau and his second wife, Ilse, entertain Ottawa's leading citizens at a party held around their indoor swimming pool in their mansion on the Ottawa River. Last year's guests included Prime Minister Pierre Trudeau and Justice Minister Jean Chretien.

There have been charges throughout the years that Campeau has benefited from excellent political connections with the federal Liberals, who have been in power most of the time during which Campeau built up his business. In the 1979 (latest available figures) Chief Electoral Officer's report on political contributions of more than $100, Campeau Corp. is listed as giving $11,397.28 to the federal Liberal party. No personal donations by Campeau himself were made.

"I have supported friends in politics, but I have never leaned on

Robert Campeau, chairman and chief executive officer, Campeau

them to get anything special," Campeau says. "If I believe in people, I will help them. If not, I fight them."

Recently, Campeau has attracted public attention mostly because of the controversies in which he has been involved, the most notable of these being his unsuccessful takeover bid in August 1980 for Royal Trustco Ltd., Canada's largest trust company. Campeau emerged smelling like a rose when an investigation by the Ontario Securities Commission bore out his claim of a "conspiracy" by Royal Trustco and its corporate friends to thwart Campeau's bid.

Campeau is described by associates and government officials as "mercurial," "emotional," "very strong willed," "abrasive," and "hardnosed in negotiations." In his younger days, it was not unusual for Campeau to jump up and down at zoning hearings with deputy chairman, Jean Paradis, described by acquaintances as "diplomatic and elegant," tugging at him to sit down and be quiet.

Some attribute Campeau's outbursts to a Gallic temperament. Others say it stems from a disciplined, driving determination to win that is as evident when he golfs, plays tennis, or swims for an hour or more without getting winded. Just over five feet tall, with wavy gray hair, Campeau even walks decisively.

Business associates say he is "ruthless, although not dishonest." "He knows what he wants and goes for it, and if he doesn't get it, he fights back," says a longtime associate.

Others say that Campeau is "always full of suggestions," even when they are not particularly wanted. "Some suggestions improve the process and others frustrate it, because he can become preoccupied with such things as corner windows," says Ottawa architect and town planner Timothy Murray. "But he always listens to your argument. He is a straightshooter who will bargain you into the ground, but once he signs an agreement, he will honor it all the way through."

It is possible that Campeau's penchant to, as one associate says, "leave no doubt as to what is on his mind" may be a bit staged to get results. Bearing this out is Campeau's controlled behavior under pressure. "He was very calm and collected during the Royal Trustco takeover battle," says a member of the company's Board of Directors.

In many ways, Campeau is the personification of the self-taught man. Like many people who could not afford to finish school, Campeau is a voracious reader, especially of ancient and modern history. He is also proud of his ability to do carpentry around the house.

The youngest of seven children of a French-speaking family living in Sudbury, Ontario, Campeau dropped out of school after grade eight and was apprenticed as a machinist at Inco Ltd. The international nickel giant has its principal mine at Sudbury. Campeau's first job was sweeping floors for 57 cents an hour.

During World War II, Campeau job-hopped at various Ontario

and Quebec plants, working as a machinist. In 1948, at the age of 24 and living in Ottawa, Campeau decided to build his first house, hoping to cash in on the post war scramble for housing. He took this gamble even though his first child had just been born.

It cost Campeau $5,000 to build the house and he sold it for $7,300. "That was my first big break," he says. By 1949 Campeau had 40 houses under construction and decided to quit his job as a supervisor at a Canadian International Paper Co. plant near Ottawa and concentrate on homebuilding.

Longtime acquaintances of Campeau say he always had a driving ambition to be the biggest and best. "He had tremendous ambition and worked night and day," says Senator George McIlraith, who has lived in Ottawa for more than 50 years and who knew "all the engineers, lawyers, and construction people." McIlraith proposed the toast to Campeau's daughter at her wedding.

"Although he did not have a formal education, Campeau had high native ability and was very aggressive," McIlraith continues.

Adds Ottawa Judge Kenneth Fogarty, another early acquaintance of Campeau, "He had no great depth in formal education and was untrained and unsophisticated in many ways. But at the same time, he was and is an intelligent, clever, and imaginative man.

"The degree of sophistication which he lacked was often an advantage for him because he would be bull-headed, impatient, take far-out positions, and was easily given to expressions of his opinion — often jumping up and down — whereas more sophisticated people are inclined to be less vocal."

Fogarty met Campeau 25 years ago when Fogarty was representing the mortgage companies from which Campeau was obtaining financing to build a group of low rise apartments in Ottawa. "It was a big project for Campeau then and he was just assembling his staff," Fogarty recalls. "He asked me to draft the invitations for guests to come to the opening of the apartments since he hadn't had much education."

Later on, Fogarty and Campeau continued, as Fogarty says, to be "in contact and collision a few times" when Fogarty became a city councillor (1961-1972), chairman of the planning board, and then mayor of Ottawa (1970-1972).

"Campeau was impatient and often vocally critical, but he also was a good force in helping develop the city," Fogarty says. "He was the first big successful residential developer in Ottawa, which is a tribute to his ability to take risks and be imaginative."

Nor was Campeau leery of taking on City Hall, which in the early days of his company was headed by Mayor Charlotte Whitton, an equally tough and fiery personality. To say that Whitton and Campeau did not get along is to put it mildly.

Ronald B. McCartney, president, Campeau   *Jean Paradis, deputy chairman, Campeau*

The province of Ontario lacked comprehensive zoning legislation until the early 1960s. When Ottawa's was drawn up in 1964, Whitton and Campeau clashed bitterly over its wording and coverage. Later, after she was no longer mayor, she stood in the path of a bulldozer in a vain attempt to delay a Campeau project.

Campeau's ties to the Liberals have always garnered attention. For example, deputy chairman Jean Paradis was appointed by the Liberals to serve as head of the Ottawa branch of Canada Mortgage and Housing before joining Campeau in 1954 as secretary and general manager. Liberal Senator Louis Giguère, a prominent figure in the so-called "sky shops" affair, was on Campeau's Board from 1970 to 1974. (Giguère was charged with, and acquitted in 1978, of accepting a $95,000 bribe in return for using his influence in obtaining a lease extension for a duty-free shop at Montreal's Dorval Airport.)

Campeau has also employed people with ties to the Progressive Conservative Party. Pierre Benoit, head of the company's western U.S. land operations, is a former Ottawa mayor and unsuccessful Progressive Conservative candidate in Ontario.

And Champlain Towers, a 243 unit Campeau apartment project located on the edge of Ottawa's Rockcliffe Park district, home of most politicians, has become a prestige address among politicians from all parties, even though its architect says there is "nothing uniquely superior about it. Chief Justice Bora Laskin, several Liberal cabinet ministers, and former Progressive Conservative minister George Hees live there, even though there is nothing special about the design of the place," says Timothy Murray, senior partner, Murray and Murray and Partners. The architectural and town planning firm has done work for Campeau for 20 years.

Although Campeau Corp. has capable professional management, the firm remains largely a one-man show. "Successful developers like to make all the decisions themselves," says a member of the company's Board.

Now seven years from the normal retirement age of 65, Campeau says that he has no plans to step down when he reaches that age. One of his children, 23-year-old Daniel, is already at the firm, working as executive assistant to president Ronald McCartney.

Although he suffered from the handicap of knowing virtually nothing about real estate, Campeau has built up a highly successful operation in a relatively short time.

Since 1976 the company's assets have doubled from $544.8 million to $1 billion, and it has $3 billion in projects planned over the next five years. They include a two million square foot, $450 million new head office in downtown Toronto for the Bank of Nova Scotia, Canada's fourth largest bank, a $400 million, 29 acre residential and commercial project, called The Vineyard, in Dallas, a $250 million, 80-story office tower for Houston, possibly another 80-story skyscraper in Dallas, and a $400 million redevelopment project in San Jose.

Seventy-five percent of the projects will be built in the U.S., primarily in Florida, Texas, and California. The company is also scouting the New York, Boston, Washington, Denver, and Seattle markets.

Today, Campeau estimates that the pre-tax value of Campeau Corp. stock, of which he owns 84 percent of the common shares, is $50 a share, after a four for one split in May 1981.

Campeau's wealth is not evident at Campeau Corp. offices. Both the head office in Ottawa's west end, located a half hour from downtown, and the executive office in Toronto are very modest. Friends describe Campeau's Ottawa home as "good quality, but not ostentatious or lavish."

He also has a winter home at Jupiter, Florida (near Palm Beach), where he lives during the first part of each year. Business can be mixed with pleasure at Jupiter, since Campeau Corp. is constructing three condominium apartment towers there.

In keeping with his individualistic nature, Campeau has always tried to avoid joint ventures. However, the rapid expansion of the company has forced him to share the decision-making with senior management. Although still largely a one-man show, Campeau has had, since 1978, a four-man senior management team consisting of Campeau, president Ronald McCartney, and two executive vice-presidents, David King and William (Don) Carroll.

Because McCartney deals with the residential side of the business (land and housing) and King with the commercial side, they are, in effect, on an equal footing. So is Carroll, who is responsible for finance.

With Campeau remaining in Ottawa while all the other executives have moved to Toronto, it is logical to wonder if he is taking a less active role in the company. But other members of the management team say that even now they are each away several days of the week and, therefore, meet all over North America and not just in Ottawa.

The Toronto relocation will put the company in eyeball to eyeball contact with Canada's financial community which is centered there. Campeau's headquarters will be in the new Bank of Nova Scotia building at the hub of the financial district at King and Bay Streets.

Its downtown site, as compared with its suburban Ottawa headquarters, is symptomatic of the increasing trend by developers to be located in the central core, now that they are more involved in commercial development. The suburban headquarters were fine when the firm's main interest was homebuilding.

"Many people still view Campeau as an Ottawa housebuilder and a lessor of office space to the federal government, but this is just a minor part of what we're doing and it makes me so annoyed that people are unaware of this, " says Don Carroll. The Bank of Nova Scotia building, although just one of the four or five major projects the company has planned for the next few years, should help spotlight, to Canadians, its move into commercial development.

Moving downtown will also eliminate the tiresome plane change that must be made in Toronto for flights from the U.S. en route to Ottawa by Campeau executives. Although regional management is given substantial authority, the strings are pulled by the top four executives who insist on being kept fully informed of all developments on major projects. "The magnitude of projects is so great that one project can destroy you," Carroll says.

In its early days, Campeau Corp.'s close knit management group was known among critics as "le maudit (wretched) gang Alfred." Many Campeau executives came from Alfred, Ontario, a small community with about 1,000 people in the early 1950s, located approximately 45 miles from Ottawa.

The Alfred people consisted of Campeau's first wife, Claudia, Alban Cadieux, who had married Claudia's sister, and two friends of Cadieux, Marcel Lalande and Raymond Larocque. (Alban Cadieux is not related to Clément Cadieux, senior vice-president, special projects, at Campeau Corp.)

The Alfred "gang" is no longer close knit. Marcel Lalande, who had become senior vice-president, housing and land development, left in June 1977 over a "disagreement" that he will not discuss. He now manages the Ottawa branch of Costain Ltd., a Toronto-based development company (assets $264.7 million).

Alban Cadieux now runs Blue Bonnets Raceway, a Montreal harness horse racetrack, which Campeau Corp. owns. According to the Canadian Trotting Association, Blue Bonnets had the largest attendance (2,460,913) of Canadian harness tracks in 1980. The runnerup, Toronto's Greenwood track, had an attendance of 1,309,950.

Raymond Larocque remains at Campeau Corp. as vice-president, building products, a division that is being phased out by the company now that it has pulled out of single family housing. Larocque plans to stay with the firm, but says he is not as close to Campeau as in the early days.

Another early team member was Jean Paradis, who had worked at Canada Mortgage and Housing Corporation since its founding after World War II. As manager of CMHC's Ottawa branch, he became acquainted with Campeau, then "a budding, very promising homebuilder."

Paradis decided to join Campeau in 1954, even though the company was still so small that it had fewer than ten people in management and operated out of a storefront office on Bank Street in downtown Ottawa. "I joined on a hunch," he says. "Campeau seemed so confident and a comer. Although he was not all that polished, he was a hell of a pusher and very aggressive and dynamic. If things did not go his way, he would get very mad.

"His English was fairly limited, but his aggressiveness did not deter him from speaking it. In the early days of the company, he was its heart and soul. As he has gotten older, he has mellowed — somewhat."

Paradis is credited by many as having been Campeau's Professor Higgins, who, as in Bernard Shaw's *Pygmalion*, has been responsible for giving Campeau polish and cooling down his flareups at public meetings. "I plead guilty to a degree," Paradis says.

Paradis was corporate secretary from 1954 until 1968. Subsequently he became senior vice-president (1968-1971), executive vice-president (1971-1972), president (1972-1974), and deputy chairman (1974 to date).

Today, Cadieux, Larocque, and Lalande have been replaced by a new inner circle of president Ronald McCartney, 52, and executive vice-presidents David King, 44, and Don Carroll, 39. Paradis, now 60, has been semi-retired since 1978 when he suffered a heart attack. He goes to the office three afternoons a week and is a member of the company's executive committee.

McCartney joined Campeau in 1970 when Campeau acquired Canadian Interurban Properties of which McCartney had been vice-

Harbour Square Condominiums and Harbour Castle Hotel, Toronto

president and general manager. McCartney deals with the residential side of the business and King with the commercial end. "We like a very personal approach in acquiring new opportunities and the splitting of duties has allowed more direct management," McCartney says.

King joined Campeau in 1974 after working for six years as vice-president in charge of development at Cambridge Leaseholds Ltd., a major Canadian shopping center developer. Previously he was in charge of shopping center development at Simpsons-Sears Ltd. He decided to leave Cambridge during the time that Trizec made an aborted bid to take it over.

King has played a pivotal role in Campeau's diversifying out of its geographic roots in Ottawa and operational base of housing and government buildings into a North American commercial developer. "We were three to six years behind competitors in entering markets in western Canada, California, Texas, and Florida," he admits. "But these markets are growing so aggressively that it didn't matter when we came to town."

Like other Canadians, King finds it easier dealing with U.S. than Canadian regulators. "The intent of U.S. governmental bodies is to have projects happen, whereas some Canadian jurisdictions attempt to not have projects happen."

Although Carroll was named William John, he goes by the name Don, which has stuck to him since childhood when his younger sister could not pronounce John. A chartered accountant, Carroll turned down four job offers from chartered accountants' firms upon graduat-

ing from Dalhousie University in Halifax in 1965 because their acceptance letters were addressed to him as "Bill" instead of "Don," which he
had told them he preferred.

He opted for a fifth job offer at Peat, Marwick, Mitchell and Co.
which had used "Don" in its acceptance. There, Carroll met Campeau
in 1970 and soon found he was devoting half his time to Campeau
Corp.'s business affairs. Campeau Corp. was — and is — one of Peat
Marwick's largest clients.

Carroll specialized in taxation at Peat Marwick, starting in
November 1969, one week before the revolutionary Benson White
Paper (named after the Finance Minister Edgar Benson) was intro-
duced.

"As a result, I dealt with chairmen and presidents, explaining the
White Paper," Carroll recalls. "But by the late 1970s the new income tax
act was several years old, so that I was no longer dealing with the top
management at companies. Instead, I was dealing with corporate tax
managers and the work wasn't as exciting."

Therefore, in December 1978, Carroll accepted a long-standing
offer from Campeau to join his firm. "He has an extremely high level of
personal and business integrity as well as entrepreneurial flair mixed
with pragmatism, loves to do transactions, works hard, and has tremendous personal drive," says Ross Walker, senior partner in Toronto at
Peat, Marwick. He is the audit partner for Campeau.

Carroll's drive to excel is evident in athletics, too. He runs four to
five days a week and has competed in, and finished, marathon races in
New York and Toronto. He is also a former tournament bridge player.

Walker says that Campeau and Carroll make a good combination
because Campeau's passion is making deals whereas Carroll enjoys the
nuts and bolts of framing the agreements. "Bob Campeau has no
interest in paper work and as soon as he has completed one transaction,
he is on to the next, whereas Don will do all the documentation that will
give the company the best deal," Walker says.

Campeau, Cadieux, Larocque, and Lalande started out in a one-
room office. In their favor was the post war demand for housing and
Campeau's ability to buy well-located farmland. During the 1950s
housing boom, the firm built 1,000 or more units a year and soon
became Ottawa's largest developer.

Financing was obtained from the Bank of Nova Scotia (still the
company's lead banker). A major boost came from the winning of a
Department of National Defence contract to build 134 housing units
for members of the Canadian Air Force. The contract was paid for in
stages, providing cash flow to expand the business.

To make sure that it had sufficient building materials, the company started its own prefabricating plant for roof trusses and wall
panels in 1957. Sales were made both in-house and to other contractors.

At first Campeau Corp. bought 70 percent of the output and later there was a 50/50 split between in-house and outside customers, Larocque says.

"We developed several new products, including metal connectors for the roof trusses, which were a lot cheaper and faster to attach," Larocque says. Gradually, sales of the connectors and other building supplies were extended throughout Canada and into the U.S. and Europe. A do-it-yourself outlet, Allied Building Supply, was also opened in Ottawa.

The building products division never exceeded $30 million in revenue, although it made a profit until two years ago. Now that the company has moved into office and condominium development and out of single family housing, it plans to divest itself of the building products business.

The European and U.S. operations were sold in 1978 and the Canadian operations were sold this year (1981) to Automated Building Components of Markham, Ontario, one of the world's largest roof truss producers.

One of the most significant events in Campeau Corp.'s development occurred in 1970 in a $45 million deal in which Campeau sold a controlling 52.5 percent interest in his firm to Power Corp.

Power, headed by Paul Desmarais, a native of Sudbury as is Campeau, is a holding company with interests in financial services, transportation, and newsprint. Among the companies it controls are Great-West Life Assurance Ltd., Consolidated Bathurst, and Montreal Trust.

In return for selling control of Campeau Corp. to Power, Campeau gained control of Canadian Interurban Properties Ltd., a real estate developer. Its main assets were shopping centers in Ontario and Quebec and the then fledgling community of Kanata, located just west of Ottawa. Kanata had been started by William Teron, whose firm, William Teron Ltd., was acquired by Canadian Interurban in 1967. Teron later became head of Canada Mortgage and Housing.

The arrangement between Power and Campeau did not last long, and that period was a difficult time in Campeau's personal and business life. Between May 1970 and February 1971, he suffered a nervous breakdown due to the pressures of the year-long negotiations with Power and the breakup of his first marriage. During those months, he went away to recuperate and, associates say, "bounced back."

On his return, he negotiated the buyback of his company. Power sold back its interest to Campeau in May 1972 for $28.5 million, $16.5 million less than it had paid for the holding.

The breakup had two causes. First, Campeau disliked the loss of total autonomy. Second, the link to Power did not provide greater access to funds which he had anticipated.

As Campeau explained in the company's 1971 annual report, issued in April 1972: "We entered into the transaction with Power Corp. because we were able to acquire substantial real estate assets and it was anticipated that substantial financing benefits would accrue to the company from the various financial institutions in which Power Corp. had a major interest.

"Although our relationship with Power Corp. has been pleasant and beneficial, the financing benefits have not materialized because the indirect relationship which has been created between ourselves and the financial institutions (a reference to Great-West Life and Montreal Trust) which are also subsidiaries of Power Corp. make it inadvisable, if not impossible, for us to enter into financial arrangements."

Campeau does not avoid fights, and he has been embroiled in several over the years. Some concerned company projects and others takeover attempts.

In 1968 the company took its first major step into office building development with the $100 million Place de Ville project at the west end of Ottawa's downtown district. Covering six acres on the equivalent of two city blocks, Place de Ville has two hotels with a total of 959 rooms—the Skyline and Holiday Inn—and one million square feet of office space. Located in what Campeau then described as "no man's land," the proposed site consisted of rundown buildings up to 100 years old. The controversy over the project centered around the planned height of the second tower, which broke the city's height restrictions.

Campeau wanted the tower to be 450 feet tall, three times higher than the 150 limit on height. That restriction had been set by the federal government to prevent obstruction of the view of the Peace Tower on Parliament Hill.

The National Capital Commission, the federal agency which had jurisdictional authority over Ottawa's appearance, was willing to allow the tower to be 325 feet high. The Ottawa Planning Area Board supported the NCC.

Campeau agreed to scale the project down to 375 feet, and the haggling over the remaining 50 foot difference delayed the start of construction by months. Eventually Campeau agreed to reduce the tower's height to 342 feet.

Critics of Campeau argued that he bought the land for Place de Ville at a lower price, based on the 150 foot height (9 to 10 floors) restriction, and then got the height jacked up, yielding him substantial profits. They also blamed him for sparking the subsequent construction of skyscrapers in Ottawa.

Supporters said that the federal government was equally at fault in the 150 foot ceiling being broken by such tall buildings as the two 20-story Department of National Defence Towers completed in 1972. Moreover, Place de Ville was positioned so that it would not impinge on the view of the Peace Tower.

The Spires, a 39-story condominium adjacent to the Houston Medical Center, Houston (Artist's rendering)

Ten years later, in 1978, Campeau was again embroiled in controversy over a project for the federal government which the company was awarded without a public tender. It was the $160 million, 1.9 million square foot Les Terrasses de la Chaudière in Hull, Quebec, across from Ottawa. Construction of Les Terrasses took place during a hotly argued move by the federal government to house civil servants both in French-speaking Quebec and English-speaking Ontario to reflect the country's bilingual origins.

Campeau had not promoted the idea of government development in Hull and was a late entrant, following early bird Cadillac Fairview. Because Campeau was slower in going into Hull, the site for Les Terrasses was slightly removed from the center of activity. The federal government and Campeau both said that since he already owned a portion of the land, it would be unfair to expropriate it and award the Les Terrasses project to another developer. But an investigation by the Ottawa *Citizen* said that Campeau had controlled none of the key properties when planning for Les Terrasses started. According to the *Citizen*, government planning for the project started in 1973 and Campeau Corp. did not make its first purchase until March 1974.

Campeau was also accused of pressuring the National Capital Commission to proceed with a planned $3 million land beautification development project across the street from a hotel, L'Auberge de la Chaudière, which Campeau was building adjacent to the government office project. Campeau charged that the NCC was breaking an agreement for the beautification program by placing a two year moratorium on the demolition of housing units and a motel on the site. He threatened to stop construction of the hotel until what he termed "an acceptable solution" was found. Construction had already been suspended for six months.

As evidence of Campeau's alleged pressuring of the NCC, Conservative Members of Parliament released a copy of a February 20, 1978, letter from Campeau to the NCC chairman, Pierre Juneau. It said: "I received a letter from the Deputy Minister (of Public Works) and calls from the Minister of Public Works and from the Minister of State for Urban Affairs. They were all very anxious to have the hotel open its doors in July 1978.

"We have resumed construction in good faith believing that the problem would be solved. I then asked the NCC to abide by its agreement instead of renovating old buildings which will be demolished in two or three years.

"I can understand your problems, especially the matter of the lease for the Diplomate (motel), but I believe that you could go into litigation and that the Diplomate would have to prove its need for compensation. I do not believe they would be very high because this company is probably in debt at this time, or experiencing losses at this time.

However, I do not want to be implicated in that situation.

"I only want the NCC to abide by its agreement. I am taking the liberty of sending a copy of this letter to the Minister of State for Urban Affairs."

The curious circumstances surrounding Les Terrasses prompted some Conservative Members to press for a Royal Commission inquiry, but the Liberal government rejected this request. The Conservatives may also have been grandstanding since their evidence, according to House Leader Walter Baker, who had asked for the inquiry, was circumstantial.

However, Les Terrasses still received a public spanking in a September 1978 report of the Senate Committee on National Finance, "The Accommodation Program of the Department of Public Works." DPW is responsible for housing government civil servants.

The report criticized the federal government for paying above normal rents in Les Terrasses and three other so-called lease-purchase contracts for government occupied buildings in the Ottawa-Hull area. (Under a lease-purchase arrangement, a tenant pays a fixed rent, with an option to purchase the property some time in the future, normally at a predetermined price.)

The Senate Committee said that the government was paying $13.67 or $14.67 per square foot, depending on prevailing interest rates, at Les Terrasses, whereas the current market rate was only $10.70 per square foot. The government was also paying above market rents at two Olympia & York projects and one Cadillac Fairview project, although the spread was not as large as at Les Terrasses.

At Les Terrasses, the rent per square foot was $2.97 to $3.97 above the current market rate. Olympia & York's L'Esplanade Laurier was $1.48 higher, its 240 Sparks Street was $1.02 higher, and Cadillac Fairview's Place du Centre was $1.23 higher.

The report went on to slam the government for awarding both Les Terrasses and Place du Centre without tenders. "In entering into them the Department (of Public Works)...failed to observe precautions taken as a regular course in all other projects for the acquisition of space," the Committee said.

"Given the circumstances of that time—the intense demand for space by the federal government—the lack of capital funds to permit Crown construction and the legitimate desires to obtain firm costs in a highly inflationary environment and to control the architectural development of the National Capital Region—it is understandable that DPW entered into the four Ottawa-Hull lease purchase agreements.

"However, DPW, with the approval of the Treasury Board, failed to observe precautions taken as a regular course in all other projects for the acquisition of space.... These agreements have committed DPW to pay rates for the space involved well beyond the prevailing private sector level." The Committee recommended that future rents in lease-purchase agreements be competitive with the general market rate for straight leases.

Ironically, the report was issued three days after Les Terrasses was officially opened. At that ceremony, Campeau said the project was "a good deal for the federal government and a good deal for Campeau Corp." An editorial in the September 30, 1978, Ottawa *Journal* disagreed, saying, "At least he (Campeau) was half right."

Robert Campeau is used to getting what he wants, but he has never succeeded in takeover attempts of other companies. The unsuccessful 1980 bid for Royal Trustco was just the latest in a series of takeover flops.

The first such try occurred in October 1973 when Campeau attempted to purchase Toronto-based Markborough Properties Ltd., then Canada's tenth largest developer (it still is among the top 15). Markborough's chief attraction was Meadowvale, its 3,000 acre residential development just west of Toronto. Moreover, Markborough's revenue from land operations, cash flow, and net income were all soaring and showing signs of continued steep increases. In 1972, Markborough's land operations revenue doubled from $3.4 million to $7 million. Cash flow was 70.3 cents a share, compared with 44.4 cents in 1971, and net income was $984,000 compared with $540,000 in 1971. By the end of 1973, land operations revenue quadrupled to $29.4 million, cash flow jumped to $3.15 a share, and net income had increased six-fold to $6.1 million.

In addition, Markborough's widely held share ownership made it a sitting duck for a takeover bid. Nobody held more than 10 percent of the company. The major shareholders included Aluminum Co. of Canada, Air Canada pension trust fund, Canadian National Railways pension trust fund, T. Eaton Co., A.E. LePage Ltd., and several life insurance companies.

Peter Langer, Sr., now president of Markborough and then executive vice-president, says "Campeau's offer came out of the blue. He had talked to Brian Magee (then Markborough's president) prior to the offer, but never to management, which we found rather unusual."

Markborough executives were concerned that the company would disappear as an entity and become just a part of Campeau Corp. They also regarded Campeau's price of $16 a share as being too low. According to their evaluations, the pre-tax asset value of the shares was $27 and the after-tax worth $17. Magee recommended that shareholders reject the bid.

A few weeks later, just before Campeau's bid was due to expire, Hudson's Bay Co. made a counter-bid of $17.50 a share. Not only was its bid higher, but also, since The Bay is primarily a department store chain, it meant that Markborough would continue to operate on its own as a real estate subsidiary. That bid was neither opposed nor supported by Magee. Subsequently, Campeau raised its bid to $18.50 and the Bay to $19, the winning offer.

Defeat rapidly followed defeat. An attempt in 1974 by Campeau to buy a major broadcasting firm, Bushnell Communications Co., for $10 million also ran into a stone wall. The Canadian Radio-Television Commission (CRTC), which must approve such transactions, rejected Campeau's bid.

Campeau did not help his cause when he told the CRTC that he was interested in Bushnell only as an investment. The CRTC was also concerned about a possible conflict of interest—Campeau, Ottawa's dominant builder, would own the city's dominant local television station, CJOH.

For the next six years, Campeau made no further acquisition efforts. Then, in August 1980, he bid $453 million for Royal Trustco Ltd., touching off one of Canada's most strident takeover battles.

The battle was viewed by many as the outsider (Campeau) versus the insiders (the Canadian business establishment). Campeau regarded it more as a struggle between an owner-manager (himself) and professional managers (Royal Trustco). Part of the animosity may also have stemmed from Campeau's combative, bare-knuckle reputation, although Royal Trustco showed itself to be an equally tough scrapper.

Royal Trustco defeated Campeau's bid but in the process damaged its reputation. Campeau's allegations that Royal Trustco staved off Campeau by turning to its "friends" to buy Trustco stock and keep it away from Campeau were borne out in a subsequent Ontario Securities Commission hearing.

Campeau's bid for Royal Trustco was in line with the trend among real estate developers to diversify. Because developers have an insatiable need for cash, they are looking more and more toward acquiring financial services companies with which they can do joint ventures through participatory mortgages held by the financial institution.

Moreover, Royal Trustco is Canada's largest trust firm, administering assets of $25.8 billion, including $19 billion in clients' trust funds, in the year Campeau made its bid. The company also is a leading residential real estate broker across Canada, owns a data-processing subsidiary, Computel Systems Ltd., and has banking outlets in Florida, England, and Ireland.

Campeau management regarded Royal Trustco as an ideal fit with Campeau operations. "It would have been the best of all worlds because we wouldn't have been involved much in management and the yield on the Royal Trust shares would have serviced a good part of the debt (arising from the purchase) and Royal Trustco could have aided our real estate expansion," says Don Carroll. "We could see Royal Trustco getting into commercial real estate, participating mortgages, and the acquisition of properties."

At 7:00 a.m. on Wednesday, August 27, 1980, seven hours before Campeau Corp. announced its bid and four days after he requested an appointment with Royal Trustco chairman, Kenneth White, Campeau visited White at White's country estate near Sherbrooke, Quebec.

He announced his intention to buy Royal Trustco, even though Royal Trustco's assets of $7 billion were nearly ten times those of Campeau Corp.'s $866 million. Campeau offered $21 a share for Royal Trustco, which from January to August had been trading between $12 and $16⅛ on the Toronto Stock Exchange. The deal was to be financed through Campeau's longtime banker, the Bank of Nova Scotia.

As Campeau later told the Ontario Securities Commission hearing in vivid detail, White reacted furiously:

"He said, 'I'm telling you right now I won't work for you and if this bid is successful I'm going to quit, and I really don't like you, Campeau, and I don't like Paul Desmarais (head of Power Corp.) and I don't like Conrad Black (head of Argus Corp.) and I don't like Edgar Bronfman. I don't like all these guys making bids for public corporations and I wish to hell you would stay where you are and don't bother us. This is really going to complicate the Bank Act and it is really not helping the French Canadian and English Canadian situation.'

"I said, 'What do you mean by that?' I said, 'Our money is money, isn't it?' I said, 'I don't see the point in that at all,' and then he said, 'Look, I'm telling you now, that you should pull this bid.'

"I said, 'Look, I came down here to tell you that we are going to make a bid and the bid is going to be announced by noon. I wish I could have told you a week ago or four or five days ago ... but we are certainly going to go ahead with it.'

"'Well,' he said, 'it will not be successful.'

"I said, 'You may want to go and get a White Knight but,' I said, 'I have known you for a long time, and you may not get a White Knight. Of course, if a White Knight bids more money, we would have to examine this, but I think we have concluded here that the price is fair and, in other words, I feel there is no reason why we couldn't get along very well.'

"He said, 'There isn't going to be any White Knight.' He said, 'I'm going to stop that. I'm going to call my friends and I am going to lock up fifty-one percent of this stock before you can turn around,' and, he said, 'you may think or you may tell me money talks and really, in the end, shareholders are going to make up their minds, but I'm telling you that I have got ways to persuade these friends of mine to go along with me and they will.'

"He said, 'You know, I think the conversation is pretty well over. I don't want to say any more. I'm going to escort you to my gate,' and I

Proposed 80-story office tower in downtown Houston (Artist's rendering)

went out, and he escorted me to the gate and, before he entered the house, he said, 'You should pull that bid. Pull that damn bid.'

"I said, 'I'm sorry, Ken, but we are not going to pull the bid. The bid is going to go ahead,' and he said, 'Well...' and as he started to walk toward the stair, he turned around, and he said, 'I'm getting on the phone now, and I'm getting all my team together and we are going to stop you,' and that is exactly what he did."

Royal Trustco's August 28 minutes submitted to the OSC hearing of a special meeting of the company's executive committee summarized the August 27 session between White and Campeau in a more restrained fashion:

"The Chairman (White) informed the Directors that early in the morning of 27 August 1980, he had been telephoned at his country home by Mr. Campeau, who indicated an urgent need to meet him immediately. Although he had previously arranged to meet Mr. Campeau at 1:00 p.m. on Friday, 29 August, he consented to see him later in the morning of 27 August.

"The Chairman described the discussion with Mr. Campeau, the disclosure by the latter of his intention to bid for all the shares of Royal Trustco and the request of Mr. Campeau for the Chairman's support and assistance on the basis that he could 'name his own price.' The Chairman stated that he informed Mr. Campeau that he would oppose him and asked him to leave his property immediately."

In its bid, Campeau said it planned no changes in Royal Trustco's management. But it did say in its offer: "If the Offer is successful, the Purchaser intends to conduct a review of the Company's businesses with the assistance of the Company's senior management. The review will focus on ways in which the skills of the Purchaser in the development, brokerage, and management of real property could assist these businesses and will also focus on opportunities for the Company's businesses during the 1980s. Such review may identify areas for the development and improvement of the Company's businesses and could lead to changes in those businesses."

On September 8, Royal Trustco's Directors rejected Campeau's bid on these grounds:
• Royal Trustco is the parent company of Canada's largest group of trust companies and has been entrusted with the management and investment of $19 billion of its clients' assets and funds. The confidence of these clients in the impartial investment of such trust funds should not be jeopardized by placing such assets under the control of a person whose business is in constant demand for funds. In addition, the Royal Trust Group holds in excess of $7 billion of funds held for depositors.
• The Directors have received the opinion of McLeod Young Weir Limited dated September 5, 1980, stating that in its opinion the terms

of the Offer are inadequate from a financial point of view. McLeod Young Weir Limited is a financial adviser to Royal Trustco and is one of Canada's leading investment dealers.

- A significant number of the clients of the Royal Trust Group, including many with substantial assets held in trust by Royal Trust, have indicated that they will withdraw their business from Royal Trust should the Offer succeed. Such withdrawals would have a substantial adverse effect upon Royal Trustco and the Royal Trust Group.
- A successful Offer likely would result in a forced divestiture of Royal Trustco's substantial investment in its United States banking operations as Campeau Corporation has not received the prior approvals required by United States law to acquire control of Royal Trustco.
- Control of Royal Trustco ought not to be in the hands of a single individual or corporation which would then be in a position to influence policies and decisions to the potential disadvantage of the Royal Trust Group of companies and its clients. Independence from such influences must not only exist but be seen to exist in the operations of the Royal Trust Group.
- The experience and competence of Campeau Corporation has little relevance to the ownership and management of Royal Trustco and the Royal Trust Group.
- Based on publicly available information concerning Campeau Corporation and the financing arrangements it has made to fund the Offer, Campeau Corporation would be unable to repay its indebtedness without the sale of substantial assets or acquisition of a substantial new source of revenue.
- The Offer is defective and deficient in providing material information and disclosure. Royal Trustco has authorized counsel to commence appropriate legal actions. It is intended that proceedings be launched on September 8, 1980, to enjoin the Offer and to declare it invalid.
- A shareholder who accepts the Offer may be liable to pay income taxes on one-half of any capital gain.

The four-day Ontario Securities Commission hearing between January 15 and January 20, 1981, found that Royal Trustco was active in trying to stop Campeau well before it issued its September 8, 1980, rejection of the bid.

According to evidence presented at the OSC hearing, Royal Trustco did "approach various companies and institutions with the purpose of either inducing them to hold onto the shares they had in their possession, or going into the market and buying shares and not tendering those shares under the bid."

The hearing found the following purchases were made by some of Canada's biggest corporations after Campeau made its August 27 bid:

ROYAL TRUSTCO LIMITED
SHARES PURCHASED DURING BID PERIOD
(August 28–September 30, 1980)

PURCHASER	COMMON	PREFERRED	CONVERTED PREFERRED (X 1.425)	TOTAL	SHARES HELD AS OF AUG. 27/80	TOTAL HOLDINGS	%
Sun Life Assurance Co. of Canada	408,656	194,600	277,305	685,961	244,633	930,594	4.76
Bank of Montreal	300,000	153,715	219,043	519,043	1,243,666	1,762,709	9.01
The Toronto Dominion Bank	1,611,417	239,990	341,985	1,953,402	0	1,953,402	9.98
Oxford Development Group Ltd.	1,599,518	210,349	299,747	1,899,265	0	1,899,265	9.71
National Trust Co. Ltd.	100,000	0	0	100,000	0	100,000	.51
Commercial Union Assurance Co., Ltd.	110,000	7,700	10,972	120,972	95,833	216,805	1.11
Noranda Mines Ltd.	401,890	69,200	98,610	500,000	0	500,000	2.56
Canadian Pacific Ltd.	81,200	0	0	81,200	—	—	—
	51,000	0	0	51,000	—	—	—
Canadian Imperial Bank of Commerce	516,000	0	0	516,000	0	516,000	2.64
Midland National Bank (Newark, N.J.)	79,281	55,180	78,631	157,912	—	—	—
Deutsche Bank (Frankfurt, West Germany)	350,000	0	0	350,000	150,000	500,000	2.56
Hong Kong and Shaghai Banking Corporation (Hong Kong)	546,200	0	0	546,200	—	—	—
Olympia and York Investments Ltd.	1,518,547	184,100	262,342	1,780,899	0	1,780,899	9.10

Source: *Ontario Securities Commission hearing in the matter of Royal Trustco Ltd.*

On October 2, 1980, Campeau withdrew his bid for Royal Trustco, having been unable to accumulate sufficient shares. True to form, he bowed out fighting. In the company's press release announcing the withdrawal, he said: "Normal market action was obviously disrupted. We should all know who did it and how they did it."

The takeover battle did more good for Campeau Corp. than if it had hired a team of public relations experts to polish up its image, which had suffered from the Place de Ville and Les Terrasses projects and the company's buyback of its stock in 1977 at $7 a share. That price was $3 less than the stock's issue value in 1969, which caused some analysts to label it "a disgrace and an insult."

"We couldn't have bought the publicity that the Royal Trustco takeover offer brought us in the U.S.," says Don Carroll. "At least 85 percent of the publicity was positive for us.

"I was clearing U.S. customs at Toronto International Airport recently and the Customs officer noticed the Campeau sticker on my briefcase and said, 'You're the guys who got burned on the Royal Trustco affair,' which shows how well known we've become. But actually, we didn't get burned and instead made a few million dollars."

That money was made in March 1981 when Campeau sold its eight percent interest in Royal Trustco to Olympia & York for $22 a share, $3 more than it had paid. Campeau made a $5.1 million gain on the sale because of the higher price it got for the stock. But the $2 million it cost the company, primarily in legal fees, in the takeover battle reduced that $5.5 million gain to only $3.3 million.

"We felt that Royal Trust, as the largest trust company, should be making a far better profit and that its potential had not been realized," Don Carroll says about the decision to pull out of the trust company. In the year ended December 31, 1979, Royal Trustco had a profit of $27 million, $3 million more than the number two trust company, Canada Trustco Mortgage Co., which had one-third less revenue than Royal Trustco. (1979 figures are used for comparison because the Royal Trustco takeover battle occurred during 1980 before the 1980 results were completed.)

"As a minority shareholder, we had no input and Kenneth White was unlikely to consult us. We canvassed the market thoroughly to see if we could buy shares and when it was clear that Olympia & York was not going to sell, we sold to them because we couldn't see being stuck with $33 million worth of shares if we had no input."

In its early years, Campeau Corp.'s unique feature, distinguishing it from other developers, was its self-sufficient, integrated operation. It manufactured its own roof trusses and wall panels and had its own lumber yards and sawmills. The self-sufficiency had both benefits and drawbacks. On the plus side, the company was always assured of ready supplies. On the negative side, it meant each division in effect operated as a separate business, with separate management and financial systems.

Campeau Corp. also stood apart from most of the developers in its development of hotels. Most developers avoid operating hotels because of the rollercoaster cycles in profits. Campeau, however, operated two—the 963 room Harbour Castle Hilton in Toronto and the 243 room L'Auberge de la Chaudière in Hull. In 1980, Campeau had a $2.5 million profit from its hotel operations, representing a $1.5 million loss from L'Auberge and a $4 million profit from the Harbour Castle, which opened in 1975 just as Toronto was suffering from a glut in hotel rooms. The Harbour Castle never really recovered, despite that 1980 profit.

As the company moved, in the 1970s, more and more into commercial development and away from housing, and as the hotel market flattened, Campeau's profit from these ventures dropped.

In 1980 profit from the hotel and building materials operations was $2.5 million, or one-seventh of total corporate profit of $14.5 million, compared with $3.4 million, or one-half of total profit in 1979. In addition, these operations are labor intensive. The Harbour Castle employs 600, L'Auberge 300, and the building materials operation 600. By contrast, all other Campeau divisions employ only 600 people.

Campeau has decided to discontinue its direct involvement in hotel, building product, and lumber operations. "We have leased L'Auberge for $1 million a year (compared with last year's $1.5 million loss) plus 75 percent of the profits," Don Carroll says. Negotiations are underway to sell the Harbour Castle to Saudi Arabian investors for $90 million. The interest on that alone would be three to four times last year's $4 million profit.

However, while it is dropping out of hotels and building materials, Campeau will be diversifying into oil and gas, just as other developers such as Nu-West, Carma, and Olympia & York. And although its takeover attempt of Royal Trustco failed, Campeau is still interested in moving into financial services.

"We won't diversify for the sake of diversifying, but only if we can make money in it and bring management expertise to it," Campeau says.

In Canada, Campeau is primarily active in Ontario and Quebec. Last spring (1981), it enhanced its Ottawa presence by buying, for $70.3 million, Admiral Leaseholds Ltd., one of the largest industrial companies in the Ottawa area.

It has just opened its first major office building in western Canada, the 400,000 square foot Principal Plaza in Edmonton. However, it has no projects in Calgary, where most other developers are very active. The company considered entering the Calgary market about three years ago but ruled it out because it thought it was too late. Since then, the boom has continued in Calgary. "We underestimated its strength," Don Carroll says.

Even in Ontario and Quebec, though, Campeau until recently has concentrated on smaller secondary markets rather than the big cities. Its planned Bank of Nova Scotia building in Toronto will be its first office tower in that city. It also has only relatively small regional shopping centers in the city. By contrast, Toronto has been the principal market for most of Canada's developers. With the major ones mostly shunning smaller communities such as Timmins and Oshawa, Campeau had these markets to itself.

Much of the company's emphasis in recent years has been on development in the U.S., although it is a comparatively late entrant. It did not go south until 1978, three years after most Canadian firms headed into the U.S.

But Campeau is rapidly catching up. Proportionately, its U.S. assets are growing at a faster pace than its Canadian assets. In 1978 the U.S. market accounted for 5.3 percent of company assets; now it accounts for 23.7 percent. By contrast, Ontario, the company's biggest geographical sector, has dipped from 56.5 percent of total assets in 1978 to 44.3 percent in 1980.

Campeau's U.S. projects are centered in Florida, Texas, and California. Most are $200,000 and up luxury condominiums, even though that market has softened because of high mortgage rates. Florida was selected because there is interest across the U.S. and Canada in having a Florida condominium in which to spend the winter season or retirement years. California is attractive to overseas investors as well as domestic buyers, and Texas is undergoing a tremendous boom.

"The market will ride the crest of demand," Campeau says. "In the next 10 to 15 years there will be more demand for condominiums than single family housing.

"People's habits are changing and they attach much more importance to their time. Now that they earn $25,000 a year, they are far more reluctant to spend two hours traveling to work than when they made $8,000 a year. They want much more leisure time."

In Toronto, for example, the company has a waiting list of 1,600 names for the 492 units in an addition to its Harbourside condominium apartment project.

The company's philosophy is to be a major presence in a select few markets rather than a small player in huge markets. However, it is moving into the highly competitive luxury condominium market in the Boston-New York-Washington corridor and plans to enter the commercial development scene in Denver and Seattle, also very popular markets.

"Not only is the market larger in the U.S., but it is easier to do business than in Canada because most government authorities are more cooperative in the U.S. with developers than in Canada," president Ronald McCartney says. "For every month it takes to get approval in the U.S., it takes a year in Canada."

One example of the company's shrewdness is its proposed 80-story buildings in Houston and Dallas. Campeau had to get the approval of the Federal Aviation Agency to exceed the 70-story limit on buildings.

"By adding ten storys, those ten floors will be the best for rental, but it will not cost one-seventh more to build them," Carroll says.

In Dallas, Campeau plans two towers with a total of 120 floors. The company is considering first building a 40-floor tower, which is faster to rent, and then an 80-story building.

While it has investigated the Saudi Arabian and European markets, it has ruled out any participation because the distance and difference in time zones would make its hands-on management style very difficult to apply. In addition, it would mean learning a host of regulations in each country.

Campeau's ambitious development plans are increasing its hunger for financing. "We would like to do them all with borrowed money, but that is difficult in these times because lenders want a piece of the action," Carroll says.

The company's lead bank in Canada is the Bank of Nova Scotia. In the U.S., it deals primarily with Bank of America.

Campeau Corp. also decided to get relisted on the Toronto Stock Exchange in May 1981 to be in a position to issue more shares if it needs the money to finance deals.

The company also has installed a more sophisticated system of monitoring its finances and the progress of projects. "Like many businesses, Campeau had not been developing reliable information fast enough regarding where it was, or sufficiently reliable forecasts to make intelligent decisions," Carroll says. "It was getting historical information far too late. As a result, budget projections were largely based on wishful thinking."

Carroll has implemented a more frequent financial reporting and forecasting system. Its main theme is the comparison of actual versus forecasted monthly performance. "It forces managers who are over or under budget to keep head office better informed," Carroll says. "Thus, if the market is weak in one spot, but strong in another, we can push more in the better market."

The monthly summaries, headed by a one-page summary, itemize cash flow, revenue, net assets employed, the return on those assets, the average selling or rental price, and the amount of space being leased. The figures are compared with the year before and with the budgeted forecast.

The financial reports also enable the company to determine

whether the profitability of a project is waning to the point where it should be sold. "In the old days, developers would hold onto shopping centers and office buildings, but now we are taking a much harder look at the continued viability of our assets," Carroll says.

"If those assets have matured and the rate of growth is less than from other assets, we will take a more aggressive posture in selling them than in the past. It's like a stock portfolio — if you wouldn't sell shares in a company, then they are worth keeping."

One thing is certain, though. Campeau will continue to grow rapidly like all the other developers. Whereas it has taken 32 years for the company to reach $1 billion in assets, those assets will likely quadruple within the next five years. Not bad for a man who started at 57 cents an hour.

Chapter Nine

BRAMALEA LIMITED

"Developing a new town is like burying a huge box of gold bullion and getting nothing out for ten years."

ALAN TAYLOR
PRESIDENT (1962-1971)
BRAMALEA

BRAMALEA LTD.

SENIOR MANAGEMENT TEAM

Chairman and Chief Executive Officer:	J. Richard Shiff
President:	Kenneth Field
Executive Vice-President:	Benjamin Swirsky

UNITED STATES OPERATIONS

Executive Vice-President Bramalea California Inc.:	Peter Perrin

OPERATING DIVISIONS

Senior Vice-President:	Bruce Pattison *(Shopping Centers)*
Vice-Presidents:	William Bodrug *(Office Buildings)*
	Myron Boltman *(Industrial)*
	Stewart Davidson *(Finance)*
	Douglas MacKinnon *(Commercial)*
	Cyrus Motahedin *(Marketing)*
	Gordon Deson ⎤
	Gordon Lavis ⎟ *(Construction)*
	David Ptak ⎟
	Edward Tyityan ⎦

OFFICES

Canada
Toronto
United States
Newport Beach, California; Houston

On Thursday, August 1, 1974, Arthur Armstrong resigned the presidency of Bramalea Ltd. Management was taken over by its two major shareholders, J. (Joseph) Richard Shiff, then 48, and Kenneth Field, then 31. Shiff, who had been Bramalea's commercial and real estate lawyer for ten years, and Field, who had been a director since September 1973 and vice-president since early 1974, owned 35 percent of Bramalea. Shiff had also been Armstrong's personal lawyer.

"The gentleman who took over was my own personal lawyer, executor of my estate, and trustee of my children's trust," says Armstrong. "If you derive any implication from that statement, you're welcome to do so." As for Field, Armstrong calls him Shiff's "protegé."

Field says that he and Shiff originally bought shares in Bramalea strictly as an investment and then became concerned about what they viewed as an over-extension geographically and operationally and too loose management. "We never anticipated having control, but once we did, we decided to turn Bramalea into a major company doing major office building projects."

When Armstrong left Bramalea, so did 17 other top executives, according to Shiff. At the time, it was said Armstrong had resigned to go into business on his own. He stayed in the Toronto area for three years and then moved to Phoenix, where he is involved in residential and commercial real estate investment and development through his own firm, Armley Investments, and as vice-president of Hearley Homes. That company was started, and is headed, by Frank Hearley, who was vice-president, residential, at Bramalea and left Bramalea with Armstrong. The Homebuilders Association of Central Arizona describes Hearley Homes as a "medium size" builder.

The 1974 shakeup was the third management upheaval at Bramalea since it was started in 1957. All the changes revolved around questions of management style. Since 1974, all has been calm in the executive suite.

Despite the behind-the-scenes problems, Bramalea has done very well for its stockholders, especially since 1974. The stock has increased 12-fold in value, from $2.23 to $25, since 1974 when Field and Shiff took over. Between 1963, when Bramalea went public, and 1974, the stock ranged from $3 to $7, except for a brief stay at $15.50 back in 1967.

Armstrong, who was 51 in 1974, had nominal shareholdings. According to Field, Armstrong had brought in Field and Shiff as investors in 1973, appealing to them to buy the shares of a major shareholder who was planning to sell out in order to prevent a takeover by another developer.

Although there is a 17 year age difference, Field and Shiff are longtime friends. They have known each other since Field's childhood because Shiff was the lawyer for Field's father. They had disagreed with Armstrong's management style. They were also concerned about the extension of Bramalea into ventures in western Canada, the United States, the Bahamas, and England at a time when the company was heavily involved in the massive 8,000 acre development of the community of Bramalea, a satellite city 16 miles northwest of Toronto. "We never considered walking away; besides, we didn't know if the company was salable," Shiff says.

But Armstrong says Bramalea, started in 1957, had had its most profitable year yet in 1973. Bramalea's annual reports bear this out. In fiscal 1973, the company had a $3.3 million profit, compared with $1.9 million in 1972, its previous high. Prior to that, Bramalea had either recorded losses or a razor thin profit.

Although Bramalea had got off to a slow start and was virtually bankrupt in 1962, new management under Armstrong, then executive vice-president, and Alan Taylor, then president, turned the company around.

Since Shiff and Field took control, the company has been managed efficiently and diversified from strictly residential into commercial properties, a much more stable form of real estate development than housing, which is more vulnerable to cyclical demand.

Among Bramalea's major office projects is a five-block, $400 million project, to be called Main Center, in Dallas. Construction on the venture, the largest in that city's history, will start next year. The Center will have two 70-story office towers, a 600 room hotel, and retail space. About 40 percent of the first tower, scheduled for completion in 1984, will be occupied by the First National Bank of Dallas. Field regards it as the culmination of Bramalea's seven year drive to become a major office developer.

Since 1974, when Shiff and Field took over Bramalea, its assets have risen six times from $165 million to $1 billion, typical of the spectacular increase in real estate developers' assets in the boom that started in the late 1970s and is still continuing. Revenue has jumped from $66 million to $170 million, and net income has nearly quadrupled from $2.4 million to $9.2 million.

All this has been reflected in Bramalea's trading on the Toronto Stock Exchange. Taking stock splits into account, Bramalea's shares have risen from $2.23, at the time of the management change, to around $25 in 1981.

This has made Shiff and Field "paper" millionaires many times over, with their shareholdings now worth around $50 million each. Shiff and his family own 2,014,663 shares, or 23.3 percent, and Field and his family own 1,980,765 shares, or 23 percent.

J. Richard Shiff, chairman and chief executive officer, Bramalea (Photo: Susan Goldenberg)

However, the problems in its early days and the heavy financial demands of the new town of Bramalea kept the company out of two hot areas pursued by other Canadian developers—western Canada and the United States. In 1975 Bramalea purchased a number of prime shopping centers, a Vancouver hotel (the Hyatt Regency), a Toronto hotel (the Four Seasons), and three Edmonton office buildings from another developer, the then troubled Trizec.

Since 1975, however, Bramalea has done little development in western Canada, although it is building an addition to one of the Edmonton buildings. It has no office towers in Calgary, Canada's oil capital and the site of a tremendous boom in construction and demand for space. By contrast, the Edmonton market is not as strong. According to a 1981 survey of the Canadian real estate market by A.E. LePage Ltd., pre-leasing of office space, due to come onto the market this year in Calgary, is 100 percent compared with only 30 percent in Edmonton.

"We didn't move soon enough to get into Calgary and it's hard to find land, although the bloom is off now because of the oil price differences between the federal and Alberta governments," says John Taylor, chairman of Bramalea's executive committee and formerly chairman of the Board. No relation to Alan Taylor (Bramalea's president from 1962 to 1971), John Taylor is also chairman of North American Life Assurance Co., Canada's 11th largest life insurer.

Bramalea had become involved briefly in the U.S. in the early 1970s under Armstrong, but that venture, although successful, was dissolved by the co-partner, Kaiser Steel, which wanted to curb its diversification. Bramalea did not re-enter the U.S. market until 1979.

It now has only five percent of its assets in the U.S., whereas most Canadian developers have at least half their assets south of the border. But it is moving fast to catch up. Shiff predicts that half of Bramalea's assets will be in the U.S. by 1985. Also, Bramalea is one of two of Canada's top ten developers (Nu-West is the other) to have Americans as outside members on its Board. They include Texas oil baron Clint Murchison, Jr., who joined Bramalea's Board in the spring of 1981.

Bramalea is certainly not the only Canadian developer to have had problems and dissension in its early days. Trizec was near bankruptcy when it was taken over by Peter and Edward Bronfman, who subsequently swept out the previous management. Oxford lost its principal backer, Great-West Life, because of disagreements over financing and expansion policies.

In most of these cases, the decisive hand has been held by the people holding the most shares. Bramalea was no exception. Although Armstrong made a handsome salary of $91,250 in 1973, he owned very few shares. Neither did his predecessor as president, Alan Taylor, who had become vice-chairman and was earning $72,100 in 1973. Both had been hired as professional managers by the British investors who were

Kenneth Field, president, Bramalea

the largest shareholders of Bramalea until Field and Shiff bought into the company in the early 1970s.

Because Bramalea was a widely held company and the British had only 13 percent, it was easier for Field and Shiff to increase their shareholdings in the open market than if Bramalea had been closely held by one or two investors. The largest British investor was Eagle Star Insurance, one of the world's largest insurance companies. One of its subsidiaries, English Property, owned a controlling interest in Trizec until 1976.

Field was already considerably wealthy. His father had owned a photo-finishing business that eventually was sold to 3M and became 3M's Canadian photographic operation.

As Field tells it, he and Shiff started to buy shares in Bramalea in 1973 at Armstrong's request because Armstrong was worried that the planned sale of shares by a major shareholder, Robert Hunt of London, Ontario, would make the company vulnerable to a takeover. (Hunt held 140,000 shares of the total 7,123,114 issued in 1973.) Field had met Armstrong when they were involved in a joint venture housing development project east of Toronto.

"Senior management had no (substantial) financial stake in the company and were worried they might lose their jobs after a takeover," Field says. "There were rumors that Cadillac Fairview Corp. and Denison Mines, among others, were interested in acquiring the company.

"Armstrong asked us to keep away the rumored contenders for Bramalea by buying Hunt's shares," Field says. To buy Hunt's shares, Field and Shiff formed the Field Syndicate in which Field, his brother, and sister held 57.5 percent and Shiff, his wife, and children had 42.5 percent. Subsequently, the Field Syndicate increased its Bramalea holdings to a 35 percent interest.

On September 12, 1973, Field became a director of Bramalea. On January 1, 1974, he became vice-president. He says he found "a number of managerial decisions and operating methods were troublesome. Dick and I had a number of meetings with Arthur Armstrong about this.

"We always had high regard for Arthur Armstrong. He was an honest, capable officer, but his management style was different from that we envisioned. Some companies are managed successfully by remote control....Our approach is much more hands-on for significant decisions."

On June 27, 1974, Armstrong announced the election of Shiff as vice-chairman and Field as executive vice-president. "We weren't satisfied, nor were the English shareholders, with the company," Shiff says.

"I took a six months' leave of absence from my law firm (Shiff & Gross of Toronto). The vice-chairmanship was a title to get me in to start working. The company was not liquid at that time and had serious financial problems which required management changes and we asked for them to be made."

What was making Field and Shiff unhappy was Bramalea's geographical expansion.

Bramalea was ahead of its time in that it was the first major eastern Canadian developer to move into western Canada and the first Canadian firm to branch into the southern U.S. and overseas, although only briefly. But its timing was bad since it coincided with a downturn in U.S. and British real estate. Also, the boom in western Canada was still several years in the future.

The diversification occurred at whirlwind speed. In 1969 the firm purchased a controlling interest in the Crown Colony Club, a resort at Chub Cay in the Bahamas. That was followed by a string of new ventures in 1971.

Bramalea formed a joint venture — Kaiser-Bramalea Corp. — with Kaiser Cement and Gypsum Corp. of Oakland to pursue community and land development in the U.S. Kaiser and Gypsum, part of the Kaiser's empire, had building operations on both the west and east coasts of the U.S.

In addition, Bramalea established Bramalea Overseas Ltd. for residential, commercial, and urban renewal projects in England and Bramalea Wescorp Developments, a joint venture for projects in western Canada.

Unfortunately, none of these deals worked out. The firm became embroiled in a lawsuit over the management of the Bahamian resort. The houses built in England cost double their budgeted amount. Moreover, although during construction the British pound fell dramatically, the project did not benefit because it had been financed in Canadian dollars. Thus, Bramalea was battered in two directions by losses in the English venture. The partnership in western Canada was having problems and Kaiser decided to withdraw from the joint venture in California. "The whole exercise of this expansion was viewed at that time as being poorly executed and ill-conceived," Field says.

"Everybody was having problems in 1973, but the Bramalea people didn't handle them as well because they were inexperienced and pioneers. Also, their managerial knowledge had not been built up."

But Armstrong and his predecessor, Alan Taylor, under whom the expansion had begun, maintain that it was essential in order to finance the vast undertaking of the new town of Bramalea. "It took about ten years for the Bramalea new town area to be profitable," Taylor says.

"The initial profits of the company were made from other activities — building shopping centers plus housing across Canada and in England.

"The Bramalea new town was the type of project that required what is called patient money, in which investors are willing to wait for

The Renaissance, Cumberland Avenue, Toronto (Artist's rendering)

rewards which normally are far greater than those obtained by impatient money."

Armstrong says that moving into western Canada and the U.S. was "a direction the company should have stayed in." He says that Bramalea, which was "virtually bankrupt" when Taylor became president and Armstrong executive vice-president in 1962, was turned around by doing "land development elsewhere to finance (the community of) Bramalea."

Field says that the conflict simmering between him and Shiff on the one hand and Armstrong on the other came to a dramatic head in the summer of 1974 over Armstrong's proposal that a new apartment project be started in Bramalea. "We felt the company would be in error to build rental apartments at that time without long-term financing," Field continues. "When we discovered the construction department was starting to issue construction orders to sub-contractors, we wanted to call a meeting of the senior management.

"Arthur Armstrong happened to be in San Francisco and the other senior executives were also away on business. With regard to protecting our investment and deciding whether to maintain or dispose of it, Dick and I called Armstrong in San Francisco and asked to meet him there. We set up a meeting for two days later.

"When we arrived, we found that he had assembled all the other senior executives to confront us," Field recalls. Armstrong says only two other executives were present.

"The basic tenor of the meeting was who was in charge of Bramalea—them or us," Field continues. "They said if it was to be us, they would resign en masse."

Because Field and Shiff owned part of Bramalea and the others had only a nominal financial stake in the company, Field and Shiff held the winning hand. "We accepted their ultimatum," Shiff says.

Armstrong says that "until the very last minute, the gentleman was my personal lawyer and knew everything about me and Bramalea."

Alan Taylor says that the situation was a matter of "incompatibility. Armstrong didn't get along with the new people and they agreed to part company. It's a normal happening."

Field and Shiff both vividly remember the day after the management change, arriving at Bramalea's 11th floor headquarters in its then two-year-old head office in mid-Toronto, and speculating about the contents in the bank of filing cabinets.

"I'll never forget standing with Dick in the doorway of Arthur Armstrong's office—or rather, former office—and looking at the rows and rows of filing cabinets and wondering what was in them," Field says.

But while Shiff and Field certainly could not have known all the nittygritty details, Shiff's ten years as one of Bramalea's lawyers and Field's vice-presidency and Board membership undoubtedly had made them very knowledgeable about the company. Nor was Bramalea in an organizational mess. In 1972, the firm had moved from a manual to a computer accounting information system which was used until 1981 when the company outgrew it because of its increasing assets.

Executives who joined the firm say that the transition was fairly smooth. This was the case in Bramalea's then biggest business sector—land development, according to the person who took over the division, Morris Smith, formerly a lawyer in Brampton, a city adjacent to Bramalea.

"I didn't inherit a dog's breakfast," he says. "Projects were not behind or in a mess. My predecessor, Murray Hardisty, stayed on for several months to acquaint me with agreements and negotiations and I frequently consulted him after he moved to western Canada."

Still, with most of the executives departing (a key and important exception was Stewart Davidson, now vice-president, finance), Shiff and Field had to find replacements. Field placed a full page advertisement in Toronto's *The Globe and Mail*, saying Bramalea was under new management and needed senior executives. He says he was inundated with telephone calls and letters. "I conducted breakfast interviews at 7:00 a.m., 8:00 a.m., and 9:00 a.m., held meetings the rest of the morning, and then gave lunch interviews at 11:30, 12:30, and 1:30. But most of the people weren't as senior as we wanted.

"Many of them, however, had worked for Bruce Pattison, then senior vice-president in charge of shopping centers at Cadillac Fairview. They kept saying Pattison had taught them everything they knew. I decided to call Pattison. He was reluctant to join but liked the challenge of building up a shopping center division from scratch.

"So I called Eph (Allen Ephraim) Diamond, then chairman at Cadillac Fairview and said I would like to hire away Pattison. Diamond said he understood, that we should do what we had to about staff, and wished us well." Later, Field hired several other Cadillac Fairview executives as well.

There may have been something of an ulterior motive behind Diamond's seeming generosity. Cadillac and Fairview, formerly separate companies, had just merged and Diamond had to integrate the two managements. Bramalea's hiring away of people served to ease Diamond's task.

One of the key slots that had to be filled quickly was the vice-presidency of land development. "Our lifeblood in terms of cash flow was the release of housing lots and we needed somebody with expertise in negotiating with the municipalities to get zoning approved for housing construction," Field says.

He hired Morris Smith, who had been the City of Brampton's solicitor between 1963 and 1970. Subsequently, Smith went into private practice and did work for the Township of Chinguacousy (*pron*. Chincousy), home base of the new town of Bramalea.

Smith had drafted many of the regulations covering the new town's development. Moreover, not only did he know all the rules; he also knew all the politicians and civic administrators.

Smith had met Field and Shiff only casually once or twice, but he did not hesitate to join Bramalea despite the management shakeup. "It was a challenge, a mountain to climb, and a gamble," Smith says.

"But people I contacted about Shiff and Field spoke highly of them. Unlike the previous management, which had little financial stake in the company, Shiff's and Field's ownership gave them a vested interest in the company. Moreover, I had the opportunity to be in charge of one of the largest land banks in Canada."

Smith left in June 1980 because he felt that with Bramalea concentrating on commercial development and having only one new land bank in California, there was "no more mountain to climb." But he retains a connection with the firm. Bramalea is a client of a land development consulting business he established.

When Smith joined the firm, Bramalea's major holding was the new town of Bramalea, but it also owned land north of Toronto at Unionville and east at Pickering.

"Bramalea was the farthest ahead," Smith says. "It had a population of 35,000 (versus 62,982 in the 1980 enumeration), a shopping center, and a municipal building. But some agreements had to be renegotiated because regional government had just been introduced in January 1974, nine months before I joined the company."

Field and Shiff offered two attractive incentives to management — autonomy and share ownership. "I never had to phone them during a Council meeting to get their approval for agreements," Smith says.

In addition, senior executives can obtain interest-free loans to purchase Bramalea shares. Not only does that mean the probability of getting rich, but it also gives the management an incentive to make the company successful.

"Everyone who started with us in 1974 is a millionaire today," Field says. The value of the stock has soared from $2.23 to $25 after a two-for-one split.

Although Shiff and Field control Bramalea, directors say they are amply consulted and not regarded as rubber stamps. "Even though they control the company, they do not regard it as their personal corporation," says a Bramalea director. "They handle it the same way as a widely-held public company is run."

Shiff says that there are no plans to make Bramalea private, as has happened with Oxford and, to a large degree, with Campeau. "Our policy is definitely to keep public," he says.

Although there is a 17 year age difference between Shiff and Field, mutual friends say their relationship is more like that of brothers or friends than father and son.

After Field, who holds degrees in business and law, graduated from Toronto's Osgoode Hall Law School, Shiff asked Field to join his law firm, Shiff and Gross, as a junior partner.

"He told me he liked law, but that he would rather be on the other side of the desk as a client," Shiff recalls. Field, unlike Shiff, has never practiced law.

Field did not article for Shiff after completing his law course. Instead, he articled at the Toronto law firm of Goodman and Goodman, lawyers for Cadillac Fairview.

"That was during the time that Cadillac and Fairview, then separate companies, were discussing merging their operations (completed in 1974) and proceeding with the (8,000 acre) Erin Mills new community west of Toronto," Field recalls. "The experience proved invaluable."

After being called to the Bar, Field worked as executive assistant to the president (George Mann) of newly formed United Trust, which

Toronto Star Building, Toronto

later bought Bramalea's Ontario real estate brokerage business once Shiff and Field took over Bramalea.

When Field and Shiff took over Bramalea, Shiff says he "wanted a young person directly involved in the operating end. My plan was to sit in my backyard, look at my swimming pool, and set policy," he jokingly adds.

Today, Shiff as chairman, Field as president, and executive vice-president Benjamin Swirsky, 39, act as an interchangeable triumvirate. "There are no specific duties or areas of responsibilities," Shiff says.

"Instead, there is a constant overlap, so that when one of us is away, the others can assume the responsibilities. We work by consensus, with each of us acting as a devil's advocate."

The trio work in adjacent offices on the 11th floor of Bramalea's modest headquarters in mid-Toronto.

There are paintings by Toronto-born abstract painter Jack Bush, whose work was influenced by Picasso, in Bramalea's waiting room along with old magazines. Field's, Shiff's, and Swirsky's offices are spacious but sparsely furnished. Field has huge blown-up pictures, which he took, of his beautiful blonde second wife and children on the walls of his office.

However, while there is no formal division of authority among the three men, Swirsky, a lawyer and accountant by training, heads Bramalea's operations on a day to day basis, with the company's vice-presidents reporting to him.

Shiff and Field have no line responsibilities regarding management. Field generally deals with acquisitions and spent a year in California in 1978 scouting opportunities there for the company in preparation for Bramalea's 1979 move into the U.S. market. Shiff concentrates on general policy matters and dealings with government authorities. But it was Field who cancelled and later rescheduled an interview with Shiff for this book.

Bramalea's triad is becoming the rule rather than the exception in the real estate development industry. Expansion geographically and operationally has made the burdens of traveling, administration, acquisition, and diversification too much for one person to handle.

Other firms with multiple top management are Olympia & York (brothers Albert and Paul Reichmann), Cadillac Fairview (chairman John Daniels and vice-chairmen Neil Wood and Bernard Ghert), and Genstar (the positions of chairman and president rotate between Angus MacNaughton and Ross Turner).

"By reputation I am supposed to be conservative and Ken is the aggressive one," Shiff says. "But I don't think it always works that way. Sometimes, I am more of a gambler. Ben's (Swirsky) accounting background makes him more of a leavener. He provides the meat and bones to the ideas Ken and I have."

Bramalea is the only developer among Canada's top ten firms where the three top executives are all lawyers. "The legal background has given them training in logical thinking, the ability to do instant research, to call on resource people, and to see what their goals are and how to get there," says Bramalea director Enid Hildebrand, who is a lawyer in the Toronto brother-sister firm of Gold and Hildebrand.

Bramalea is the only one of Canada's top ten developers with a woman on its Board of Directors. Mrs. Hildebrand and her brother, Peter, were childhood acquaintances of Field.

Although Shiff, who was a partner for many years in the leading Toronto law firm of (now Senator) David Croll and Norman Borins, no longer practices law, he has not entirely left the field. He holds a Masters in Law degree in land development and estate planning and teaches a winter semester in land development problems to the third year class at Osgoode Hall Law School.

Shiff started to teach because his five sons' opinion of him dropped when he gave up law in 1974 to head up Bramalea. "Developer was then a dirty word, with the image of a desperado, someone with a big fat cigar, a speculator," Shiff says. "I felt that responsible development companies do not destroy communities and that this message had to be got across at the student level. A lot of young lawyers go into government and they were going in, I thought, with a distorted view of the industry and this was causing problems. So, I started to make speeches, as did other developers, and to teach land development.

"I think there has been a turnaround in the general public's attitude toward the industry, including the attitude of those in government. Also, students are increasingly interested in development and not from a negative standpoint."

Shiff also hopes that his five university-age sons will eventually join Bramalea. Two are studying law, another is in engineering, the fourth in architecture, and the fifth is learning Middle Eastern languages.

Shiff is more quiet-spoken than the high pressure Field who, when he recounts Bramalea's colorful and turbulent history and subsequent management changes, waves his arms in infectious enthusiasm. When Field required a new secretary earlier this year, one of the qualifications listed in the newspaper advertisement was the need for a sense of humor.

A heavy smoker of Cameo cigarettes, Field paces back and forth as he talks. Like Shiff, he works in his shirt sleeves.

Ben Swirsky, the third member of the executive trio, and Field have been friends for 15 years, dating back to college days. Swirsky attended Queen's University law school and met Field through mutual friends.

"Ben intended to become a lawyer, but is so brilliant that Peat Marwick (one of Canada's top eight accounting firms) wanted him to join them instead," Field says. "Ben was interviewing at law firms in Toronto and Peat Marwick asked him to please just drop into their Toronto tax section."

The ploy worked. "Ben soon became a senior partner in charge of Peat Marwick's Toronto operations," Field continues. "He was the youngest person ever to be appointed to Peat Marwick International."

Among the deals Swirsky negotiated was the acquisition in 1973 of Markborough Properties Ltd., then Canada's tenth largest developer, by Hudson's Bay Co., Canada's oldest and biggest department store chain.

"We relied on Ben for taxation and business advice and kept telling him we wanted him to join Bramalea. During one of my trips home in 1978 from California, where I was investigating opportunities for Bramalea, I told Ben the expansion possibilities for the company and he decided to join."

In the seven years since Shiff and Field took over, Bramalea has broadened from homebuilding and land development into a major developer of office buildings and shopping centers from which the company now derives more than half its revenue.

The competition among developers for prime locations is intense. Who wins out is often due to an element of luck. Whoever hears of something first, frequently by chance, is often the winner, provided the company has the capability and money to follow up the lead with lightning speed.

Field and Shiff readily admit they have had their share of good luck. Such was the case, for instance, with the company's $400 million Main Center project in Dallas.

"The Murchison family (an enormously wealthy Texas oil dynasty) had assembled five blocks in downtown Dallas 20 years ago, across the street from the building that J.R. Ewing (the villain in the popular television program *Dallas*) is seen entering to go to his office," Field says.

"Douglas MacKinnon, our vice-president of marketing, overheard at a cocktail party that Clint Murchison, Jr. (head of the Murchison clan) wanted to sell the land. MacKinnon called me and I took the next plane to Dallas." Murchison has now joined Bramalea's Board, which should give the company prestige and clout in its quest for further expansion in the U.S. southwest.

Another recent major land assembly along Broadway Street, Denver's widest thoroughfare, was also due to chance. Part of the property was owned by a cousin of a Bramalea executive. Bramalea plans to build two million square feet of office space on the site in a joint venture with Cadillac Fairview.

Together, these two projects, both strokes of good fortune, will increase Bramalea's assets by $750 million, Field says. The significance of this can be best appreciated when placed in perspective. It took 24 years, up until the beginning of 1981, for Bramalea to reach $750 million in assets. Current assets are now around $1 billion.

Although the community of Bramalea now has 63,000 residents compared with about 15,000 in 1971, and the amount of industrial space has grown from 140,000 square feet to three million, its contribution to overall corporate profit has dropped as that of other sectors has risen. In 1971, according to Stewart Davidson, vice-president, finance, the new town contributed 75 percent of profits; today, it is still the single largest contributor, but its share is down to 50 percent of company profits.

In its early days, the Bramalea community was a jinx as all its managements ran into financial difficulties and were either bought out or replaced. This happened three times before the last episode, the 1974 resignation of Armstrong.

Bramalea was Canada's first and only satellite city and the first one to be developed in North America by private enterprise. There are now several in the U.S., but there have been no successors in Canada.

The reason is spelled *money*. It costs a lot to develop a new town and it takes years to get a payback. "It's like burying a huge box of gold bullion and getting nothing out for ten years," says Alan Taylor, Bramalea president from 1962 to 1971.

The history of Bramalea stretches back nearly 30 years to the scheme of three southern Ontario real estate brokers to build a new town northwest of Toronto. They picked as their site the Township of Chinguacousy.

In its 1951 Official Plan, the Township said: "The township has no available sources of water and those now drawn on by the (nearby) Town of Brampton indicate that they will be strained to provide for the normal expansion of that town.

"In addition to the absence of a suitable water supply, the flat clay plain lying around Brampton presents a major drainage problem for any contemplated urban use.... It is important that anyone contemplating development should be forewarned of the impracticability of providing ordinary drainage except for farm purposes.

"In view of all these circumstances and after careful study of the problems presented, the whole of the Township of Chinguacousy is hereby designated as a rural area in which the density of population shall be such that it will not require the provision by the municipality of a public water supply, storm, or sanitary sewerage."

But the Plan then went on to leave the door open to development. "While no urban development in any form will be undertaken, no obstacle will be placed in the way of any land owners who wish to have their lands annexed to the Town of Brampton or who wish to incorporate so as to assume the full responsibilities of urban development."

Three years later, ignoring what had been said, three local real estate brokers, Tom Spriggs, Magnus Paulson, and Donald Kerr, began to assemble land for a "satellite city" to Toronto.

Their land assembly, seemingly in the middle of nowhere, was not really a harebrained idea because the site was three miles from the Toronto airport and several aircraft manufacturing plants, including that of the Avro Arrow long range fighter plane. But the Avro Arrow project was cancelled in 1959 by the federal government, just as Bramalea was getting underway.

Sprigg, Paulson, and Kerr set in motion a chain of events which would see the establishment of Bramalea Ltd., management swings from Canadians to English to Americans, and controlling ownership changes from Canadian to British and back to Canadian. Most of the time, the basic problem was that there was too little money to back such a grandiose scheme.

Caught in the turmoil were the young families who moved to Bramalea, lured by the low prices and promises of an integrated community life with shopping, a civic center, and a hotel. Because of Bramalea's financial and management problems, it took almost 15 years to get many of these amenities.

Salesmen would point out where regional shopping centers and other community services would be. Bramalea advertising promised these services, too, but nothing happened for years. Besides living in what they regarded as a barren wasteland, residents also were incensed by such other inconveniences as a lack of public transportation and having to pay long distance charges to phone Toronto, whose outskirts were just a few miles away.

Sprigg, Paulson, and Kerr assembled 2,000 acres of farmland. Then, short of money, they sold out to three local investors — James Sihler, Ralph Henson, and George Clarke. This trio formed Bayton Holdings Ltd. with the purpose of creating a new town. Such an undertaking was a daring first for Canada, although the concept had been popular in England and tried in the U.S.

A new town is a planned community started from scratch in an area with no other significant development. Unlike a large subdivision, the size and eventual population of new towns are planned in advance and are usually located some distance, as Bramalea is, from the nearest built-up area.

New towns also are meant to be self-contained and self-sustaining communities which provide the same cultural, social, recreational, and work opportunities that are available in a city. Usually, they do not have a university or theater, as a city does.

In addition, new towns differ from conventional large "bedroom" (residential only) subdivisions by including factories to provide local jobs for residents, a town center to provide community focus, and more controlled land use planning. Housing density often is greater than in subdivisions in order to allow for more community open space for recreation.

Although located some distance from big cities, new towns seek to have an urban flavor through a mix of housing styles ranging from high rise apartments to townhouses and single family homes.

The concept of new towns dates back at least to the sixteenth century when Leonardo da Vinci (1452-1519 A.D.), dismayed at living conditions in Milan, proposed a group of ten cities in which pedestrian and horse traffic would be separated and in which the population would be limited to 30,000. His idea was never acted upon.

The idea was revived in 1902 by a British court reporter, Ebenezer Howard, who sought to relieve the congestion of his native London by building a series of new towns. Like da Vinci, Howard suggested a planned population of 30,000. However, his proposal was denounced as socialistic because he suggested that the land be held in common and the profits resulting from improvements be shared by the residents.

Howard's idea later caught on in Europe as a result of the devastation of many cities during World War II and the subsequent problem of how to house the population, despite the scarcity of land and housing.

European new towns, however, unlike those in the U.S. and Bramalea, are government planned. The first North American new town was Radburn, New Jersey, which was completed in 1929.

Building a new town is an ambitious and costly project, and the three founders of Bayton Holdings soon found that like their predecessors, they needed more money since they wanted to double their land bank to 4,500 acres. In 1956, Bayton sought help from Arthur Martens, a former Canadian who had become chairman of Close Brothers Ltd., a British merchant bank, and was visiting Toronto at the time.

Martens formed a syndicate of three British firms — Eagle Star Insurance Co., Cayzer Trust (a holding company for the investment interests of the Union Castle and Clan Steamship Lines), and British Electric Traction. The three British firms, well acquainted with the success of new towns in England, decided to buy out Bayton for $5.5 million.

They then changed the company's name to Bramalea Consolidated Developments Ltd. and gave the same name to the new town. *Bra* came from the neighboring community of Brampton, *ma* from the nearby Malton airport (now called Toronto International Airport), and *lea* from the British word for meadow, which described the farmland from which the new town would grow.

In 1960, one of the backers, Eagle Star Insurance, also obtained a major interest in another Canadian developer when it co-founded Trizec Corp. in that year. This loose connection between Bramalea and

Trizec would become significant many years later. In 1975 Eagle Star engineered the sale of many prime properties owned by the then financially troubled Trizec to Bramalea. That sale catapulted Bramalea into the big league.

In May 1958 Bramalea Consolidated issued its first advertising brochure filled with pride and promises about its mammoth undertaking. "Through the creation of the satellite city, the name Bramalea will become a familiar one," it said. "It will identify a new and thriving Canadian community and stand for all that is best in contemporary living.... To complete the satellite city, Bramalea Consolidated Developments itself will spend at least $50 million.

"This will cover the purchase of land, the construction of public utilities, a share of school costs and overhead expenses for engineering, marketing, sales, public relations and administration. Hundreds of millions more dollars will be spent over the next decade by builders, industries and other interests contributing to the satellite city's completion....

"The completed satellite city will contain about 20,000 homes and some 200 miles of paved roadway. It is estimated that its construction will utilize 240,000,000 board feet of lumber, 180,000,000 bricks, 32,000,000 square feet of roofing materials and 100,000,000 square feet of sodding.

"Some 8,000,000 cubic feet of concrete will go into basements and walls and over 135 miles of sanitary sewer pipes will be laid along with 140 miles of water mains. About 240,000 tons of asphalt will be used to pave the streets which will also require some 3,000,000 cubic yards of gravel and grading materials."

Soon, just like the two previous sets of owners, the new Bramalea Consolidated Developments found itself in financial trouble. Shields & Co., a New York underwriter, agreed to bail out Bramalea with a $12 million stock issue in 1960 on the condition that the English backers put up half the money and install U.S. management. As a result, John Galbreath, who had built company mining towns in the United States, was hired as president.

Two years later, the British, dissatisfied with the lack of progress at Bramalea, terminated Galbreath's contract and brought in a new team. Alan Taylor, commercial manager of Close Brothers, the merchant bank that had formed the three-way British syndicate ownership of Bramalea, was made president.

Arthur Armstrong, who was British, had come to Canada in 1948 and had a background in real estate and importing. He was made executive vice-president. He had joined Bramalea in 1958 as secretary-treasurer.

Taylor retired early from Bramalea as president in 1971 at the age of 61, but he remained as vice-chairman for two years. Still residing in

Toronto, Taylor, a yachtsman "all my life," was chairman of C&C Yachts Ltd. of Toronto from 1971 to 1978.

"I was sent to Bramalea, originally on a two year assignment, to see what could be done to make the company go forward or sell the assets, if that was impossible," Taylor says. "When it was apparent there wasn't management available to replace me, I decided to stay on and manage the company."

Taylor describes himself as one of Close Brothers' "firemen who were sent around the world to put out financial fires." Before coming to Bramalea, Taylor had never managed a real estate firm, but he had turned around both a troubled meat packing firm and an engineering company in Europe. "Management is management," he says.

One of Taylor's first moves was to diversify the company into other ventures — shopping centers and homebuilding across Canada and in England. The company's slogan was "Building across the nation."

"The company's initial profits came from activities outside the Bramalea community," Taylor says. Eventually, Bramalea had holdings in Alberta, British Columbia, Quebec, Oklahoma, Georgia, California, and Colorado. This was close to a decade before other Canadian developers went into the U.S.

When Taylor arrived at Bramalea, only 20 houses had been built at the new town, he says, even though the project had originated five years earlier. Further development was stymied by a lack of servicing. Without water and sewage trunk lines, building houses is not feasible since few potential homebuyers want an unserviced house.

"It was a chicken and egg situation," Taylor says. "Such a project requires both housing and industry. It especially needs industry to provide the industrial taxes that the municipality can use to pay for installing servicing.

"But industry won't come unless there are people living there. So we gave the land away to attract big industries."

According to Bramalea's 1963 annual report, the company sold land for plants to three companies — Northern Electric Ltd. (now Northern Telecom Ltd.), Thomas J. Lipton Co., and Chrysler Air Conditioning for $37,617, or $310,546 less than the cost of the land. In addition, Bramalea bore the $361,000 cost of developing the land.

Taylor says it took about six to 12 months to sign up the three firms, but that it was worth it because the Township of Chinguacousy then started to install servicing.

By 1972, Bramalea had 7,600 houses, 510 rental units, and several small neighborhood shopping centers.

Despite the growth in size, an easy street system prevents visitors from getting lost. Houses are grouped in alphabetical sections, with all streets in each section beginning with the same letter. For example, "M" section streets include Mandrake, Mallard, and Montrose.

Trinity Square, Denver

Early residents found low prices of $16,000 and low monthly payments of around $175. The same house would sell today for $65,000. At the same time, residents found that none of the services promised by Bramalea and typical of new towns, such as a town center and shopping, were materializing.

"Taylor and Armstrong treated us like colonials," recalls Terry Miller, a member of the Chinguacousy Council at the time. He was one of four councillors elected in 1969 on a platform criticizing Bramalea for lacking shopping, a hotel, local phone rates for calls to Toronto, and better public transportation.

"They were very difficult people with whom to deal," Miller continues. "They never said they wouldn't do something, but they wouldn't say when they would do it."

In addition, as the only developer, Bramalea was able to impose its design goals, which included stipulating the size of fences and prohibiting television aerials. On the other hand, Miller points out that Bramalea did donate land for Bramalea's first school as well as space for a library and sponsored local hockey and baseball teams.

"We started a newspaper (*The Guardian*) which was later sold to the Inland Publishing Co. (a chain of papers put out in Toronto's suburbs)," Taylor says.

"We also started a bus service and police, fire, and engineering departments in addition to a fullscale school system to replace the little red schoolhouses," Taylor continues proudly. "By 1965, Bramalea had all the trappings of a proper municipality."

Taylor and Armstrong both say that Bramalea first had to reach a population level which retailers would regard as sufficient to locate there before a shopping center could be built and that in the meantime there were small shopping centers. "Until 1964 or 1965, Bramalea Road, the center line of the community, was a dirt road, and Highway 7 (which bisects the new town) was the only paved road," Taylor says.

"You can only attract merchants as the market grows. You don't get a major department store coming in just for fields and cows and what is now downtown Bramalea was then fields and cows."

Preliminary work on the 100 acre Civic Centre, including a town administration building and major shopping center, started in 1968. "We purchased land on which the Centre sits in the 1950s for $1,500 an acre and now it is worth $300,000 an acre," Taylor says.

A promised hotel was not started until Shiff and Field took over. It is located near a newly opened major amusement park, which should help boost occupancy.

One of the most controversial deals under the management of Taylor and Armstrong centered around a transaction between Bramalea and the Ontario Housing Corp., a provincial Crown corporation, for the provision of housing under the province's new Home

Ownership Made Easy (H.O.M.E.) plan.

Under the 1967 to 1977 H.O.M.E. plan, the province bought land and leased it to homebuyers for 50 years at an annual rent of 7¹/₄ percent of the government's purchase price. The purpose was to make it easier to buy a house because it eliminated the price of the lot from the house mortgage and reduced the down payment. The H.O.M.E. plan was pioneered at Bramalea.

In late 1967 and 1968, Bramalea sold 1,666 serviced housing lots in the new town to the H.O.M.E. plan for $10.7 million and in return got an option to lease back half of the lots on which it could build houses under the H.O.M.E. program.

In March 1969 a second agreement was made with OHC for the sale, at $18.4 million, of 390 acres for 4,602 townhouse units. In return, Bramalea received 1,398 lots on which it could build.

Taking into account the price it was paid for the land and what it would make on the total 1,529 lots on which it could build houses, Bramalea executives calculated that the firm could make a $20 million profit.

"Ontario Housing is getting a good deal, the municipality is getting a good deal, and Bramalea is getting a hell of a good deal," Bramalea executive vice-president Arthur Armstrong was quoted as saying in the newspapers following the second deal.

Critics, however, said Bramalea was getting too good a deal because it was being paid $72,000 an acre on land for which it had paid about $1,000 an acre—albeit 12 years earlier—and invested about $20,000 on services.

The H.O.M.E. project also introduced zero lot housing to Bramalea. Zero lot line means a house can be built on the lot line itself. Positioning houses this way provides the buyer with one large yard at the front, back, or side.

It also means more houses per acre—12 as compared with the usual four. The first view of these houses is claustrophobic because of the zigzagging arrangement of the homes and also because they are so close together.

The smaller lots and H.O.M.E. plan kept average lot prices in the project called Central Park to $5,000 below the usual price. The average house cost $17,000 at the outset. As a result, there were long lineups for the houses.

The Township of Chinguacousy Council, hoping to keep a lid on prices and speculation, passed restrictions stipulating that homeowners could not sell at a profit until five years after they bought the houses. Not surprisingly, residents were furious at this restriction. They pressured their Ontario Member of the Provincial Parliament, William Davis, who had just become Premier, to lift the ban. He did—and prices immediately doubled.

Shortly after Shiff and Field took over Bramalea, the new town, while still significant, became part of a broader development plan. The plan encompassed "Canadianizing" the company through buying out the English shareholders and diversifying into commercial properties.

Field and Shiff had two pieces of Canadian legislation in their favor. First, the federal government's Foreign Investment Review Agency made it difficult for Bramalea, as a foreign controlled company, to make acquisitions in Canada. Second, the Ontario government had implemented a 20 percent land transfer tax on foreigners buying land in the province.

Also in Shiff's and Field's favor were the difficulties Eagle Star's British real estate subsidiary, English Property, was having due to a slump in the British real estate market. At the same time, Trizec, which English Property controlled, was having problems in Canada.

Selling its Bramalea shares to Field and Shiff would give Eagle Star some much needed cash and so it agreed to sell its holdings. They got a good deal, paying about $5 a share, which Field says was about 20 percent of the real worth then.

Shiff's and Field's goal of creating an income properties division of shopping centers and office buildings was something that would normally take years. In their case, they amassed a huge portfolio within the space of a year through acquisitions, at bargain prices, of some of Canada's best shopping centers.

Their good fortune was due not to their hunting out properties, but to Bramalea's ties with Eagle Star Insurance which was concerned about the dismal financial condition of its other Canadian subsidiary, Trizec.

"My first wife and I had gone on a trip to Israel in the summer of 1975 and on our way back made a courtesy call on Sir Brian Mountain, chairman of Eagle Star," Field recalls. "What was supposed to be a brief stop turned into a four hour meeting.

"Sir Brian asked me what Bramalea's plans were and I explained that we intended to start developing or purchasing revenue producing assets to balance the housing side. He asked how much money Bramalea could raise to buy some revenue producing properties. Off the top of my head, I said I could raise $25 million which would give us the capacity to buy $100 million worth of property. (The $25 million would be used as leverage to borrow the rest of the money.)

"Sir Brian said that although he had no questions about the long-term viability of Trizec, he would sleep better if Trizec had an additional $25 million in the bank. He suggested that we work together with English Property and Trizec to put together a package of properties valued at about $100 million.

"But Trizec chairman James Soden and president William Hay had developed these assets and regarded them as their children; therefore, they were absolutely against their sale. We had been promised financial statements on their various assets and went to Montreal to Trizec's head office to get them. We had to wait from Monday until Friday to receive them, although it was just a matter of photostating.

"We took the information to Calgary, from where Trizec's shopping centers were being managed, and went through every lease and operating expense. We found many discrepancies between our financial statements on the shopping centers and theirs.

"Subsequently, Dick (Shiff), Ben (Swirsky), and I returned to Montreal after selecting which assets we wanted. We went on a Tuesday and didn't take any change of clothes since we expected negotiations to be completed that day.

"There was an army of Trizec people in the boardroom and they excused themselves, saying they wanted to have a conference. That was at 11:00 a.m. and at 4:00 p.m. they hadn't come back. I'll never forget that boardroom — it had no windows and poor air conditioning.

"Every night we went back to the Château Champlain and begged to have our rooms again. We had to buy shirts and underwear because we hadn't taken any luggage. Finally, on Friday afternoon, we settled all the terms and on Sunday completed the letter of intent for the transaction."

That should have been the end of the Trizec deal but, instead, its completion on October 28, 1975, was only the start because Bramalea suddenly found itself without backing from its bank, the Bank of Nova Scotia. It was not the first clash between the two. Some members of the Bank had opposed Bramalea's borrowing to buy back shares from Eagle Star.

Share buybacks were not as common then in real estate as they have become in recent years. When a loan is made for a building, the building is used as collateral by the bank, but in the case of share buybacks, there is no security on which the bank can fall if there is a default on the loan.

Thinking they were assured of the $25 million loan they needed to finance the deal, Field and Shiff announced the acquisition before going to the Bank on October 30, two days after the papers had been signed with Trizec. But the person with whom they regularly dealt at the Bank was away, and instead they saw an executive who had been opposed to the share buyback.

"He pulled out a recent issue of the *Financial Post* which had an article saying shopping centers were no longer a good investment," Field recalls. "Actually, it said building new shopping centers was unprofitable because of rising construction and mortgage costs, but it did not say buying existing centers was a bad investment."

(Although Field did not mention it when being interviewed for this book, that article had been written in May 1975 by the author of this book. As Field says, it predicted shopping center construction would slow down, but that developers would renovate and expand existing centers, as has since happened.)

The Bank of Nova Scotia executive rejected Field's and Shiff's loan application. "At 5:15 p.m. we walked out of the Bank and Dick (Shiff) was so upset, he didn't put on his raincoat even though it was pouring," Field continues.

Field and Shiff had both had personal loans from the Canadian Imperial Bank of Commerce, and so they crossed from the northeast corner of King and Bay Streets, where the Bank of Nova Scotia had its headquarters, to the southeast corner, where the Canadian Imperial Bank of Commerce has its head office.

"Fortunately, I had met Charles Laidley, then senior vice-president, loans and investments (and until he resigned in the spring of 1981, vice-chairman, corporate banking), and his wife Barbara while vacationing in England and we had gone sightseeing together," Field recalls. "So, we asked to see him, even though banking hours were over.

"It happened to be the night of the Bank's annual dinner for its directors and senior officers and Laidley was dressed in his tuxedo for the occasion. While we were explaining the situation, Barbara Laidley came into the office to fetch her husband to the dinner.

"When she saw me, she came over and kissed me on the cheek. Chuck Laidley then said that anybody who had that warm a friendship with his wife couldn't be all bad and gave us the money.

"The next day we withdrew all our business from the Bank of Nova Scotia and gave it to the CIBC." Since then, Bramalea and the Bank of Nova Scotia have resumed dealing with each other, although the Commerce remains Bramalea's lead banker.

Neither executives at the Bank of Nova Scotia nor the Canadian Imperial Bank of Commerce will comment on the incident, saying that business dealings with clients are strictly confidential.

The tension involved in getting the Trizec properties was well worth it. Included were Trizec's 75 percent interest in the Vancouver and Toronto Hyatt Hotels, nine shopping centers in British Columbia, Alberta, Saskatchewan, and Manitoba, and the IBM building, a major office tower, in Edmonton. (The Toronto Hyatt Hotel is now known as the Four Seasons Hotel.)

The deal was the largest exchange of real estate assets in Canada. The properties — most of them new — were then worth about $150 million and are now worth about $250 million. The impact on Bramalea's balance sheet was both instantaneous and substantial.

Net income in Bramalea's fiscal year, ended January 31, 1977 (covering 1976), was $6.4 million, or $1.15 per share, compared with $3.5 million, or 57 cents a share, a year earlier. "It accelerated our aspirations by five years," Field says.

Moreover, it was a great morale booster at Bramalea. "It showed that things were starting to roll," ·recalls Stewart Davidson, vice-president, finance. Davidson, who had joined Bramalea in 1972, was one of the few members of the previous management team to remain.

Davidson is also the reason Bramalea's year-end changed in 1975 from November 30 to the end of January. Officially, the reason for the switch, according to the 1975 annual report was that: "The mid-winter is a slow period in our industry and we can devote more time to the completion of the financial statements without being distracted by the normal end-of-season rush in development activities." Also, the change made it possible to squeeze the Trizec acquisition into the 1975 fiscal year. But another major factor was that the newly married Davidson wanted to take his bride to his home country of New Zealand at Christmas.

"If the year-end had still been November 30, we would have been preparing the annual report in December (annual reports are released several months after a company's year-end)," says Davidson. "But even so, I had to come back from New Zealand for three days because of the Trizec acquisition."

The revamping of Bramalea from a homebuilder into a diversified developer with a growing interest in shopping centers and office buildings kept the firm from going into the U.S. in the mid-1970s as other Canadian developers were doing. By 1978, however, the company felt secure enough in its re-organization to scout out the U.S. market.

Field was assigned the task of sniffing out opportunities and started by going to Los Angeles for a three week reconnaissance. "It seemed like a natural place to become involved because it was similar to the development business in Toronto," Field says. "A tremendous number of Canadian developers were there and the large Canadian banks all had representative offices.

"On a Sunday afternoon I returned to Toronto and went to see Dick Shiff at his home. I told him the only way for Bramalea to become involved in the U.S. was for me to move to California for a year. Dick went to the telephone and dialed Information to ask if the operator knew the name of a good psychiatrist.

"Later in the week we happened to have lunch with Chuck Laidley of the Canadian Imperial Bank of Commerce.

"Dick asked Chuck what he thought of my moving to the U.S., expecting him to say it was not a good idea. But Laidley had been the officer the CIBC had sent to California to establish its operations there and so he supported my proposed move."

Other Canadian developers have managed to enter the U.S. market very successfully by sending down key executives other than the president or by hiring knowledgeable local talent. Moreover, Field's

Main Square, Dallas

departure gave rise to erroneous rumors that he and Shiff had quarrelled. Bramalea director Enid Hildebrand also jokes that Field's going to the U.S. had a detrimental effect on the food served at Board meetings. "Dick (Shiff) is a health nut and during that year served health food, cheese, and bananas at the meetings. We couldn't wait for Kenny to return!"

Field felt that the on-the-spot investigation was necessary because "real estate is a very personal and complex business. It's very difficult to get a feel of what is a good property and how a particular market operates without knowing it as a resident.

"Moreover, California is very complex because of the large population (equal to that of all of Canada), environmental considerations, varying land prices, and competition, and it is easy to go wrong. By living there and studying it first-hand, I figured our chances of success were much greater. Also, I didn't want to rely on a hired hand who didn't know the company well enough to commit it to a big investment.

"When I went to California, I wasn't sure in what type of real estate we should be involved. We started out in industrial because it is the easiest area and acquainted us with the local laws. Then we moved into residential and office buildings."

Last year Bramalea bought a 65 percent interest in 1,520 acres in Rolling Ridges Estates near Los Angeles for $15 million. Over the next ten years, Bramalea plans to build 3,500 housing units and a large regional shopping center on the site.

The interest in the land was held originally by Cadillac Fairview in what is called a buy-sell arrangement in which either partner has the right to buy out the other. The local partner, Creative Communities, which had assembled the land, approached Bramalea to buy out Cadillac.

The importance of the Rolling Ridges purchase is twofold. First, it is the first large land bank Bramalea has acquired in several years. It has not been enlarging its Canadian holdings significantly.

Second, such purchases are unusual for Bramalea now that it has changed its emphasis from land development to office buildings and office towers. In fiscal 1981, ended January 31, 1981, the company bought only 115 acres of land.

The expansion of Bramalea is forcing the firm to update its nine-year-old financial systems. The new system, which will be in place sometime in 1982, will introduce such features as calculations in Canadian and U.S. dollars, information on the different accounting practices in both countries, construction progress, and historical data. "We will use the historical data to make projections and evaluations regarding proposed ventures," Stewart Davidson, vice-president, finance, says.

Now that Bramalea has broken the rarefied $1 billion level in assets, it is looking at diversification into oil and gas, as are other Canadian developers. In June 1981, it bought a 27 percent interest for $18.5 million in Coseka Resources Ltd. of Calgary. In its fiscal year ended July 31, 1980, Coseka had net income of $5.1 million on revenue of $17.5 million, compared with $3.3 million on $11.9 million a year earlier.

But acquisition and inflation are such powerful forces in real estate development that assets are constantly growing. Bramalea is no exception. Between its January 31, 1981, year-end and the release of its annual report in May, the company's assets climbed from $679 million to $1 billion.

Chapter Ten

DAON DEVELOPMENT CORPORATION

"It is an error for a company to have a quantitative goal, because it places a cap on the ability to grasp opportunities."

JACK POOLE
PRESIDENT
DAON

223

DAON DEVELOPMENT CORPORATION

CORPORATE MANAGEMENT

Chairman:	Graham Dawson
President and Chief Executive Officer:	John ("Jack") Poole
Executive Vice-President:	William Levine
Senior Vice-Presidents:	Mac Campbell *(Chief Financial Officer)*
	James Findlay *(Administration)*
	Mitchell Gropper *(Syndications; limited partnerships)*
	Russell Nunn *(In charge of Canadian operations)*
	Rodney Schroeder *(Shopping centers and corporate acquisitions)*

OPERATIONS (BY FUNCTION)

Shopping Centers
Senior Vice-Presidents: Donald Milliken
    Alvin Poettcker

Office Centers
Senior Vice-President: John Harris
Pacific Northwest
Senior Vice-President: Kenneth Bellamy
Daon Management
Senior Vice-President: Donald Weber

GEOGRAPHICAL DIVISIONS

Canada
    President: Russell Nunn
    Senior Vice-Presidents: Donald Schweitzer *(Office development)*
    Brenton Siddons *(Industrial)*
    James Whitehead *(Land)*

United States
    Executive Vice-President: Thomas Rielly
    Senior Vice-Presidents: Warren Colton III *(Land)*
    Jeffrey LeHecka *(Commercial/industrial)*
    Michael Shatsky *(Residential marketing)*
    Vice-Presidents: Jonathan Feucht *(Joint ventures)*
    Daniel Liddiard *(Commercial/industrial)*
    Michael Ryan *(Land)*

OFFICES

Canada
Vancouver *(Head Office)*, Calgary, Edmonton
United States
Newport Beach, California *(Head Office)*, Seattle, San Francisco, Miami

There are few businesses that have as many plants in the head office as developers have. Nowhere is this craze for plants, plants, and more plants more in bloom than at Daon Development Corp. All the greenery is somewhat ironic, considering Daon co-founder and president Jack Poole once said he found it "much more beautiful to look at the manmade things in Vancouver at night than at what used to be a national forest."

With the exception of Cadillac Fairview, Daon has the most luxurious and lovely head office of Canada's major real estate developers. Its new 19-floor building with its gold-colored windows, located on Vancouver's waterfront, has huge containers of plants, the size of two sandboxes for children, in every reception area and potted tropical plants throughout the executive suite. In addition, Daon has one of the finest West Coast Canadian art collections outside of an art gallery. It was largely selected by Mimi Hudson, a fine arts graduate who is secretary to chief financial officer Mac Campbell. The collection includes works by E.J. Hughes, Jim McKenzie, Maureen Enns, and Alan Wood.

The executive offices, located on the 18th floor, are each decorated in the taste of the occupant and could easily win an interior decorating award. Jack Poole's suite, done mostly in blues, has a sitting room with an antique cash register in an alcove, a dining room off the office, and a wraparound multi-window view of Vancouver's harbor.

Daon's appearance of a highly successful business is backed up by its balance sheet. Its revenue has gone from $12.69 million in 1969, when the then five-year-old company went public, to $697.9 million. Its assets have risen more than 5½ times since 1976 to $1.6 billion, and they should top $2 billion by the end of this year.

This growth is even more remarkable when stacked against the performance of Cadillac Fairview. Cadillac's assets have doubled since 1976; Daon's have jumped more than 5½ times. Cadillac's net income in its latest fiscal year (ended February 28, 1981) was one-quarter of what it was four years earlier, whereas Daon's increased almost sevenfold between 1976 and 1980. Last year Daon's net income of $51 million was 13 times Cadillac's $3.9 million. Between 1979 and 1980, Daon's net income shot up 21.4 percent, whereas Cadillac's dropped 55.5 percent.

Daon's meteoric rise has made its youthful executives (most are in their 30s or early 40s) proud to the point of being supremely confident and engagingly boastful. Nor are they ashamed of occasional mistakes and problems, which they candidly admit they either did not anticipate or did not handle properly.

Daon executives are not the only ones enthused about their company's track record. Real estate investment analysts whom Daon encourages to examine the company frequently — unlike other more wary firms — tend to exhaust every superlative in praising Daon.

"They are young, aggressive, very hard-driving, gutsy people who are thinking all the time and have a strategic sense," says James Cripps, real estate investment analyst at Pemberton Securities Ltd. of Vancouver. "They are willing to redeploy money and people and take losses in both big and small deals. They swing at everything that comes by and generally they bat .300 and several they hit over the fence. They don't care if it rains or snows or interest and mortgage rates are high. They are the superstars of the real estate business. They really understand the whole Canadian development business."

If you think that Cripps is speaking overly kindly because Daon is a hometown Vancouver firm making good, you have only to listen to analysts in Toronto who have equally nice things to say. "Daon's track record is truly superior to most companies in real estate or industry in general," says Ira Gluskin of Brown, Baldwin & Nisker Ltd. who is known for his acerbic criticisms of companies with poorer performances.

Daon's climb to the top is based on its ability to identify and then grasp opportunities and to shift quickly to new regions and product lines.

Daon concentrates on land development, condominium conversion, shopping centers, and office buildings, primarily in western Canada and the United States. It was one of the first Canadian developers to enter the California market. At one time, Daon had a Toronto office.

"Sometimes what you don't do can be your smartest moves," says one of Daon's directors, William Corcoran, president of W.J. Corcoran Ltd., a Toronto investment house. He was executive vice-president of McLeod Young Weir Ltd., Daon's investment dealer, when he joined Daon's Board in 1974.

"It's a lot easier working up and down the west coast. The time zones are the same, there is less time spent traveling, and there are fewer differences north-south than east-west in architecture, cities, and approaches."

Daon knows what to avoid. It does not build homes, a wise decision considering the decline in homebuyers due both to fewer people in the homebuying age group and higher mortgage and interest rates putting buying a home out of the reach of many.

Profit margins are higher in other types of real estate, such as office buildings and shopping centers. Housebuilding also requires much more staff than these other real estate venues. By contrast, condominium conversions take less time than building from scratch and, therefore, bring in cash more quickly.

Graham Dawson, chairman, Daon (Photo: Susan Goldenberg)

However, Daon's condominium conversions, most of which are in the U.S., have largely been stalled because high mortgage rates have frightened off potential buyers.

"Every company decides on the areas of business for which it feels it is best suited and ours is as a supplier of lots rather than home-building," Poole says.

It knows what it wants to avoid: diversification into other fields, such as oil and gas. "Our expertise is in real estate in which there are sufficient opportunities," Poole says. Nor has Daon grown through acquisitions as have other developers such as Nu-West; instead it has swollen through moving into new geographical areas.

Conversely, it knows what not to avoid. It pioneered condominiums and was quick to see the opportunities in the California market. In just the five years since Daon went into California, its U.S. assets, now also located in Florida, Washington, Colorado, Maryland, and Georgia, account for 46 percent of total assets, 69 percent of revenue, and 57 percent of operating profit. It has zeroed in on areas where population growth is above the national average.

John W. (Jack) Poole, president and chief executive officer, Daon

Early in 1981 Daon beefed up its U.S. land holdings by buying 3,500 acres of land for $100 million in San Diego, where population growth in the 1970s was three times the national average. It also bought 1,000 acres for $12 million in Denver, another high growth area.

And finally, it is flexible about going into geographic and product areas that it has said in the past it would absolutely never touch, if those areas turned out to match the industry's adage for success: location, location, and location.

Thus, early this year, Daon, which had always maintained that its bailiwick would be the west coast and that it would never go east or into the hotel business, did both in the space of a few weeks.

- It acquired a 50 percent interest for $24 million (U.S.) in the Omni International project in Atlanta, Georgia. The total purchase price was $47 million. The other half is owned by an Atlanta firm, Cousins Properties Inc. The Omni has a 471 room luxury hotel, 230,000 square feet of retail space, and 500,000 square feet of office space.
- It purchased for $4.6 million (U.S.) a 55-year-old hotel in Tulsa, Oklahoma — the Mayo, which is considered a landmark. The required restoration is similar to condominium conversion with which Daon has had extensive experience.
- It bought the Place Victoria Stock Exchange tower in Montreal in a joint venture with a Vancouver investment group. Daon's share of the price was $40 million. The total price of $85 million was less than 50 percent of estimated replacement value.

It was Daon's first purchase in each city, but in every case Daon was getting an excellent deal, with the Omni and Mayo both being bought at rock-bottom prices and Place Victoria having the potential of higher-yield rents.

"These purchases were not inconsistent with our philosophy of going anywhere in North America for the right quality of acquisition," Poole jubilantly told shareholders a few weeks later at Daon's annual meeting. "We will have to expend $18 million on rehabilitating the Mayo Hotel because of its age, but since it is a historic building, half the cost will be tax write-offs. Not only that, there also is a 220 car garage, an adjacent 17,000 square feet that can be developed, and the new headquarters across the street of Cities Service Co. with close to 20,000 workers. All this will generate business for the hotel and it should become worth $50 million. Moreover, when Mike Shatsky (senior vice-president, residential marketing for the U.S.) gave a reception for Tulsa's business elite, the Mayor asked everyone to give us a standing ovation and we're not used to that.

"While we were sitting around after the Tulsa deal congratulating ourselves on how clever we are, the same person (a California architect) who had told us about the hotel reminded us about the Omni which he called the biggest real estate sleeper in the world. At the moment, though, it was the biggest turkey in the world, a spectacular failure (the hotel had high occupancy and the office and retail areas low occupancy) that had been in litigation for seven years and every other real estate developer that had been approached had turned it down.

"But the deal had its attractive features. Because the banks were sick and tired of the property, which was in foreclosure, they were willing to accept an all cash, unconditional offer. The limited partnership owners were willing to sign since if they didn't they would face a tax liability after the banks' threatened foreclosure went through in January (the Daon deal was completed December 31, 1980).

"A lot of maintenance and upgrading are necessary, but we bought 1.6 million square feet of spectacular architecture and Atlanta's most successful hotel which generated enough cash in 1980 to justify our having bought office space that was 50 percent vacant and exhibit space that was 100 percent empty. All it needs is creative and aggressive management and we are considering converting one of the office towers into hotel use.

"The *Atlanta Journal* said it was the biggest real estate bargain in Atlanta's history, but more than that it was a downright steal and we believe that. It couldn't be replaced for $160 million today and in three to four years will be worth that.

"As for Place Victoria, it is a fine, fine property. Most of its leases mature in five years and just by bringing the rents up to market value, it should produce $17 million in net cash flow."

Whether Poole's exuberance over the three deals is justified, time will tell. But Poole is absolutely sure that "each one could be called the finest acquisition Daon has ever made although they will not contribute to earnings this year at least."

As these acquisitions show, Daon is quick to seize opportunities which reflects the risk-taking nature of president and chief shareholder 48-year-old Jack Poole, an engineer turned door-to-door salesman turned real estate developer. He is backed up by two able lieutenants — 38-year-old William Levine, executive vice-president responsible for corporate strategy, office building and shopping center divisions, and Daon's Pacific Northwest subsidiary, and 37-year-old Mac Campbell, senior vice-president and chief financial officer.

Levine joined Daon in 1970, after answering a box number advertisement in the *Financial Post*. An economics graduate of the University of British Columbia and an MBA graduate of Harvard University, Levine says "It wouldn't have mattered if the ad had identified Daon by name, since I hadn't heard of it. But I was impressed by the fast growth of the firm and Jack Poole is a hell of a salesman."

Campbell is an MBA graduate of the University. of Western

Ontario. He had been a sales manager for the T. Eaton Co. in Edmonton and a real estate analyst at both Canavest House Ltd. and Greenshields Inc. During that period he helped sell Paragon Properties Ltd., an Alberta firm, to Daon and initiated Robert Campeau's unsuccessful bid for Markborough Properties Ltd. of Toronto. In 1974 Daon asked Campbell to become its treasurer and he joined because as an analyst "I had got to know all the companies and really admired what Daon was doing.

"When I joined, Bill Levine was vice-president of finance and there was a company secretary, an accounting group, and me as treasurer," Campbell recalls. "There was no corporate finance department, though. Today, there are 180 people (out of a total of 900 employees) in the financial area, including accounting. Seventy of those are in project and corporate finance and treasury."

Employees say that the terse Levine is soft-spoken, quiet, and extremely bright. "People are uptight when they are called into meetings with him because he asks probing questions that put you on the spot," says one employee. "He gets to the essence of a situation. Although he's quiet, he's very influential and the fact that he is in charge of office and shopping center developments means these areas will come into higher profile now."

The more outgoing Campbell is described as "very energetic. He works at a very high level of intensity up to 11:00 p.m. speaking to bankers or the media. He runs at a very fast pace but is very fair." Other employees say that Campbell "is a genius whom you can't always understand. What he doesn't know about corporate finance and real estate investment, you don't need to know."

Campbell has been a pioneer in what the real estate industry calls "creative" or "innovative" financing — finding new ways of financing projects. One of his most admired methods has been his technique of spreading the costs and risks by selling limited partnerships in specific projects to the public. About 35 percent of Daon's profit in 1981 is expected to come from its sale of limited partnerships in three new Alberta shopping centers.

Still, while Poole relies heavily on Levine and Campbell, he remains the one who is pulling the strings, taking an interest even in such matters as the selection of pictures for the annual report. He expects stellar performance and rewards it bountifully with bonuses equal to as much as an individual's salary.

"While Daon has become a much bigger company, it doesn't have the feel of a big company because Poole has kept it non-bureaucratic," says Daon director William Corcoran. "Besides having terrific business judgment, Poole has a very good relationship with important and junior people. Everybody at Daon has profit responsibilities and not just titles, and so everybody can relate to one another."

Matinee idol handsome (fellow male executives say he turns women's heads in elevators), Poole is the only developer of the big ten to wear his hair curling modishly over his shirt collar. (He dresses conservatively, however, as the others do.) He maintains his brawny physique from wrestling at college by playing racquet ball on the courts in the Daon building, although Daon employees say he is only an average player.

The son of a grain buyer, Poole was born in Mortlach, Saskatchewan (1976 census: population 278), a tiny community best known for its pre-historic animals archeological dig and situated about 80 miles west of Regina.

He got into real estate in a roundabout way. In his youth he worked on highway and construction jobs and then, at the age of 17, after marrying his childhood sweetheart from Mortlach, he studied civil engineering at the University of Saskatchewan. Upon graduating, he became a management trainee in Calgary at Gulf Canada and, finding that boring, he became a door-to-door salesman for the Fuller Brush Co. on weekends and evenings. He liked selling, and this led to his answering an advertisement for salespeople at Engineered Homes Ltd., a major Calgary homebuilder now owned by Genstar. Engineered asked him to be an assistant manager in Edmonton. Poole recognized that there was a lucrative market in building instant housing for the resource-related towns springing up in northern British Columbia such as the one Engineered was building at Fraser Lake for Idaco Mines. As it happened, Dawson Construction Ltd., a family-owned heavy engineering firm founded in 1922 and specializing in bridges, roads, and dams, was installing roads and sewers for the project.

Poole expressed to Dawson's on-site manager his frustration at Engineered's not pursuing opportunities in British Columbia because Engineered had run into cash flow difficulties. The manager suggested that Poole, then 31, meet Graham Dawson, the second generation president of Dawson Construction. The idea was that with Dawson in every type of construction except housing, Poole would round out the firm's capabilities. Dawson, who is eight years older than Poole, says, "My impression today of Jack hasn't changed much from back then. He's dynamic, aggressive, intelligent, enthusiastic, competent, and a great motivator."

The two formed a firm called Dawson Housing Developments Ltd. with 50/50 ownership. Today, Poole owns a slightly larger proportion — 22.75 percent, or 8,109,000 shares, worth $57 million on paper — and Dawson 19.03 percent, or 6,784,387 shares, worth $47 million. The balance is publicly held.

At the outset, it was decided that Dawson, who wanted to continue running his own business, would be chairman and Poole would be president. Another factor was that Poole was the one going out to drum up business and, as Dawson says, "Being president of a firm gives a better entrée."

"The trend in western Canada has been to foreign ownership and I didn't want my company, that my father had founded and which is now the largest in Vancouver and one of the largest in British Columbia, to fall into outside hands," Dawson says. He estimates his firm does $100 million in business annually.

It has worked on such projects as building the Trans-Canada highway through the mountainous Fraser Canyon and Kicking Horse Pass in British Columbia, the Peace River dam in northern British Columbia, and Robson Square (a government and court complex in Vancouver). The firm's Sceptre Dredging division has one of the world's largest portable dredging fleets and has worked for Imperial Oil, Cominco, and MacMillan-Bloedel Ltd.

Dawson Construction and Daon have an arms-length business relationship. Graham Dawson does keep a downtown Vancouver office, with a number but no firm name on the door, in Daon's headquarters. Dawson has done some construction for Daon but on a competitive tender basis that has been made public knowledge. The most recent was the $14,686,000 Daon Centre head office in Vancouver, for which Dawson was paid over a three-year period.

The evolution of Daon shows how a small developer can start out in one area and end up in another based on adaptability to new trends. As the company reflected in its 1979 annual report: "The principal reason for our growth has been our ability to respond to changing market conditions and take advantage of opportunities when and where they arise. We have tried to avoid becoming permanently wedded to any one market or product line. We have grown by moving selectively into larger projects and by expanding geographically."

For the first five years, Dawson's and Poole's new firm, initially called Dawson Housing Developments Ltd., concentrated on building 14 instant towns for up to 500 people in British Columbia and the Yukon. Almost at the outset, though, the company branched into condominiums, then a new housing concept, because it was in the right place at the right time. One of the towns was Port Alice, at the north end of Vancouver Island, for Rayonnier Ltd., a forest products firm.

"The costs of clearing the land and construction were very high," Dawson recalls. "British Columbia had just passed (in 1965) Canada's first Condominium Act and we decided a condominium project at Port Alice would be a good idea. It would lower our site costs and provide ownership and individual mortgages for employees." That launched Daon's reputation for rapidly grasping innovative opportunities since the project became the first of its type in Canada.

"With that learning experience, we decided to branch into urban development and bought land in Port Moody, also in British Columbia, and built a second condominium there, which was very successful," Dawson continues. "Subsequently, we re-examined where Dawson Housing was going and decided to place less emphasis on instant towns and more on urban housing," Dawson says.

To finance this more expensive type of construction and give it more clout with financial institutions, Dawson went public on the Toronto and Montreal Stock Exchanges in 1969. The strategy worked. Prior to 1969 Daon's mortgage financing sources had been limited to the federal government's Canada Mortgage and Housing Corporation and two insurance companies. By 1970, it was also getting financing from two national trust companies, three banks, and an acceptance company.

In 1971, having dropped "Housing" from its name, Daon entered the commercial real estate market, building a 12-story head office in downtown Vancouver, a suburban shopping center and warehouse in Vancouver, and a 23-floor office tower in Calgary. In just six years, the company had changed from a homebuilder into concentrating, as its 1973 annual report later recalled, "on building a portfolio of quality income-producing properties because the ongoing revenue from them will have a stabilizing effect on overall income."

In 1973, faced with confusion of its name with that of a Dawson construction company and a Dawson real estate firm, the company decided to change its name. Although Poole was by then the largest shareholder and the firm's active head (with Dawson opting to stay at his own construction business), changing the firm's name to Poole was never considered. Instead, the company's advertising agency, Cockfield Brown, suggested the low-cost solution of dropping the "w and s" in the middle of the name to form Daon.

Daon's development has been a combination of good timing, good positioning, and seizing opportunities. Unlike eastern-based developers, like Cadillac Fairview, Daon was next door to what would become Canada's fastest growing province of Alberta and closer to the U.S. growth regions of California and the southwest states. Consequently, it had a bird's-eye view of the burgeoning boom in both areas and capitalized swiftly on this knowledge.

Back in 1969, Poole made a deal which became the golden egg for the company's future growth. He acquired a 1,450 acre land bank, called The Properties, in northeast Calgary—enough land for the next ten years. Between 1973 and 1979, Daon acquired another 4,250 acre tract, called The Homesteads, in southeast Calgary for development between 1980 and 1985. Thus, Daon was well-positioned to benefit from the enormous demand for housing in the 1970s as people flocked to Alberta to cash in on the boom in the oil-rich province following the 1973 Arab oil embargo.

Most of the Alberta activity was at first in the Calgary area, the financial and oil center of the province, but recently Daon has stepped up its presence in Edmonton, Alberta's manufacturing and industrial center, with the purchase of 1,200 acres.

In turn, the money Daon was stacking up from its Alberta coup provided it with the funds to get a flying start on most other Canadian developers (except Genstar) in the California market. California is an ideal market — it's near Daon's head office in Vancouver, its population is equal to that of Canada, and it is one of the fastest growing states in population and wealth.

Back in the mid-1970s, California and, indeed, the entire U.S. real estate market had another attraction — land was dirt cheap as a result of the 1974-75 recession which had sent the real estate industry reeling. In 1976, when despite its Alberta venture, Daon was still a relatively small company with $278 million in assets compared with Cadillac's $1 billion, it plunged into the California market.

"I think we hit that market about six weeks ahead of time," Mac Campbell later told the 1978 industry outlook conference of the Canadian Institute of Public Real Estate Companies (CIPREC). "Of the existing development industry in California as we started in there in 1976, only about 25 percent survived the 1974 to 1976 crunch. And those who did survive are strapped with liabilities and their banks have no confidence to lend them any money.

"And so the slightest suggestion you gave about a buying interest, you were swamped with vendors. For the first year you were able to negotiate very low cash, in many cases no cash, since the escrow or the title company put up all the cash they needed to tie something up in escrow. You had very long closing periods and you could put enough subjects into the deal so that you eliminated in most cases all the development approval risk, if not the construction and market risks, because a great volume of our production in California is the double escrow-process, as they call it down there (we haven't owned the asset until we have sold it).

"Now (1978) it is a much more competitive environment, and we are actually pleasantly surprised to see improving deals being brought to us and I think that's a result of the fact that we've performed on the deals we've committed to buy in the past."

Daon's entry into California had rapid-fire results. A year later, by 1977, the company's U.S. operations were generating 35 percent of total profit and accounted for one-third of its assets. Buy by 1978, just two years after Daon moved into California, the market had become so competitive — and Daon had made enough money — to warrant expanding into other states.

All told, Daon now has a land bank of 26,000 acres in Texas, California, Oregon, Washington, Colorado, Alberta, and British Columbia. But despite the geographical expansion, Alberta and

California remain its strongholds, expected to provide two-thirds of predicted land sales of $140 million this year (versus $120 million in land sales in 1980).

Good timing, good planning, and hard work have made Daon's road a smooth one, but there have been some bumps along the way. Unlike some developers, Daon readily admits its mistakes and will pull out, even at a loss, to avoid worse difficulties.

One area where Daon recently has been having some problems is with condominium conversions, despite its familiarity with the business.

This could pose a problem for Daon because condominium conversion had been the largest contributor to its profits for several years. In 1980, however, profit from this sector dropped from $50.8 million to $34 million, and the slippage is expected to continue. Consequently, condominium conversion dropped from providing 40 percent of profits in 1979 to only 21 percent last year.

Its difficulty is three-fold. First, the market nosedived because of high interest rates. Consequently, the company is predicting sales will drop by close to one-third from 5,200 units at $320 million in 1980 to 3,600 units at $250 million this year.

Second, there was competition and increasing consumer and government objections to conversion. Daon, however, had made a point of aligning itself with government legislators drafting laws to protect tenants, including the provision of relocation allowances to tenants who could not afford to buy a unit. This is rarely necessary, however, since Daon first surveys the tenants' buying power.

Third, Daon bombed out in the Dallas-Fort Worth condominium market because it did not do its homework. "They thought the Fort Worth and Dallas markets were the same because they are so near each other," says John Staples, president of John Staples Real Estate Management Ltd., a condominium sales agent in Fort Worth. "But the cities are like two millionaires who made their money in different ways — one in oil (Dallas) and the other in financing and cattle (Fort Worth).

"Their residential tastes are different, too. Dallas likes two-story walkup garden apartments, with a pool and garden in the center. Fort Worth likes one-story or high rise buildings.

"Daon's limited success in Dallas colored their approach to Fort Worth. They converted a two-story building into a condominium next door to an apartment that had tried conversion, failed, reverted back to rental, and had 100 percent occupancy.

"In addition, Daon had financing problems. They gave commitments to buyers for 10.5 percent interest on mortgages and then the rates went to 17 percent, so that they were caught in a crunch." (Texas had passed anti-usury laws, imposing interest rate ceilings during this period of rising interest rates.)

Daon fared equally poorly in Dallas. "They did no preliminary market studies on prices and so they purchased properties at ungodly high prices and then tried to sell them at more than the market price," says Patricia Davis, president of Real Condominiums Ltd., a leading Dallas agent.

"On the other hand, they figured if they lowered their price, they would lose money. Some of their locations were bad, too. Daon upset the marketplace because Dallas is a small community and word gets around. Daon's problem in selling condominiums helped soften the market and made it difficult to sell condominium projects of other firms."

Daon executives candidly admit that they goofed, although they place most of the blame on the Dallas manager. It pulled out of Texas in line with Jack Poole's oft-expressed philosophy that "in business, two things are important: when to start and when to stop."

While some developers (such as Nu-West and Oxford) have stayed with the same financial sources throughout the years, Daon has made a point of diversifying its sources. In 1974, when Mac Campbell joined Daon, all its banking sources were 2,000 miles away in Montreal at the Mercantile Bank, Bank of Montreal, Royal Bank, Sun Life and Standard Life insurance companies, and Royal Trust. The lone exceptions were Toronto-based National Trust and the Toronto Dominion Bank's real estate investment trust (REITS). Campbell broadened these sources to the Toronto Dominion Bank, Bank of Nova Scotia, and Canadian Imperial Bank of Commerce, as well as western institutions like the Bank of British Columbia.

In the U.S., 75 percent of its financing has come from the Canadian banks represented there and the rest from U.S. banks, primarily New York-based Citicorp. "Canada's banks are among the top 75 worldwide in size and operate nationally, whereas the U.S. has a localized banking system in which some banks have only one branch," Campbell says. Consequently, Daon found itself in the unusual position of checking the credit standing of its U.S. lenders, instead of the normal reversed situation.

Campbell's goal, however, is to switch from the 75:25 Canadian:U.S. bank ratio for financing for U.S. projects to obtaining 25 percent of the financing from Canadian sources and the balance from U.S., English, European, and Japanese markets. This accounted for Daon's decision this year to become the first Canadian developer listed on the London Stock Exchange. Eventually, Daon will also be listed on the over-the-counter market in the U.S.

"The LSE is the most mature property stock market in the world, and English financial institutions are very attuned to property," Campbell says. "In the United Kingdom, about 32 percent of pension fund money is invested in real estate, compared to only one or two percent in Canada.

444 Market Street, San Francisco. A Daon joint venture office tower with Cadillac Fairview.

"We need more financing sources because Daon's average annual compound growth rate over the past five years has been 50 percent and it is continuing at that pace, whereas the average growth rate of the financing institutions has been 10 percent to 20 percent. In one year we may build six or seven shopping centers and most financial institutions are lucky if they can finance two or three of those."

Still, Daon does not regard itself as having a bottomless source of cash and it wants to know where every penny is going. Daily cash reports are required from its Canadian and U.S. operations. Weekly forecasts are prepared on the outward and inward flow of funds, and a 12-month computer projection is done on cash flows from every project.

Campbell is now in the midst of turning this system into an historic base from which projections can be made and to interrelate corporate and project cash flows on the computerized system. Much of this work had been done manually before.

Such close attention is essential if Daon is to complete projects on schedule and on budget. Its importance is highlighted by an example. Two years ago Daon won out over 17 other applicants to build a large shopping center by the spring of this year in Red Deer, Alberta. The terms of the agreement entitled the city to charge Daon a $1 million penalty if the project were not completed on time, including landscaping, and a further penalty if not designed as promised ($100,000 on plants in an inner garden court below a skylight).

Furthermore, if the project had not been ready by the spring, the tenants would likely have had to wait for the fall opening, because the summer is a slack shopping period. Daon's tracking system resulted in the center's opening on schedule.

As in any well-run business, Daon takes into account the worst possible scenario and does contingency planning. In March 1979, in view of money's getting tighter and interest rates inching up, Campbell and his staff began to debate "what if interest rates rise to 20 percent?" As it turned out, their crystal ball gazing was dead on, but at the time, Campbell says, "We thought that was ridiculous and that it would never get there."

Campbell's solution, like that of his counterparts at other Canadian development firms, has been to build up a stormy weather fund of $25 million each quarter in liquid assets, even if it has meant deferring or refinancing some acquisitions. The money is invested in short-term securities, including shares of other real estate companies. At one time, Daon held one million shares of Cadillac Fairview, which it bought at $10½ a share and sold last year for $17 after a Cadillac Fairview stock split gave two new shares for every two held. It now owns 14 percent of Edmonton-based Melcor Developments Ltd. and under 10 percent of S.B. McLaughlin Ltd., an Ontario-based developer.

"There is nothing like having cash for getting business and better financing terms," Campbell says. "Previously, we had to pay up to five percentage points over the prime rate (in interest charges), but now we pay a point under prime to a point over prime."

Not only does the nest egg put Daon in a defensive position; it also gives an offensive capacity. For example, Daon was able to pay cash on a few days' notice for the Omni project in Atlanta and get it at a bargain price.

In recent years, Daon, apparently dissatisfied with Richardson Securities Ltd. as its lead underwriter for share issues and public debentures, replaced it with McLeod Young Weir Ltd. Its secondary underwriter, used primarily to ensure that Daon gets competitive rates, is Greenshields Inc., Canada's largest underwriter of real estate issues. In the U.S., Merrill Lynch guided Daon's application to be on the NASDAQ (North American Securities Dealers Association's Quotations) over-the-counter market.

In 1977, Campbell brought in a policy of using 10 percent of earnings to purchase common shares of the company in the marketplace. The procedure was started to provide liquidity because in 1977 real estate shares were being snubbed by large institutional investors in the wake of the 1974-76 recession in the U.S. Daon's buyback of its shares accounts for about two to three percent of the total trading.

Last year Daon rocked the real estate industry with what has come to be known as "creative" or "innovative" financing. The idea was to sell limited partnership units to the public to finance a particular venture. Its first offering was 68 percent of its new Daon Centre headquarters in Vancouver. The other 32 percent would have been footed by Daon. The end result, though, was a 50:50 split and a Daon decision to make further such offerings to large corporate partners.

Here is what happened. With developers facing record mortgage and interest rates at the same time that investors were becoming increasingly aware that property values were soaring, Daon decided to match the two needs. It got the necessary funding by having the public foot much of the bill, thus limiting Daon's outlay when interest rates were sky high. Moreover, the units would be held by passive investors who would not interfere in day to day matters.

The concept of limited partnership units is not new in North America, having been around for about 15 years. However, Daon was the first to get all the outside money from the public and none, as had been customary, from mortgage companies because in 1980 mortgage money was too expensive. Since it was a local project and the building had a high profile, Daon decided to use Vancouver-based Pemberton Securities, western Canada's biggest investment dealer, as its underwriter. Coincidentally or not, Jack Poole and Pemberton president Robert Wyman are nextdoor neighbors.

The deal, offering $25 million in units to the public, was the largest syndication of its type ever in Canada and the fourth biggest ever to be done in North America. This did not mean, however, that the average person could afford to participate, since the minimum investment was $20,000 for 20 units.

Nor was the return such that would appeal to those wanting a quick buck. Each year an investor would get a fixed seven percent, less than if the money just sat in a savings account accumulating interest. It was a good investment only for those interested in a hedge against inflation. If, as seems inevitable, inflation continues, the building will appreciate and an investor could conceivably almost double the investment in the long run.

The idea, however, turned out to be a qualified success, with $18³/₄ million worth of units sold, $6 million short of the original goal. What went wrong? Both Daon and Pemberton place the blame largely on the slowness in getting approval from regulatory agencies.

"In the first week, we got $40 million in requested orders, but we could not sell any because the offer first had to get approval from the British Columbia and Ontario Securities Commissions," says Donald Steele, vice-president, finance, at Pemberton's and the pilot of the offer. "So we had to stop both selling and the road shows promoting the units. By the time the approvals came through six weeks later, public interest had waned."

Unfortunately, Daon and Pemberton encountered the unexpected at the time they got the go-ahead to sell the units. The idea was conceived in January 1980 and a prospectus was filed in February while mortgage rates were sky-high. But by the time regulatory approval was received, the rates had dropped and the units no longer seemed that attractive. The long delay in approval also raised doubts as to whether it would ever be approved.

Then, too, Steele says, some accountants and lawyers felt threatened by the units because selling real estate had been the preserve of the real estate industry, whereas investment dealers had always sold real estate stocks. "So some of these people advised clients not to buy the units." And, as Steele concedes, neither Daon nor Pemberton ever "quite succeeded in educating the public" about this innovative concept. "Maybe a half dozen people understood it," Steele says.

Another lesser factor was that since both Daon and Pemberton were Vancouver-based, there was a lack of knowledge and interest in the deal in eastern Canada. As a result, 80 percent was sold in Vancouver and only 20 percent elsewhere.

At the same time with mortgage financing coming down out of the stratosphere, it was to Daon's advantage to sell a smaller share in the building to the public than initially intended. So it capped off the deal at 50:50 with the public in June of 1980 because this way it would own

Woodcroft Place, a 6-building, 1,222-suite residential community in North Vancouver

more of the project—and reap more of the profits—and it could pay for the outstanding $6 million not bought by the public at inexpensive rates.

This test run was followed by selling limited partnership units for each of three major shopping centers in Alberta—at Edmonton (Heritage Mall), Calgary (Sunridge Mall), and Red Deer (Bower Place Shopping Centre). But some significant modifications were made. Much larger units were offered—a minimum of four units at $125,000 each—to private investors through real estate, rather than financial brokers. They charged half the commission—three percent—than was charged for the office building, although it should be kept in mind that fewer and larger units were being sold for the shopping centers.

The total offering was for $177.5 million, of which $144 million was sold within weeks. The $177.5 million covered land acquisition plus development, construction, initial leasing, interim financing for the centers, and $18,497,000 for expenses incurred by Daon in developing them.

The outside partners will have a 52 percent interest in the malls and Daon will have 48 percent. On the plus side, the arrangement reduces Daon's borrowing costs. On the negative front, shopping centers are such money-makers that some real estate observers question the wisdom of Daon's giving away a piece of the action.

All three were more than 90 percent leased several months before opening this year. For long-term investors, the partnership promises healthy returns in the long run according to Daon's projections:

	1981	1985	1990	1995	Last Year of Projections 1997
			Projected Income $ Thousands		
Net Income From Malls Distributable	$ 9,514	$24,964	$34,668	$54,063	$ 66,772
Net Income to Limited Partners	8,807	16,324	22,669	35,352	43,662
			Projections Per Investment of $500,000 (4 Units)		
Distributable Net Income Before-Tax	$24,791	$45,951	$63,811	$99,513	$122,905
Return on Investments	10.82%	9.19%	12.76%	19.9%	24.58%

"They were very imaginative in how they financed these centers," says Fredrik Eaton, president, Eaton's of Canada, which has department stores in all three malls. "Daon is an aggressive, dynamic company that makes decisions really fast."

In the coming years, Poole says Daon will continue to concentrate in British Columbia and Alberta, as well as the western United States, although if another Omni International crops up, "It doesn't mean we won't look at opportunities elsewhere on this continent." Recently, for example, Daon bought a 40-story office tower in Philadelphia for $50.5 million.

With Daon's amazing growth record and skill in making deals, Poole is reluctant to predict how large Daon will be by the middle of this decade because "real estate investment is a series of transactions" which can double or even triple a firm's assets overnight." But Poole is not thinking small. "It's an error for a company to have a quantitative goal, because it places a cap on the ability to grasp opportunities." And grasping opportunities has always been Daon's style.

Chapter Eleven

GENSTAR CORPORATION

"The differences between regulations in Canada and the United States are mind-boggling. There is less uniformity in the U.S. than in Canada. In Canada it is reasonably uniform and uniformly difficult."

WALTER BANNISTER
EXECUTIVE VICE-PRESIDENT
GENSTAR

GENSTAR CORPORATION

Executive Office: San Francisco
Head Office: Vancouver
Chairman*: Angus MacNaughton
President*: Ross Turner

*Starting in May 1981, MacNaughton and Turner are rotating on an annual basis as Chairman and President.

OPERATING DIVISIONS
Executive Vice-Presidents:
Walter Bannister *(Land and Real Estate)*
J. Leonard Holman *(Canadian building materials and construction services)*
Bernard Johnson *(Canadian cement and gypsum manufacturing and chemical operations)*
Nicholas Liberatore *(Marine, international, and heavy construction activities)*
George Michals *(Chief financial officer)*
Gregor Peterson *(Financial services)*

LAND AND REAL ESTATE
Executive Vice-President: Walter Bannister
(Based in San Francisco)

HOUSING
Canada
GENSTAR PROPERTIES LTD.
  Head Office: Calgary
  President: C.D. Wilson
Operates in Alberta, British Columbia, Manitoba, Ontario
United States
GENSTAR PACIFIC CORP.
(Holding Company)
  Head Office: San Francisco
Operates in Washington State, Oregon, California, Texas, Florida

Engineered Homes
  President: G.H. Magnussen
Keith Construction
  President: L.H. Frodsham
Housing Components
  President: Lou Luini
Commercial Development
  President: C.D. Smith
Broadmoor Homes
  President: B. Smith, Jr.
Broadmoor Homes Northern
  President: R.B. Menard
Genstar Homes of Texas
  President: J. Thompson
Sutter Hill Ltd.
  President: M.D. Couch

LAND DEVELOPMENT
Canada
GENSTAR DEVELOPMENT CO.
  Head Office: Vancouver
  President: V.S.G. Lewis

United States
GENSTAR PROPERTIES
  Head Office: San Diego, California
  President: F.D. Dembinsky

Genstar Corp. is both Canada's most resolutely unique developer and at the crest of the wave of the future for the real estate industry.

It is the only one with its top 25 executives located about 1,000 miles from the head office, a prince as deputy chairman, whose ancestors include Austrian Empress, Maria Theresa, a European company 7,000 miles away as the chief shareholder, and worldwide operations extending through Asia, Africa, Europe, and North America. The executive office is in San Francisco and the head office in Vancouver. Until May 1981, the head office was 2,500 miles away in Montreal. The founder and largest shareholder, the 159-year-old Société Générale de Belgique, one of the world's largest holding companies, is in Brussels.

Genstar is also a pioneer in having the titles of chairman and president rotate annually between the two senior executives, although their duties and responsibilities do not switch. The executive musical chairs plan started in May 1981 with former vice-chairman Angus MacNaughton getting first dibs on the chairmanship, to be followed by president Ross Turner. Company executives call them "the Siamese twins."

Genstar executives do not draw attention to it, but historical records show that Prince Charles de Bar, Genstar's deputy chairman based in Brussels, has a famous family tree. The name *de Bar* stems from the city of Bar le Duc in Lorraine, France. The name was brought into the family by François de Lorraine when he married Austrian Empress Maria Theresa (1717-1780).

Maria Theresa was Empress when Frederick the Great of Prussia invaded Austria in 1740, seeking the rich territory of Silesia. That touched off a European war, with France supporting Frederick and England supporting Austria. Frederick acquired Silesia in 1742, but despite this loss, Maria Theresa was a popular ruler in Austria. The same cannot be said of one of her daughters, Marie Antoinette, who was beheaded during the French Revolution.

Genstar is also the only Canadian developer listed on the New York Stock Exchange. Other Canadian firms have avoided the NYSE like the plague because listing would mean revealing officers' salaries and providing more information in annual reports under the 10K disclosure requirements of the Securities and Exchange Commission. But Genstar, with more than 50 percent of its revenue now coming from the U.S., is stalking U.S. investors and indirectly oiling up new banking sources through advertisements in financial publications and speeches by executives to investment dealer analysts. The ploy appears to be working. Last year, 45 percent of the stock market trading in Genstar was done in the U.S. versus 17 percent in 1979. Sensitive to questions about whether the company is then really American and not Canadian, executives hasten to say that trading would be higher in the U.S. because it has a ten times greater population.

Genstar has achieved the diversification from the cyclical nature of real estate that other Canadian developers are seeking. In 1980, one-quarter of its $2.3 billion revenue came from land and real estate development and the rest from such other businesses as marine transportation, personal financing, waste management, asphalt production, and wallboard production. That compares with real estate accounting for one-third of total revenue in 1979.

But real estate is still the largest contributor to Genstar's net income, accounting for 46.4 percent in 1980, and has the largest return on net assets—14.9 percent—compared with 12.1 percent in the second ranking category, marine services.

It is the only developer with a financial services arm. The division is involved in mortgage banking, financing Genstar real estate joint venture activities, title insurance, and escrow. Real estate analysts say Genstar will likely place more emphasis on its financial services because this reduces its reliance on outside financing sources, many of which are competitors for real estate projects.

Moreover, with pension fund money increasingly being invested in real estate, having both real estate and financial services under one umbrella is a natural evolution for developers. That reasoning was behind Genstar's offer in the summer of 1981 for Canada Permanent Mortgage Co., Canada's third largest trust company with 1980 assets of $5.5 billion plus $9.4 billion in assets under administration. "Genstar looks like what other developers are going to look like," says Harry Rannala, real estate analyst at Walwyn Stodgell Cochran Murray Ltd.

Canada's largest producer of pre-cast concrete structural and architectural components such as wall panels and stairs, Genstar is also the third largest manufacturer of cement in Canada, in the top 15 U.S. cement and lime producers, the largest operator of tugboat and barge equipment in Canada, and North America's seventh largest real estate company in terms of revenue. All told, it has 20 different businesses with 20,000 employees at 500 offices and plants and assets of $2.4 billion. Its activities span from Japan, collecting barge cargo, to constructing an airport in Sri Lanka, to building houses in San Diego and Calgary. While its real estate operations are now confined to Canada and the U.S., it is investigating opportunities in Brazil.

The global and operational diversification has paid off handsomely for Genstar. While other developers' fortunes have risen and declined with ups and downs in the economy, Genstar's countercyclical operations have resulted in its revenues steadily growing an average of 30 percent annually and its net income rising an average of 39 percent a year over the past ten years. Shareholders who had faith in Genstar

Angus A. MacNaughton, chairman, Genstar

Ross J. Turner, president, Genstar

*Walter S. Bannister, executive vice-president,
land and real estate development, Genstar*

have done well, too, with the share price having quadrupled since 1965, when it was listed on the Toronto Stock Exchange as an amalgamated company under its former name, Sogemines Ltd. Three eastern Canada firms had been merged — Inland Cement, Brockville (Ontario) Chemical Industries, and Iroquois Glass — as Sogemines switched from a holding company to an operating corporation.

What is Genstar, then? A conglomerate? Or a real estate company with outside interests? Certainly, the company name doesn't give any clues. Devised by corporate logo expert Lippincott & Margulies of New York in 1969 when the firm went public, the name was aimed at allowing Genstar to work in any field without having to change its moniker. The corporate logo of a square inside a stylized star, according to the firm's 1969 annual report, "represents strength and stability and the coordination of various activities into a single unit."

What does that mean in practice? One thing it does *not*, Genstar executives say touchily, is that it is a conglomerate. "It is a central holding company owning a lot of other companies which run their own operations and remit dividends in after-tax dollars to the holding company, unlike operating subsidiaries at other firms which transfer money in pre-tax dollars to the core company," says Walter Bannister, executive vice-president, housing and land development.

"Nor is it a real estate company. We try to limit real estate activities to between 25 percent and 30 percent of total revenues and assets," Bannister says. "It was up to 45 percent of the total until Flintkote Co. (a major U.S. producer of building and construction materials) was bought in 1980. Last year it was 25 percent ($589 million). It will become a smaller proportion not by reducing it, but because other areas, such as waste management, the fastest growing area, will expand more quickly." Flintkote, which was purchased for $447 million, was Genstar's biggest ever acquisition and almost equal in size to Genstar. Flintkote had 1979 revenue of $869 million compared with Genstar's $1 billion and is being credited with Genstar's steep increase in revenue to $2.3 billion in 1980.

The nature of Genstar is not the only puzzling element of the company. There is also the question of whether with its executive offices in the U.S., the company is really American rather than Canadian. The majority of its stock is Canadian-held and two-thirds of its directors are Canadian, although two of them, Genstar chairman Angus MacNaughton and president Ross Turner, are at the executive offices in San Francisco. Close to 60 percent of its assets are in the U.S. compared with only 17 percent in 1977.

Its nationality has been a subject of hot debate between Genstar and the Foreign Investment Review Agency (FIRA) and is now sitting in a sort of limbo. Genstar has a Canadian charter, but with its top executives moving to San Francisco in March 1980 and half its business and employees being in the U.S., with expectations of surpassing Canadian results, the company has come under FIRA review several times. Two years ago, it was told that it was "not a non-eligible company." In plain language, that meant Genstar was regarded as Canadian and would therefore not come under FIRA's review of acquisitions of Canadian businesses by foreign firms.

Then in June 1980, four months after the Genstar executives transferred from Montreal to San Francisco, Herb Gray, federal Minister of Industry, Trade, and Commerce and an ardent nationalist, said he no longer felt bound by the earlier FIRA opinion. Since then, Genstar has acquired a couple of small Canadian companies in Alberta without FIRA's saying anything and re-applied to FIRA to clarify its status, with the intention of going to court if FIRA said it was ineligible to be regarded as Canadian. Why should Genstar go to all this trouble? What does it really matter if it's regarded as Canadian or American, considering that its growth is coming largely from its U.S. operations?

"We don't want to be subject to review with acquisitions because some provincial planning bodies are more nationalistic than others and could react unfavorably as a result of our having to go before FIRA," says John Chase, Genstar's vice-president of corporate affairs. "By contrast, while Americans are interested and wonder about the ramifications of foreign investment, they are not as nationalistic."

However, FIRA took no action when Genstar bid for Canada Permanent.

One of the most unusual features of Genstar is its rotating chief executive duo of Angus MacNaughton and Ross Turner. In many ways they are the odd couple of the corporate world, despite having the same background — both are chartered accountants — and being very close in age. Turner was born May 1, 1930, and MacNaughton on July 15, 1931. They get the same salary ($375,400) and each owns 1.28 percent of Genstar's common shares. They also have the same size offices, located side by side in Embarcadero Center, a $300 million redevelopment project on San Francisco's waterfront, developed by David Rockefeller and the Prudential Insurance Co. Located on the site of a former rundown section of the city on landfill over what used to be part of San Francisco Bay, the Center has four office towers, a luxury hotel, and retail shops and restaurants.

After only a few months in its rather spartan premises in Three Embarcadero (one of the office towers), Genstar had grown from 25 to 150 people who spilled over four floors in the building and a couple of other buildings several blocks away. They were united this summer in the new Four Embarcadero Center, occupying the top three floors with options to lease two more floors. The atmosphere is shirt-sleeve casual.

In appearance, manner, and outside interests, McNaughton and Turner have nothing in common. The dark-haired, bespectacled, youthful-looking MacNaughton appears as the accountant he is. He is shorter and chunkier than the tall, lanky, silver-haired, suave Turner who looks like a diplomat. MacNaughton is the fourth generation of a Quebec family; Turner was born in Winnipeg. MacNaughton responds instantly in conversations and excels at mental arithmetic. Turner ponders his replies, is more relaxed, and jokes more. "He fools outsiders as a result, but then he hits them with a question that shows he understands the matter more than they do," says a Genstar executive.

MacNaughton is a crack snow and water skier for which he has a house at the Lake Tahoe resort area. Turner's sports were canoeing and working out on the local YMCA basketball court until he injured a knee in recent years.

But despite their differences, they appear to work well together, although some outside observers wonder whether there is actually a power struggle between them for supreme authority. Employees, however, say they blend together so well in business that if one tires of something, the other can immediately carry on. And employees find that with travel to Genstar's continent–spanning operations consuming at least three-quarters of MacNaughton's and Turner's time, it makes for smoother operations to have the tandem team.

MacNaughton has been with Genstar almost since its start. He joined four years after its establishment in 1951 and rose steadily through the ranks to treasurer (1961), vice-president (1964), executive vice-president (1970), and president (1973). Genstar's corporate, financial, and administrative groups report to him and the operational functions report to Turner.

Turner has worked at Genstar twice, starting at BACM Ltd., a family-owned western Canadian land developer, homebuilder, and road paving company that was bought by Genstar in 1968. He then worked at several other companies including Seaspan International Ltd., the largest west coast marine transportation firm, which supplied towing and marine equipment to Genstar as well as other clients. In 1972 he rejoined Genstar as president of a new Vancouver-based subsidiary, Genstar Western Ltd., with responsibility for coordinating Genstar's cement, building materials, heavy construction, land development, and housing operations in western Canada. A year later, Genstar bought Seaspan for $19 million.

Beneath MacNaughton and Turner (called the "two big votes" by senior executives) are six executive vice-presidents ("six little votes") — one in charge of finance and the others of Genstar's industrial categories — housing and land, building materials, construction, cement, marine, financial services, and investments (a grabbag including manufacturing chemicals and fertilizers and Genstar's acquisition of Flintkote). The six executive vice-presidents have the latitude to run their divisions without having, as Walter Bannister puts it, "to call up and say you want to start a new subdivision." Divisions are given an indefinite time to cure problem areas before shutting them down. For example, Bannister is considering closing Genstar's weak Houston operations and shifting to Dallas or San Antonio after several years of waiting for an improvement.

Although many of its operations, such as housing, construction, and building materials are related, Genstar's policy is that only 35 percent of production be sold in-house and that competitive bids should be obtained. The 35 percent is sometimes more a target than an actuality. For example, Calgary-based Genstar Housing Components, which makes stairs, walls, and roof trusses, sells 80 percent of its production to Genstar-owned Engineered Homes Ltd. and Keith Construction Co. of Calgary.

It was Turner who had the delicate task of explaining to shareholders in Genstar's 1978 annual report why the company was transferring 25 of its executives to California, while leaving 40 others at Place Ville Marie in Montreal. Later the company would say that it left primarily because an increasing amount of its activity and investment was in the U.S. ($250 million in 1978 alone). It had already sold its Quebec operations and pared down its Ontario ones to a handful of land deals.

But Genstar also was part of the exodus of businesses from Quebec following the election of the separatist Parti Québeçois in November 1976. "Montreal has ceased to be the ideal business center it once was," Turner wrote. "In addition to the negative effects on business of the uncertain political climate, the current lack of vitality and activity is a deterrent to attracting new investment to the province. It is also becoming increasingly difficult for businesses to attract and retain professional staff in Montreal. Problems are created for families with school-age children who do not happen to meet arbitrary government regulations for acceptance into the school system of their choice." The government wanted children transferring to Quebec schools to be educated in French.

But Turner went on to say that even more importantly, 90 percent of Genstar's profits, operations, and assets are located in the western half of Canada and the U.S. "An arc drawn from San Francisco as its center would encompass most of these assets and operations within a radius of 2,100 miles, whereas a similar arc centered on Montreal requires a radius of 3,500 miles."

Walter Bannister was the first to be sent to California because he could get a U.S. work permit easily (his wife is an American citizen). Genstar paid for the transplanted executives' trips to find a house, subsidized housing purchases, paid moving expenses, and picked up the bill for one year for a tax accountant to handle the taxation differences between Canada and the U.S.

But as a decentralized company, Genstar has senior executives located all over the map. It has a Canadian-based and U.S.-based treasurer, because of the differences in banking and securities laws, and a legal counsel in San Francisco and assistant legal counsel in Vancouver. The head of the Canadian housing operations is in Calgary; the Canadian land operations president is based in Vancouver. Mike Rogers, president of the eastern arm of Canadian land development, is headquartered in Edmonton because he did not want to move to Toronto.

The San Francisco executive office keeps in touch with Genstar's far-flung operations by sending mailbags daily by courier and lots of telephone calls. To cut down its phone bill, Genstar is extending its WATS service from California to the rest of the U.S. and Canada.

Whereas other Canadian development companies were the brainchild of an individual, many of whom still run the firm and own either all or most of their enterprise, Genstar is the offspring of a corporate giant and has always been run by hired professional managers. It was started in Montreal in March 1951 under the name of Sogemines Ltd. by the Société Générale de Belgique of Brussels. Sogemines is an abbreviation of Société Générale des Mines.

Formed in 1822, the Société has large-scale interests in more than 80 companies in Belgium and abroad in banking, electricity, oil and gas, diamond mining, chemicals, iron and steel, shipping, and military equipment. It owns 23.9 percent of the Société Générale de Banque of Brussels, which is the world's 45th largest bank with 1979 assets of $35.2 billion (U.S.). (The Royal Bank of Canada, Canada's largest bank, ranks 34th globally, with 1979 assets of $51.7 billion Canadian.)

It wanted a foothold in North American resource industries and chose Canada over the U.S. because it regarded Canada as more of a frontier country at that time than the U.S.

The Société has four members on Genstar's 18 member Board of Directors and a 21 percent equity interest in the firm. Charles de Bar, deputy chairman of Genstar, spends most of his time in Brussels.

Sogemines did not start out as a real estate company. At first it was active in chemicals, cement production, tug and barge transportation, and steel and rubber distribution. With the purchase in 1968 of a majority interest in BACM, the construction company where Ross Turner worked at one time, the firm, renamed Genstar in February 1969 (the same year it was listed on the New York Stock Exchange), moved into real estate.

In 1965, predating by almost 15 years the decision of Canada's other developers to diversify, Genstar laid down this strategy as corporate policy: "Our objective is to achieve a balance between our various activities and so lessen our vulnerability to economic decline. Cement is a sound business to be in and so are the related activities of building materials, heavy construction, land development, and housing. The

MAIN COMPANIES OF THE SOCIÉTÉ GÉNÉRALE DE BELGIQUE
(Besides Genstar)

Société Générale de Banque	World's 45th largest bank
Sofina	Finance company
CMB	Belgium's leading shipping company, operating 15 lines to four continents. Also operates bulk carriers supplying Belgian and Luxembourg steel industries. Subsidiaries in cargo storage, towing, ship repairs.
Société de Traction et d'Electricité	Investment in Belgian, French, and U.S. energy, chemical, and electro-chemical sectors.
BN	Manufacturing railway and urban transport rolling stock, marine containers, truck bodies, bridges, equipment for nuclear and sugar industries, military equipment.
FN	Manufacturing of arms and ammunition, sporting equipment, aircraft jet engines.
Sibeka	Production, processing, and commercial use of diamonds, such as diamond tools.
Carbochim	Ammonia, nitric acid, plastic films, fertilizers, manganese dioxide for dry batteries.
PRB	Chemicals for use in pharmaceutical and food industries.
CBR	Cement manufacturing.
CFE	Contractor for building construction, dredging, electrification, road building.

chemical business, though not outstanding, benefits from a steady demand."

Real estate investment analysts like to debate whether Genstar's success has been due to being lucky or smart, with the consensus that both have played a role. For example, Genstar entered the land development business not in the rapidly saturating central Canada markets, like many of its competitors, but in western Canada through the acquisition of BACM. A year before Genstar bought into BACM, BACM had bought Engineered Homes Ltd., a large homebuilder in Alberta and British Columbia, which allowed Genstar to be on the ground floor when the boom started in these provinces in the 1970s.

In 1976 Genstar acquired Abbey Glen Corp., then Canada's sixth largest real estate company with assets of $385 million, at a distress sale price of $179 million. Although its headquarters were in eastern Canada, Abbey Glen had most of its holdings in western Canada, as well as land in New Jersey and Florida. Cadillac Fairview had bid first for Abbey Glen but dropped out because it did not want to get into a bidding war.

Despite its good land holdings, Abbey Glen was a troubled company. Its controlling British shareholder, Capital & Counties Property Co. of London, was floundering in England due to high interest rates combined with a fall in property values. Abbey Glen, founded in 1974, was also viewed sourly by real estate investment analysts since, notwithstanding its good assets, it had a large bank debt and limited cash flow. As real estate analyst Ira Gluskin of Brown Baldwin & Nisker Ltd. stated baldly at the time, "Abbey Glen should be at the bottom of any list of real estate stock recommendations."

But while Abbey Glen did have a negative financial impact on Genstar initially, it also had all that strategically located land. The sale by Genstar of Abbey Glen's apartments, office buildings, and shopping centers paid for the purchase, leaving Genstar with what it wanted — Abbey Glen's land.

Similarly, Genstar got a head start in moving into the lucrative California market.

In 1970 Genstar acquired Sutter Hill Co. of Palo Alto, an eight-year old company, 70 percent involved in supplying venture capital to fledgling high technology firms and 30 percent in selling shopping center development packages to long-term investors, determining location, getting tenants, and supervising construction.

Over the next few years, Genstar acquired several more residential homebuilders at bargain prices because the recession had wiped out most of their business. In 1977, Genstar established divisions in Texas, Washington, and Florida. By last year, it ranked 14th among the top 200 homebuilders in the U.S. and was the only Canadian-controlled firm to be in the top 40.

Real estate investment analysts have high praise for Genstar's canniness. "Genstar is well positioned to benefit from the energy related growth of western Canada and from the rapid development of the southern and western United States which are continuing to experience a large population influx," says Harry Rannala.

"The rapid progress of these two markets has placed a heavy demand on available resources and on the ability of local companies to provide the required office, industrial, and housing units. Much of Genstar's phenomenal performance was based upon the anticipation of these developments. As a result, the company was able to secure a major position by having a fully integrated operation in place to service the exceptional growth of these markets. This exposure to two major profit centers will continue to benefit the long-term profitable development of Genstar."

Housing and land development have been Genstar's fastest growing sector in terms of revenue. Between 1975 and 1980 sales rose close to 270 percent from $156.3 million to $580 million. In Canada, Genstar builds houses from Ontario to British Columbia and in the U.S. it is in Washington, Oregon, California (its biggest market), Texas, and Florida. It holds options on land in South Carolina and is also looking at the Georgia market.

The more mature Canadian operations have a higher performance with a pre-tax profit margin of 31.4 percent in 1980 on net income

Crow Canyon Country Club, San Francisco

Antelope Hills/Broadmoor, San Francisco

of $70.9 million (in Canadian dollars) compared with an 11 percent pre-tax profit margin on net income of $45.2 million (in U.S. dollars) in the U.S. operations, many of which are still at the start-up stage. Of Genstar's five U.S. land activities, three lost money, one broke even, and one was profitable (8,500 acres at Penasquitos near San Diego). Of the four housing divisions, two made money and two lost.

"This year there will be only one money-loser and that loss should be under $400,000," says Walter Bannister. "Because of the purchase and servicing costs and then the long waiting period for government zoning approval during which no money is coming in, there is enormous debt until 50 percent is sold at which point you start to cover a good portion of the cost and reduce the debt load," Bannister says. "After you reach the 75 percent mark in sales, you start to make profits."

Genstar builds all types of housing except apartments, on which it believes the costs outpace the returns, manufactures housing components such as doors, stairs, walls and kitchen units, and does shopping center development. It develops commercial land, but does not construct office buildings.

"Apartment buildings are a lousy investment, because it is difficult with today's construction and financing costs and rent controls," Bannister says. Nor is Genstar interested in major downtown redevelopment projects. "They take a long lead time and you can lose a lot of sleep over them," Bannister says.

Genstar's housing production of 3,377 units in 1979 was about half the 6,000 turned out by Nu-West, Canada's largest homebuilder. Genstar's output has grown steadily, largely because of its U.S. operations, but it has under a one percent market share in California compared with a close to 10 percent market share in Calgary and Edmonton, making it the second largest homebuilder there after Nu-West. However, a one percent market share in California, where the population is 21.5 million, can be 10 times as large in unit volume as in Alberta (1.8 million population).

Number of Houses Sold

	1975	1976	1977	1978	1979	1980
Canada	2,468	2,446	2,707	2,534	2,199	1,757
United States	440	797	997	945	1,178	954
TOTAL	2,908	3,243	3,704	3,479	3,377	2,711

Growth in the U.S. is being emphasized partly because Genstar was unhappy about the possible political repercussions of its large Canadian presence. "Since our concentration in western Canada was so high and we were seeking approvals at every subdivision meeting, we were too visible for people to throw darts at in protesting land prices," Bannister says. His goal is to have activity split evenly between Canada and the U.S. and he is well on his way. Today, 33 percent of Genstar's houses are built in the U.S. compared with only 14 percent in 1975.

Much of the impetus for this growth can be attributed to the affable, straightforward, gentle but firm 56-year-old Bannister. Tall, with thinning gray hair and glasses he often wears over contact lenses, he is the son of a Grand Trunk Railway and then Canadian National Railway fireman and locomotive engineer. Bannister attended 12 schools in Michigan and Illinois as his father moved from place to place during the Depression. He studied mining engineering at the Michigan College of Mining and Technology.

Bannister's career, like his youth, has been a "gypsy business." The move to San Francisco was the 13th for him and his wife. They live in Hillsborough, one of San Francisco's wealthiest suburbs, conveniently located midway between Genstar's offices and the San Francisco airport from which Bannister makes frequent trips to his division's widespread operations.

The wanderlust carries over to the Bannisters' vacations. Each year they go for a two-week cruise on a cargo ship that takes passengers. "I can't take eight weeks for a full cruise, so we fly to a city and join the cruise there for a two week segment, putting our luggage on the boat in advance at San Francisco." In 1981 they started at Rio de Janeiro and went around South America. Last year they went to Alaska.

After serving in the Canadian Army in World War II, Bannister worked at three mining companies — Inco, Kerr-Addison, and Johns Manville. In 1973 he became vice-president of production at Genstar's oldest business, Inland Cement, which had been started in 1956. After nearly nine years when "things tapered off," Bannister went to Buenos Aires as president of the local operations of Lonestar Industries, a U.S. cement company.

After three years he was transferred to Lonestar's head office in Connecticut where he "didn't like it" and so was delighted when Genstar asked him to return as president of Inland Cement. He just had time to expand Inland's Edmonton plant and set up a new one in Vancouver when Genstar created a new management level of executive vice-president to oversee its vast business interests. "I thought I would be placed in charge of wallboard, but instead Ross Turner asked me to handle real estate and gave me the weekend to think it over."

In a holdover from his early days in the mines, where latecomers who missed the cage had to climb down the shaft, Bannister is at work by 7:45 a.m. and leaves by 5:15 p.m. Besides traveling, he swims (his house has a pool), golfs, and, in a reflection of his father's occupation, has a model railroad.

Until recently, Genstar's Canadian and U.S. housing and land development business was handled on a north-south basis with Toronto looking after activities in New Jersey, Florida, Ontario, and Quebec and Vancouver in charge of western Canada and the western U.S. This system was jettisoned because of administrative confusion arising from government social security, pension, and tax benefits and regulations differing widely between Canada and the U.S. So Ontario and Quebec were lopped off the U.S. operations and formed into Genstar Eastern Development. Western Canada was separated from the western U.S. operations and made into Genstar Western Development, with head-quarters in Vancouver. Genstar Eastern's president, Mike Rogers, is headquartered in Edmonton by choice, but his successor will likely be located in Toronto or Winnipeg.

Genstar's modus operandi is to let its local operations act as separate profit centers with their own president and senior management. The housing and land division, for example, has 19 profit centers, 16 of which are headed by a president, two by general managers, and one by an executive vice-president.

Each profit center is evaluated twice a year on the bases of sales, profit, inventory, return on assets, interest costs, and how fast projects are completed. From this examination, the company can determine who is doing best — or worst — and why. Formal group seminars are held occasionally to review such topics as marketing land or financing trends.

In May of each year every division does a five-year strategic fore-cast on growth rates, organization, and geographic and product line expansion. In September they prepare a profit forecast for the current and next year. Bannister then reviews each plan and inevitably finds that "all of them want to grow faster." His task is to decide, in conjunction with Ross Turner, which projects will get the go-ahead.

This encourages the individual operations to act as nearly inde-pendent entrepreneurs. For a view of how this works at the grassroots level, consider the plans of Calgary-based Genstar Housing Compo-nents, which makes wall panels, stairs, roof trusses, and kitchen units for Genstar's western Canada operations. It is not one of the housing and land development division's largest sectors, recording revenue of $22.7 million and profit of $1.9 million in 1980, compared with $27 million sales and $1.5 million profit in 1979 — or four percent of total 1980 housing and land development revenue.

Genstar Housing Component president Lou Luini, 48, typifies Genstar's predilection for promoting people from the ground up over a long, careful nurturing period. Luini took 22 years to proceed from carpenter's helper to journeyman, foreman, production manager, assistant manager, design manager, general manager, vice-president, and then president. He is encouraged to devise ways of increasing productivity, even if this involves expensive machinery. Recently, for example, Luini got Bannister to ante up $250,000 for two machines that will speed up production by 50 percent at Genstar Housing's kitchen cabinet manufacturing operation. "If you show them there is money to be made or saved, they are good to you, but they don't have an open purse — you must justify everything," Luini says.

Last year, on a bigger scale, Luini convinced head office that the Canadian housing manufacturing operations should be consolidated. Until then Genstar's two Calgary homebuilding firms, Engineered Homes and Keith Construction, each had their own lumber yards even though they were only five miles apart. "Consolidation enabled us to increase our profit last year (by $400,000) over 1979, despite the sales volume (down by $4 million) being only 80 percent of what had been projected," Luini says.

Spurred by the results of this consolidation, Luini is now gearing up to propose a $5 million consolidation on 20 acres of the housing and kitchen component operations, which are now six blocks apart. He has a district picked out but knows getting the money will take several years of pitching the idea as being more deserving of getting funds than major projects of other housing and land development presidents. Meanwhile, he is investigating ways of expanding his division both geographically and in product line. He once shipped some components for cottages to Hawaii, has received inquiries from Argentina and Venezuela, and may export to South America.

Why should the kitchen cabinets just be sold in central Alberta? Couldn't they be shipped elsewhere, too? These are thoughts that are occupying Mike McDonough, the manager of Genstar Housing Component's kitchen cabinet division. He has started shipping to northern Alberta, Saskatchewan, and Manitoba and recently set up small warehouses in these provinces and Vancouver to reduce frequency of shipments. Now, with Genstar such a major presence in California and in Ontario, McDonough is eying those markets. At the same time, he is expanding into upgrading kitchen cabinets into attractive living room, dining room, and den furniture.

With Genstar's multi-million dollar empire behind them, Luini and McDonough know that they can make into reality what most small businessmen can only dream of doing. In turn, their creativity will bring in more profits for Genstar.

With operations spread throughout Canada and the U.S., Genstar is a perceptive observer of the differences between the two countries in housing and land development. At the same time, as a manufacturer of housing components, it provides a close-up view of the how and what of housing production. "The differences between Canada and the U.S. are mind-boggling," Bannister says. "There is less uniformity in the U.S. than in Canada. In Canada it is reasonably uniform and uniformly difficult."

"It can take 11 years to get approval in Canada because no one authority is responsible in a community for producing houses, whereas several are responsible for limiting them. Also, there are many contraditions between federal and provincial housing subsidies as to the size and price for which they provide funds.

"In the U.S. it ranges from the more difficult than in Canada to the less difficult. For example, because Houston has no zoning, anybody can get into the business and everybody has. As a result, there are enough lots for the next four years and lot prices are only $9,000 and a house about $60,000. By contrast, in California, where state, county, municipal, and coastal commissions must all give approval, a lot is $120,000 and the average house price $110,000 to $250,000. The cheapest 650 square foot townhouses in the (San Francisco) Bay area are $100,000.

"The costs of municipal government shifted from the average taxpayer to the new homebuyer due to Proposition 13 (approved in June 1978 by Californians to reduce their taxload for municipal services). Proposition 13 was a publicity stunt—it focused the anti-tax feelings of people but did not reduce government spending. Whereas a building permit in Houston costs $10, in San José you have to pay $2,600 and $3,000 per house to the school board to go toward education for future homeowners. In addition the Board asks for land for a school. But future homeowners do not attend all the zoning hearings, so that they regard us as greedy so-and-sos when actually we're just passing along these costs."

If over-regulated California gives Bannister heartburn, under-regulated Houston gives him severe indigestion. "We lose money on every house we sell in Houston (200 in 1980) because with the glut of lots, you have to offer 11 percent mortgage rates and absorb the difference of $9,000 between that and the prevailing 15 percent rate." Thus, even though Houston is one of the largest U.S. markets with an average of 30,000 newcomers annually, Bannister is considering pulling out after two painful years.

And, Bannister points out, because homebuilders and land developers still want to make hefty profits, homebuyers can expect some major changes in housing design.

"Houses will be smaller and there will be more cluster housing and partner housing in which two couples share the same living and dining rooms, but have their own master bedrooms.

"Companies like Genstar will shy away from traditional land banking. In the past, land developers would buy farmland as a reserve and rent it back to the farmer; his rent would pay for the interest costs and the taxes would be at the agricultural rate. But at today's prices and interest rates you can't get hold of land for long periods of time. Consequently, there will be more joint ventures. Since more money in Canada is made on land than housing (an after-tax profit of only two percent is typical), we will place more emphasis on land there and less on housing. In the U.S. there are still new areas to enter and we will place more emphasis on housing."

"We will also be more ingenious in our acquisitions. One alternative is to exercise the option on land in yearly segments and develop just enough lots for one year instead of three to four years as we used to do. We can gauge demand from state and provincial forecasts, what type of product is selling, and how much inventory is left."

Buyers should be aware, though, that it is the configuration of a home which substantially determines the price because the components are basically the same even though luxury homes have fancier doors or window frames. The similarity in houses is evidenced by Genstar Housing Components which produces prebuilt housing parts (walls, doors, roof trusses). When Genstar Housing Components receives blueprints from Genstar's housebuilding divisions in Calgary, Engineered Homes and Keith Construction, it translates the information into computer programming as to where each wall, fireplace, and staircase goes.

Each of the 35 walls for a big house and 20 for a small one are broken down into 12 pieces of computer information. The walls are also divided into sections because otherwise they would be too heavy to lift. All told, Genstar Housing Components has 500 computer programs. They trigger machinery to saw off wood, put in nails, square walls, precut stairs, and make roof trusses automatically. The units are all coded and placed on separate trailer trucks for hauling to the construction site. "Using this method, six houses can be built in an eight hour shift, whereas it would take three men eight hours to build one house," says Lou Luini.

Obviously, this greater productivity reduces costs and Genstar is also examining other ways of shaving outlay. Like Nu-West, it is a strong proponent of storm water retention lakes which allow the use of ten inch pipes instead of the traditional 90 inch ones, because the lake retains the water as it rains. After the storm, some of the water can be released at a lower rate through the smaller pipe and the rest retained as a lake. The warmer weather of California also cuts some costs, in proportion to those in Canada, because plastic pipes can be used, instead of steel, and they only have to be buried two feet below the ground instead of seven feet as in colder Alberta.

Genstar does most of its financing through the major Canadian banks. "U.S. bankers are accustomed to specific debt for a particular project, whereas the Canadian banks are used to corporate financing (for an entire corporation which then divvies it out to projects) and so figure if they lose their shirt on one subdivision, they'll make it back on another," Bannister says. "I once met with a San Diego banker who had a fantastic title. He asked not if, but when, we would default on a loan for a subdivision. I said we had never defaulted, but if we were to, we would work our way out or shut down and pay our bills. He couldn't grasp this."

Genstar has started dealing with U.S. banks — but on its own terms. It borrows corporately from the Canadian banks and provides acquisition and construction loans internally to its divisions, then goes to outside sources for "takeout" (mortgage) loans. The U.S. banks were reluctant at first just to provide takeout financing because loans for construction are more lucrative. So Genstar hired John Chase, formerly with Trans-America (a diversified company with interests in industrial machinery, transportation, and insurance) and Itel (a high technology firm), and a longtime San Francisco resident, as vice-president, corporate affairs, to make Genstar well known in the U.S. His public relations campaign of advertising in business journals has opened bank doors.

Bannister expects a shakeout in this decade, due to the costs of doing business and competition, more so among medium builders who expand too quickly than small ones who stick to what they can handle. That will provide acquisition opportunities for Genstar. Already it has picked up one such family-owned company, Broadmoor Homes of California, which otherwise would have gone bankrupt since of the three subdivisions it planned to bring onstream in 1980, one was delayed by a protest group and a second by the community's slowness in approving it. "As a result, it was losing several million dollars, but now that the two subdivisions are underway, it will eventually be a $100 million a year business," Bannister says.

Sharp decisions like this and its astute diversification will mean that Genstar will no longer have to complain jokingly in magazine advertisements that at $2 billion in assets and growing, it is "the biggest company you never heard of."

Chapter Twelve

THE ROAD AHEAD

"Most lenders want some participation in the income or the ownership as a hedge against inflation."

NEIL WOOD
PRESIDENT (1974-1981)
CADILLAC FAIRVIEW

The outlook in Canada and the U.S. is promising for Canadian developers. But they will also have to deal with such challenges as rising interest rates and the increasing competition for projects from their lenders—the banks, insurance companies, and pension funds.

With projects becoming so vast, however, it is likely that the borrowers—the developers—and the lenders will compete on some projects in the future and link forces for more joint ventures than in the past.

So far only about two to three percent of Canadian pension fund money is invested in real estate, but this is expected to soar as pension funds seek ways to get bigger in order to make payments to their investors. According to Statistics Canada in 1979 (latest available figures), $55 billion was invested by Canadians in private and Canada Pension plans.

Canada's biggest real estate pension fund is Morguard Properties Ltd., based in Toronto. It had assets in its fiscal year ended September 30, 1980, of $503.3 million. Morguard acquires, develops, manages, and leases property on behalf of the 25 pension funds that own it. They include several provincial government funds as well as those of International Harvester Ltd., Abitibi-Price Inc., Du Pont Canada Inc., CIL Ltd., and Bell Canada.

Investing in real estate provides a tax shelter for the funds' investors. As long as their money is invested in the fund, they pay no tax on it. The pensioners pay tax only when they receive their pension. At the same time, investing in real estate provides a hedge against inflation.

Recently, for example, Olympia & York bought three buildings in West Palm Beach, Florida with $18 million from British Overseas Airway Corp. pension funds.

However, under Canadian legislation, only 10 percent of a pension fund can be invested in real estate. In the United Kingdom, about 20 percent of pension fund money can be so invested.

Morguard participates in deals ranging from $2 million to $100 million. "We only deal in office buildings, industrial parks, and retail projects," says president Roy Greiner. "We have always avoided residential and land development because of rent, fiscal, and monetary controls on that segment of the market."

On any given deal, 50 percent to 80 percent of Morguard's pension funds participate. Each fund has a pro rata share based on its size. In recent years Morguard has purchased around $100 million in assets a year.

Morguard has done well for its investors, outperforming Daon, which has had the fastest growth rate among the developers. In its fiscal year ended September 30, 1980, Morguard's total revenue rose 59 percent (to $70.3 million), whereas Daon's total revenue rose 31 percent (to $697.9 million) in its fiscal year ended October 31, 1980.

The success of four-year-old Morguard Properties has prompted the formation of competitive real estate investment funds for pension pools. They include Penlea, which A.E. LePage manages for Air Canada, Bell Canada, the hospitals of Ontario, and the Ontario Municipal Employees.

Others are run by Royal Trustco, Canadian National Railways, Great-West Life Assurance, Canada Life Assurance, North American Life Assurance, and Sun Life Assurance. So far, however, Morguard is the only fund that develops properties. The others only acquire real estate.

The insurance companies, which used to be content merely to provide financing for real estate ventures, are now becoming directly involved either through joint ventures with developers or on their own, also as a hedge against inflation. The lenders' change of attitude came from their recognition that, after the declining value of the dollar was taken into account, they were getting very little return on their loan, whereas the developers were benefiting from inflation puffing up the value of their properties.

Now lenders are either owning all or part of projects to participate in the rewards. As a result of the upward push in interest rates, 20 year, long-term fixed mortgage loans have become virtually extinct and replaced by short-term loans of as low as one year to a ceiling of five years.

The leader is Winnipeg-based Great-West Life Assurance, which pioneered this trend 20 years ago. It has a major equity interest in 16 development companies in Canada and the U.S., with assets at book value in excess of $1.2 billion. Great-West's holdings in the firms range from 15 percent to 100 percent. At one time, Great-West's largest investment was in Oxford Development Group. (It pulled out in 1979.)

Present investments include a major share in Cambridge Leaseholds Ltd., Canada's second largest shopping center developer, Bentall Properties Ltd., a major Vancouver developer, and Delta Hotels, Canada's fastest growing hotel chain.

In addition, Great-West has $1.8 billion in real estate investments in Canada and the U.S. That places it on a level with such major developers as Daon, Nu-West, and Trizec. These include major developments in Georgia, Texas, and Arizona.

Perhaps the real estate development industry's biggest headache is the cost of financing. Today's fluctuating interest rates have killed off the traditional 20 year mortgage financing and replaced it with five year maximums and often just a one year ceiling.

As projects get bigger and developers do more and more of them simultaneously, their appetite for financing will grow stronger and stronger. "The method of financing for developers is changing," says Neil Wood, president of Cadillac Fairview until the fall of 1981. "The conventional historic method has been to get mortgages from insurance companies. But now, although developers are continuing to work with insurance firms, they are turning more to pension funds and foreign sources."

The need for cash is resulting in more joint ventures between Canadian developers, Canadian and local American developers, and between the developers and financial institutions. "Most lenders now want some participation in the income or the ownership as a hedge against inflation," Wood says.

In an effort to stave off the inroads the financial institutions are making into their turf, some developers are branching into financial services. Genstar already has its own financial services division, and it was the reason largely behind Campeau's unsuccessful bid in August 1980 for Royal Trustco and Genstar's bid in the summer of 1981 for Canada Permanent Mortgage Corp.

Because developers' costs are rising, tenants can expect shorter term leases and higher rents. "There has been an enormous escalation in land costs partly because with less land being zoned, everything has to be packed into a relatively small area," says Gordon Gray, chairman of A.E. LePage.

"That has caused incredible increases in land prices. There also have been huge increases in construction costs due to inflation in wages and the price of materials.

"In addition, there has been an enormous increase in financing costs. A first class office building erected in the 1960s would have cost $25 per square foot for land, construction, financing, and leasing costs. Today, it costs $100. Consequently, tenants must pay four times more rent today than they did 20 years ago.

"The problem is further compounded by long-term financing costs. When financing used to cost eight percent, developers were happy with a 10 percent return. Now, it is virtually impossible to get sufficient rent to show a return equal to, or greater than, the current financing rates of over 15 percent."

Another area in which tenants and consumers can expect changes is in shopping centers. New shopping center construction in Canada is unlikely in the next few years because the market is already well served.

Opportunities for shopping center developers lie more in expanding and upgrading existing centers. Changing the tenant mix is another avenue.

"There will be a recharacterization of tenant mix every five to ten years, so that the center responds to new merchandising philosophies and presentations," says Kenner Ames, vice-president, shopping center development at Trizec.

"For example, early shopping centers had a shoe repair, one cinema, and a hobby store and no pet shop, library, or skating rink. Then the shoe repair did poorly because plastic products, which didn't wear out, came into vogue.

"Today, the shoe repair business is coming back because leather shoes are making a comeback. There are several hobby stores in plazas because people have more leisure time. The one cinema has grown to twin cinemas and now sixplexes and eightplexes.

"Libraries are becoming popular because, although they do not pay the market rent, they generate traffic. In the U.S., skating rinks are popular because they are a novel idea, whereas in Canada, many parks and clubs have rinks.

"To attract people to shopping centers in these days of rising gasoline prices, we will have to provide 'happenings' for the entire family, such as folk song concerts, billiard championships, and fashion shows."

But while new shopping center activity is slowing down, there are still plenty of opportunities for the developers. Chief among them is the resurgence of the downtown cores. Canadians are expert in redeveloping inner cores of communities.

And there are still lots of opportunities in the U.S., as well as in South America and perhaps other parts of the world. "The Canadians could end up four times their current size due to their entry into the U.S. market," predicts Michael Galway, executive director of the Canadian Institute of Public Real Estate Companies.

But while they are getting larger, a change in the management style of the developers is inevitable as the entrepreneurial founder-owners, who still run most of the firms, are succeeded by a new breed of competent but less colorful and dynamic professional managers, who are as much concerned with bottom line performance as expansion.

Moreover, because real estate attracts entrepreneurs who like the independence of plotting their own future, the industry has a high turnover rate. The very reasons for which a company hires a talented entrepreneur — creativity and daring — are the motives for the talent leaving and setting up his or her own firm.

Still, the companies have gained terrific momentum due to the drive of their founders, and they can only continue to do well as this momentum carries them along.

While the names of the chief executives will change throughout the years, the Canadians will continue to be among the world's largest developers.

Appendices

Appendix A

FIVE YEAR FINANCIAL RESULTS

Note:
(1) There is no table for Olympia & York, which, as a privately held company, does not disclose such data.

271

Bramalea

Year End: January 31

	1981	1980	1979	1978	1977
Revenue ($ millions)	169.9	146.4	112.4	101.9	104.0
Net Income ($ millions)	9.2	6.9	6.6	6.5	6.3
Total Assets ($ millions)	679.5	508.5	406.2	347.9	344.3
Share Price Range	$18-$7⅝	$11.88-$6.69*	$23.75-$13.38	$15.25-$7.50	$8.13-$5.13
Profit Margin (Net Income as a Percentage of Revenue)	5.4%	4.8%	5.87%	6.4%	6.05%
Return on Shareholders' Equity (Net Income as a Percentage of Equity)	21%	19%	17%	18.7%	20.1%

*Two for one stock split in July 1980.

Cadillac Fairview

Year End: February 28

	1981	1980	1979	1978	1977
Revenue ($ millions)	784.3	666.9	420.4	290.3	253.4
Net Income ($ millions)	3.9	25.6	23.5	22.5	15.2
Total Assets ($ billions)	2.7	2.3	1.8	1.4	1.3
Share Price Range	$29¼-$17	$24.25-$9.63	$10.75-$6.25	$10.50-$8.38	$11.88-$8.50
Profit Margin (Net Income as a Percentage of Revenue)	0.5%	3.7%	5.5%	7.3%	5.9%
Return on Shareholders' Equity (Net Income as a Percentage of Equity)	2%	12.8%	13.6%	14.7%	10.8%

Campeau

Year End: December 31

	1980	1979	1978	1977	1976
Revenue ($ millions)	93.4	80.9	73.4	56.1	52.7
Net Income ($ millions)	14.5	6.6	0.5	3.2	4.2
Total Assets ($ millions)	950.3	866.3	720.3	620.8	544.8
Share Price Range	$16.50-$6.00			$10¼-$7*	$5-7/8-$3.50
Profit Margin (Net Income as a Percentage of Revenue)	15%	8.1%	0.68%	5.7%	8%
Return on Shareholders' Equity (Net Income as a Percentage of Equity)	27%	17%	1.4%	9.5%	7.3%

Delisted December 1977.

Carma

Year End: December 30

	1980	1979	1978	1977	1976
Revenue ($ millions)	340.1	142.5	104.6	62.1	57.7
Net Income ($ millions)	43.8	29.8	21.9	11.4	10.4
Total Assets ($ millions)	1,030.7	398.3	281.2	179.0	127.4
Share Price Range*	$16.50-$6.00	$9.75-$4.37	$5.37-$2.06	$2.31-$1.37	$1.50-$1.06
Profit Margin (Net Income as a Percentage of Revenue)	12.8%	21%	20%	18%	17%
Return on Shareholders' Equity (Net Income as a Percentage of Equity)	33.6%	33.7%	33%	23%	33%

Adjusted for 2 for 1 splits in 1976, 1978, and 1980.

Daon

Year End: October 31

	1980	1979	1978	1977	1976
Revenue ($ millions)	697.9	531.2	347.6	155.3	123.2
Net Income ($ millions)	51.3	42.2	15.5	10.3	7.7
Total Assets ($ millions)	1,674.2	1,221.6	653.6	464.3	278.1
Share Price Range	$11.25-$4.80	$10.38-$2.69	$3.63-$1.47	$1.63-$0.44	$0.53-$0.31
Profit Margin (Net Income as a Percentage of Revenue)	7.2%	8%	4.3%	6.5%	5.7%
Return on Shareholders' Equity (Net Income as a Percentage of Equity)	13%	13%	8.2%	10.4%	10%

Genstar
Housing and Land Development

Year End: December 31

	1980	1979	1978	1977	1976
Revenue (1) ($ millions)	589.1	461.5	404.1	372.9	246.3
Net Income (2) ($ millions)	71.6	47.8	39.1	22.5	19.4
Net Assets (3) ($ millions)	597.0	556.0	497.1	434.1	390.6
Return On Net Assets (4)	14.9%	11.5%	11.2%	8.2%	7.7%

Notes:
(1) Accounts for third largest proportion of Genstar's 1980 revenue, or 25.5 percent.
(2) Accounts for largest proportion of 1980 net income, or 46.4 percent.
(3) Accounts for largest proportion of 1980 assets, or 23.7 percent.
(4) Has largest return—14.9 percent—on net assets of Genstar's six industrial categories (others are: marine services, 12.1%; investments, 11.7%; financial services, 11.5%; concrete, 10%; cement and lime, 6.4%; building supplies, 0.9%).

Five Year Financial Results

Year End: December 31

	1980	1979	1978	1977	1976
Revenue ($ millions)	2,310.4	1,264.6	1,143.0	981.1	821.5
Net Income ($ millions)	153.7	123.6	81.6	64.4	55.7
Total Assets ($ millions)	2,434.5	2,401.4	1,492.7	1,249.2	1,205.2
Share Price Range	$47.00-$25.00	$27.75-$18.38	$19.00-$12.75	$14.00-$11.19	$12.00-$9.50
Profit Margin (Net Income as a Percentage of Revenue)	6.6%	9%	7%	6.5%	6.8%
Return on Shareholders' Equity (Net Income as a Percentage of Equity)	16.5%	19%	13%	18%	18%

Results by Category
Revenue ($ millions)

Year End: December 31

	1980	1979	1978	1977	1976
Housing and Land Development	589.1	461.5	404.1	372.9	246.3
Concrete Aggregates and Construction Services	609.3	460.2	391.2	383.1	358.3
Financial Services	76.3	30.3	60.7	20.9	16.3
Investments	46.1	81.1	91.9	97.3	80.4
Marine Services	122.7	113.6	87.5	69.2	62.4
Cement and Lime	360.6	182.1	159.2	133.6	127.9
Building Supplies	608.4*	39.9	32.1	21.1	16.1

*Includes Flintkote operations.

Nu-West

Year End: December 31

	1980	1979	1978	1977	1976
Revenue ($ millions)	862.2	619.3	409.5	319.9	215.7
Net Income ($ millions)	56.7	41.6	27.1	19.4	16.2
Total Assets ($ millions)	1,986.0	1,278.5	732.5	482.8	365.3
Share Price Range*	$16.38-$6.63	$8.50-$3.16	$3.63-$1.96	$2.15-$1.21	$1.40-$0.90
Profit Margin (Net Income as a Percentage of Revenue)	6.6%	6.8%	6.6%	6.2%	8%
Return on Shareholders' Equity (Net Income as a Percentage of Equity)	19.4%	28%	24%	25.3%	32%

*Reflects all stock splits.

Oxford

Year End: March 31

	1979*	1978	1977	1976	1975
Revenue ($ millions)	121.9	71.7	48.2	40.9	20.3
Net Income ($ millions)	6.3	4.2	4.0	3.0	1.8
Total Assets ($ millions)	1,005.9	852.9	547.1	474.8	262.2
Profit Margin (Net Income as a Percentage of Revenue)	5.2%	5.4%	8%	7%	9%
Return on Shareholders' Equity (Net Income as a Percentage of Equity)	6.2%	5.4%	5.4%	6.4%	6%

*Oxford went private at the end of 1979.

Trizec

Year End: October 31

	1980	1979	1978	1977	1976
Revenue ($ millions)	249.8	225.1	201.2	173.2	162.7
Net Income ($ millions)	15.9	11.7	8.4	4.8	4.0
Total Assets ($ millions)	1,800	1,036.9	956.7	931.6	896.3
Share Price	$54-$26.50	$25.50-$15.25	$17.13-$10.25	$13.00-$9.13	$15.88-$9.00
Profit Margin (Net Income as a Percentage of Revenue)	5.4%	5%	4.2%	2.7%	2.5%
Return on Shareholders' Equity (Net Income as a Percentage of Equity)	5.2%	5.3%	4.1%	2.7%	3.4%

Appendix B

MAJOR CURRENT AND PLANNED PROJECTS

Note:
(1) There is no table for Genstar projects because it does not build office buildings or apartments. Its houses are built for immediate sale. Genstar's volume of production is given in Appendix C.

279

Bramalea
(As of December 31, 1980)

Total Square Feet

	Canada	U.S.
Office Buildings	2,013,000	1,111,700
Shopping Centres	5,707,200	3,055,700
Industrial Buildings	3,013,050	270,800

As of December 31, 1980
Land Acreage (By Size)

	Location	Acres	Bramalea's Interest
Canada	Bramalea	2,319	2,319
	Pickering	783	783
	Unionville	522	522
	Ottawa	263	136
U.S.	Los Angeles	1,520	912
	Boca Raton	274	149

Office Buildings (By Size)

	Location	Name	Sq. Ft.	% Interest
Canada	Toronto	Toronto Star Building	767,700	100
	Toronto	Avenue Rd. at Bloor St.	500,000	50
	Toronto	121 Bloor St. E.	256,000	100
	Toronto	55 St. Clair Ave. W.	245,500	50
	Edmonton	9920–108th St.	129,300	100
U.S.	Oakland	Clorox Building	488,600	80
	Dallas	The Texas Building	120,000	100

Hotels (By Number of Rooms)

	Location	*Name*	*Rooms*	*% Interest*
Canada	Vancouver	Hyatt Regency	656	75
	Toronto	Four Seasons	483	75
	Brampton	Holiday Inn	150	under construction
U.S.	Denver	Plaza Cosmopolitan	400	50

Shopping Centers (By Number of Square Feet)

	Location	*Name*	*Sq. Ft.*	*% Interest*
Canada	Bramalea	Bramalea City Centre	910,000	100
	St. Catharines	Niagara Pen Centre	874,300	100
	Calgary	Marlborough Town Square	550,000	100
	Burnaby	Lougheed Mall	491,900	50
	Burnaby	Brentwood Mall	436,300	50
	Moose Jaw	Town 'n' Country	380,000	100
U.S.	Harrisburg	Colonial Park Plaza	513,900	100
	Baltimore	Eudowood Plaza	499,900	100
	Pampa, Texas	Pampa Mall	222,100	25
	Palestine, Texas	Palestine Mall	207,300	25
	Marshall, Texas	Marshall Mall	194,300	25
	Jamestown, N. Dak.	Buffalo Mall	190,400	50

Proposed Projects

	Location	*Description*
Canada	Toronto	256,000 sq. ft. office tower in Yonge-Bloor district.
U.S.	Dallas	Main Center: two 70-storey office towers and 600 room hotel.
	Denver	2,000,000 sq. ft. commercial development on Broadway near Plaza Cosmopolitan Hotel.
	Denver	404,000 sq. ft. of office space in two nine-storey towers in Cherry Creek area.
	Oakland	12-storey office tower in city's center.

Cadillac Fairview

As of February 28, 1981
Total Square Feet*

	Canada	U.S.
Office and Mixed Use Properties		
Completed	10,067,000	2,109,000
Under Construction	506,000	1,214,000
Shopping Centers		
Completed	8,761,000	9,394,000
Under Construction	494,000	—
Industrial Properties		
Completed	2,152,000	4,919,000
Under Construction	194,000	484,000

Company's interest alone: excludes number of square feet held by partners.

Projects Under Development

	Location	Description
Canada	Toronto	Fourth tower of Toronto Dominion Centre.
U.S.	Dallas	$200 million, 50-storey office tower (major tenant: First City Bank of Dallas).
	Dallas	$45 million, 20-storey Pacific Place.
	Dallas-Fort Worth Airport District	$350 million complex of office buildings, residential units, hotel, and shopping center over 10 year period.
	Fort Worth	$135 million, 40-storey office tower; joint venture with First United Bancorporation and Southland Royalty Co. Will be headquarters of First United and First National Banks of Fort Worth.
	Houston	Continuation of development of 30 blocks for retail, hotel, residential, and leisure-time facilities.
	Denver	$300 million joint venture with Bramalea Ltd. of Trinity Center, which will have two million square feet in two office towers.
	Los Angeles	California Center: $1.5 billion project with three office towers, 400 room hotel, 800 residential units, modern art museum, shopping, and cinemas.

Chicago	750,000 square foot Hartt Shaffner Marx Building.
New York City	$130 million, 48-storey office tower at 780 Third Avenue.
Baltimore	Inner Harbor Center office building (part of City's water redevelopment program).
Washington, D.C.	$190 million office building on Pennsylvania Avenue.
Fairfax County, Va.	$360 million Fairview Park: 180 acre development of offices, shopping, 500 hotel rooms, 250 condominium units, and 400 rental units.
San Antonio	2,000,000 square foot commercial development on 11.5 acres, starting with $70 million office tower to be completed in 1983.

Major Office and Mixed Use Properties (By Size)

	Location	Name	Year Opened	Sq. Ft.*	% Interest
Canada	Toronto	Toronto Dominion Centre	1967, 1969, 1974	3,335,000	50
	Toronto	Eaton Centre	1977, 1979	2,615,000	60
	Vancouver	Pacific Centre	1971, 1973, 1975, 1976	2,436,000	33⅓
	Hull	Place du Centre	1978	1,068,000	100
	Calgary	311-321 6th Ave. S.W.	1980	546,100	100
	Edmonton	Continental Bank Building	1980	295,000	100
	Ottawa	Meriline Court	1976, 1980	331,000	50
U.S.	Houston	Houston Center 1 and 2 (acquired 1978)	1975, 1977	2,713,000	50
	San Francisco	Shaklee Terraces	1980	655,000	50
	Denver	410 17th Street	1978	399,000	100

*Includes office, retail, and parking.

Major Shopping Centers (By Size)

	Location	Name	Year Opened	Leasable (Sq. Ft.)*	% Interest
Canada	Montreal	Les Galeries d'Anjou	1968	998,000	50
	Montreal	Les Promenades St. Bruno	1978	912,000	51

Location	Name	Year	Rentable (Sq. Ft.)	% Interest
Montreal	Le Carrefour Laval	1974	870,000	51
Winnipeg	Polo Park Shopping Centre	1959	848,000	100
Hamilton	The Centre Mall	1955	678,000	100
Richmond Hill, Ont.	Hillcrest Mall	1974	566,000	100
U.S.				
White Plains	Galleria of White Plains	1980	879,000	43
Atlanta	Shannon Mall	1980	707,000	75
Hickory, N. Car.	Valley Hills Mall	1978	501,000	75
New Bern, N. Car.	Twin Rivers Mall	1979	275,000	75

Includes outlets owned by department store.

Major Industrial Buildings (By Size)

Location	Name	Year Opened	Rentable (Sq. Ft.)	% Interest
Canada				
Mississauga, Ont.	Erin Mills, Northern Business Park	1972, 1980	1,305,000	100
St. Catharines, Ont.	Cushman Industrial Mall	1975, 1980	187,000	100
Mississauga, Ont.	Erin Mills, Southern Business Park	1972, 1979	153,000	100
Toronto	Skyway Business Park	1978, 1980	121,000	50
U.S.				
Los Angeles	Los Angeles Industrial Center	1976, 1980	2,170,000	100
Los Angeles	Pacific Gateway Center	1976, 1979	1,244,000	100
Orange County	Orange County Industrial Center	1976, 1980	1,151,000	100
Houston	Clay Hempstead Business Park	1979, 1980	289,000	100

New Communities

Location	Name	Acres
Canada		
Mississauga	Erin Mills	8,000
U.S.		
Smithville, N.J.	Historic Towne of Smithville	2,000
San Diego County	Chula Vista	3,200

Campeau

Housing Operations

Cadillac Fairview has wound down its single family operations in Canada through 1980 and 1981, except in the new community of Erin Mills, Ontario, near Toronto. In the United States, its major single family housing projects are at Indian Springs, near Palm Beach, Florida; Mountaingate, a luxury development (near Los Angeles) of 133 houses priced at $500,000 and up; and in Texas, Alabama, Louisiana, and Florida through its subsidiary, General Homes, the second largest homebuilder in Texas.

In Canada, in its fiscal year ended February 28, 1981, the company sold 591 houses; during the same period, it sold 2,976 homes in the United States.

The company is placing increasing emphasis on condominium apartment construction, especially in the United States in Los Angeles, San Francisco, Washington, D.C., Philadelphia, Miami, Hawaii, the New York City area, and Seattle. In the fiscal year ended February 28, 1981, it sold 761 condominium units in the United States and 108 in Canada, of which 101 were in Toronto.

As of December 31, 1980

Land Inventory	*Acres*
Total Inventory	15,942
Total Canada	10,342
Total U.S.	5,600

Shopping Centers	*Sq. Ft.*
Total	5,709,000
Total in Canada	5,649,000
Total in U.S.	60,000

Major Shopping Centers (By Size)

	Location	Name	% Interest	Sq. Ft.
Canada	Oshawa, Ont.	Oshawa Shopping Centre	100	972,000
	Sudbury, Ont.	New Sudbury Shopping Centre	100	479,000
	London, Ont.	Wellington Square	100	413,000
	Timmins, Ont.	Timmins Square	50	359,000
	Rimouski, Que.	Le Carrefour Rimouski	50	343,000
	Longueuil, Que.	Place Longueuil	67	340,000
	Toronto	Golden Mile Plaza	100	263,000
U.S.	Santa Clara, Calif.	3 Restaurants	50	26,000
	Sunnyvale, Calif.	Oakmead Commercial	50	23,000
	Sunnyvale, Calif.	Restaurant	50	11,000

Hotels (By Number of Rooms)

	Location	Name		Rooms
Canada	Toronto	Harbour Castle Hilton		963
	Ottawa	Holiday Inn		505
	Ottawa	Skyline Hotel		454
	Hull	L'Auberge de la Chaudière		243

Office Developments		Sq. Ft.
Total		5,618,000
Total Canada		5,325,000
Total U.S.		293,000

Major Office Developments (By Size)

	Location	Name	% Interest	Sq. Ft.
Canada	Hull	Les Terrasses de la Chaudière	100	1,910,000
	Ottawa	Place de Ville	100	1,270,000
	Ottawa	Journal Towers	100	640,000
	Edmonton	Principal Plaza	100	400,000
	Ottawa	Centennial Towers	100	380,000
	Montreal	Showmart	100	182,000

U.S.

	Location	%	Sq. Ft.
Monadnock Building	San Francisco	100	166,000
Executive Park, OB-1	San Francisco	50	95,000
Oakmead Office Building	Santa Clara	50	32,000

Industrial Properties

	Sq. Ft.
Total	1,338,000
Total Canada	149,000
Total U.S.	1,189,000

Major Industrial Properties (By Size)

	Name	Location	% Interest	Sq. Ft.
Canada	Lismer Building	Ottawa, Ont.	100	69,000
	2530 Starfield Road	Cooksville, Ont.	100	45,000
	Dashwood Building	Kanata, Ont.	100	18,000
U.S.	Signetics I	Santa Clara, Calif.	50	200,000
	Manta Buildings	San Leandro, Calif.	100	199,000
	Marlin Buildings	Union City, Calif.	100	149,000
	Poly-vue Plastics	Petaluma, Calif.	100	132,000

Residential Properties (Completed)

	Units
Total	4,751
Total Canada	3,699
Total U.S.	1,052

Major Residential Properties (By Size)

		Name	Location	% Interest	Units
Canada	Completed	Riverside Court Apartments	Ottawa	100	757
		Redwood Court Garden Homes	Ottawa	100	640
		Harbour Square	Toronto	100	539
		Playfair Towers	Ottawa	100	427
		Bryden Court Apartments	Toronto	100	352
		Champlain Towers	Ottawa	50	243
		Chateau Maisonneuve	Montreal	100	242

U.S.
Completed

Name	Location	Start Date	Units
Fleetwood Park Apartments	Westchester	60	480
Netherland Gardens	Riverdale, N.Y.	33	462
Bayou Bend Towers	Houston	—	110

Canada
Planned

Name	Location	Start Date	Units
Harbour Square	Toronto	Summer 1981	492

U.S.
Planned

	Location	Start Date	Units
South Beach-Rincon Point	San Francisco	1982	600
The Spires	Houston	June 1981	476
	Jupiter, Fla.	1981	414
La Tour	Dallas	June 1981	131

Planned Integrated Development Projects

Canada

Location	Start Date	Description
Brantford, Ont.	Late 1981 or early 1982	100,000 square foot department store and 120,000 square feet retail space
Edmonton (Commonwealth Square)	1982	Office building, hotel, condominium apartments.

U.S.

Location	Start Date	Description
San Jose	1982	$400 million downtown redevelopment project.
Dallas	1981-84	3,000,000 square feet: office, hotel, residential, and retail space.
San Francisco	October 1981	1,100,000 square feet of office space on 70 acres at Executive Park.
Houston		$250 million office tower.

Carma

Year End: December 30
Total Land Holdings

Year	Acres
1972	6,115
1973	10,937
1974	10,803
1975	12,110
1976	12,637
1977	14,995
1978	13,934
1979	14,146
1980	26,408*

*Includes 10,248 acres owned by Allarco Developments Ltd. of Edmonton, which Carma acquired in 1980.

Land Held for Future Development in Canada

Location	Carma Group Interest	Acres	Planned Development
Calgary—			
Deerfoot Business Centre	50%	111.6	office park
Edmonton—			
downtown	50%	0.7	multi-use (hotel & office)
Grand Centre	100%	25.8	shopping center
Hinton	100%	25.8	shopping center

Projects Under Development

Location	Project	Carma Group Interest	Sq. Ft.	Planned Development
Calgary	Deerfoot Business Centre—			
	Building 1B	50%	157,000	office
	Deerfoot Mall	25%	516,000	shopping center
	Downtown Office Towers Tower 1 (under construction)	50%	450,000	office with some retail
	Future Stages		750,000	
Edmonton	Strand Building	50%	185,000	office

As of December 30, 1980
Development Plans (By Size)

	Location	Land Developed and Under Development (Acres)	Land Held for Future Development (Acres)	Total Land Controlled (Acres)
Canada	Edmonton	66	5,103	5,169
	Calgary	223	4,328	4,551
	Northern Alberta	14	2,253	2,267
	Hamilton/Oakville/Mississauga	68	1,484	1,552
	Red Deer, Alta.	5	1,417	1,422
	Prince George, B.C.	—	786	786
	Southern Alberta	111	503	614
	Vancouver	48	563	611
	Other British Columbia	—	221	221
	Saskatchewan	—	9	9
	Total	535	16,667	17,202

U.S.	Location	Land Developed and Under Development (Acres)	Land Held for Future Development (Acres)	Total Land Controlled (Acres)
	Los Angeles	—	3,353	3,353
	Arizona	—	1,787	1,787
	Texas	101	1,382	1,483
	Atlanta	—	750	750
	West Palm Beach	—	667	667
	Nevada	—	605	605
	San Diego	—	208	208
	Seattle	105	88	193
	Sacramento	—	96	96
	Puerto Vallarta (Mexico)	—	37	37
	Denver	24	—	24
	San Francisco	—	3	3
	Total	230	8,976	9,206

Planned Projects (By Size)

U.S.	Location	Name	Description	Acres	% Interest
	Sacramento	California Center	Office Park	52.2	100
	Denver	Point West	Office/commercial	28.7	50
	Phoenix	7th and Bell	Shopping Center	17.0	100
	Denver	Yarrow St.	Office/commercial	16.1	60
	Phoenix	Thunderbird Business Center	Office	16.0	100
	Denver	Silo Business Park	Office/restaurant	14.0	100
	Denver	Northview	Office/retail	10.0	50
	Phoenix	64th and Greenway	Shopping Center	10.0	100
	Denver	Kehl	Office	0.4	100

Daon

Office Centers (By Size)

	Location	Name	% Interest	Rentable (Sq.Ft.)	Year of Completion	Development Stage
Canada	Montreal	Place Victoria Stock Exchange Tower	50	1,000,000 (and 90,000 retail)	Acquired in 1980	
	Toronto	Toronto Professional Buildings	100	401,000	Acquired in 1977	
	Edmonton	Seventh Street Plaza	20	329,000	1978	
	Calgary	Chevron Plaza	50	267,000	1981	
	Vancouver	1050 West Pender	30	247,000	1974	
	Vancouver	Daon Centre	50	207,000	1980	
	Calgary	Daon Building	100	167,000	1973	
	Vancouver		100			Park Place (37 floors)
U.S.	Atlanta	Omni International	50	1,600,000	Acquired in 1980	
	San Francisco (Joint venture with Cadillac-Fairview Corporation)	444 Market Street	50	605,000	1980	
	Denver (Joint venture with Bramalea Limited)	Ptarmigan Place	50	402,000	1982	
	Seattle	Daon Building	100	262,000	1981	
	Sacramento	Capital Place	100	228,000	1982	
	San Francisco	Pacific II	50	213,000	1981	
	San Francisco	Pacific I	50	175,000	1978	
	Alameda County, Calif.	Heritage Park	$66\frac{2}{3}$	100,000	1980	
	Long Beach		100			Arco Center (two 14-floor towers)

Shopping Centers (By Size)

Canada

Location	Name	% Interest	Rentable (Sq. Ft.)	Year of Completion	Development Stage
Edmonton	Heritage Mall	100	779,000	1981	
Coquitlam, B.C.	Coquitlam Centre	50	736,000	1979	
Calgary	Sunridge Mall	100	646,000	1981	
Red Deer	Bower Place	100	435,000	1981	
North Bay	Northgate Square	50	285,000	1980	(Holds option on another 340,000 sq. ft.)
Trail, B.C.	Waneta Plaza	100	193,000	1979	
Portage La Prairie, Man.	Portage Mall	100	190,000	1979	
Wetaskiwin, B.C.	Wetaskiwin Mall	100	146,000	1979	
Langley	Langley Mall, B.C.	33⅓	132,000	1975	

Hotels

U.S.

Location	Name	Rooms	Year Acquired in 1980	Description
Tulsa	The Mayo Hotel	440 rooms	Acquired in 1980	Historic landmark hotel. To be renovated and upgraded.

Residential Apartments (By Number of Units)

Canada

No major projects in 1979-80.
(Has developed condominiums in British Columbia, Alberta, and Manitoba in previous years.)

Location	Name	% Interest	Year of Acquisition or Completion	Units

U.S.

(Primarily garden apartments; high rise apartments mostly in Florida; also low rise apartments.)

Location	Name	% Interest	Year of Acquisition or Completion	Units
San Bruno	The Place	50	1980	872
College Park	Westchester Park	60	1979	606
Sacramento	Woodside I-IV	100	1979	558

Location				Year(s) of Completion	
Chicago	Four Lakes Village (Phase I)	60		1980	483
Santa Clara	Woodsborough	100		1980	477
Hollywood	Hallmark	50		1979	375
Los Angeles	The Park	100		1980	350
Miami Beach	South Bay Club	100		1979	347
Miami Beach	Ocean Pavillion	100		1980	334
San Jose	Foxborough	100		1980	296
San Diego	Village Square	50		1980	288
San Jose	Meridian Woods	50		1980	282
Encino	Newcastle Manor	100		1979	280
Hollywood	The Diplomat	66⅔		1979	268
Everett	South Pointe	100		1979	249
Miami Beach	Belle Plaza	100		1979	226
Los Angeles	Porto Verde	95		1980	216
Sacramento	Governor's Square West	100		1979	200
Santa Ana	Peppertree	95		1980	184
Mission Viejo	Casa Loma	100		1980	144
North Hollywood	Briarcrest	100		1980	120
Sherman Oaks	Parkridge	100		1980	108
Seattle	Towne Square	100		1979	106
Glendale	Alpha Terrace	100		1979	101
Sausalito	Cote D'Azur	100		1979	60

Industrial

	Location	Rentable (Sq. Ft.)	Year(s) of Completion
Canada			
Developed	Edmonton	459,000	1980-81
	Edmonton	197,000	1977-80

Canada

Industrial Land

Location	Acres	Year(s) of Acquisition	Scheduled Year(s) of Development and/or Sale
Calgary	451	1973-80	1980-86
Edmonton	335	1974-78	1980-90
Edmonton	320	1980	1981-88

U.S.

Developed

Location	Rentable (Sq. Ft.)	% Interest	Year(s) of Completion
California			
Orange County	168,000	50	1980
San Bernadino County	101,000	50	1980

U.S.

Industrial Land

Location	Acres	Acres	Year(s) of Acquisition	Scheduled Year(s) of Development and/or Sale
California				
San Bernadino County	249	50% in 100 acres and 100% in 149	1980	1980-85
Los Angeles	70	65% in 26 acres and 100% in 44		

Residential and Multi-Use Properties (By Acres)

	Location	Name	Description	Acres	Year(s) of Acquisition	Scheduled Year(s) of Development and/or Sale
Canada	Calgary	The Homesteads	Multi-Use	4,147	1973-79	1980-95
	Edmonton	Project 80	Multi-Use	1,188	1978-80	1981-90
	Kelowna, B.C.	Dilworth Mountain	Residential	821	1973	1980-86
	Bonnyville, Alta.	Bonnyville Land Assembly	Residential	261	1980	1981-86
	Calgary	Applewood Park	Residential	224	1979	1981-84

U.S.	Carlsbad, Calif.	La Costa	Residential	3,304	1981	1980-90
	Denver	Castlewood Corp.	Multi-Use	1,700	1981	1981-86
	Snohomish County, Wash.	Harbor Pointe	Multi-Use	1,424	1978	1980-88
	San Diego	Miramar Ranch North	Multi-Use	1,067	1979	1980-83
	San Diego County	Shadowridge	Multi-Use	904	1976-77	1982-84
	San Diego County	Carillo Ranch	Residential	364	1979	1980-82
	Riverside County, Calif.	Corona McKinley	Multi-Use	348	1979	1982-92
	Fort Worth	Woodhaven	Multi-Use	140	1978-79	1979-82
	King County, Wash.	Newcastle Hills	Residential	100	1978	1980-82
	Portland	Mountain Park and Town Center	Multi-Use	77	1978	
	Sun Valley	Greyhawk (41⅔% interest)	Residential	60	1980	

Nu-West

Planned

Canada

Location	Name	Description
Calgary	Strathcona Town Centre	800,000 square feet
Edmonton	Atria	City's largest suburban office building (180,000 square feet) plus a 13,000 square foot atrium

U.S.

Location	Name	Description
Dallas	Quorum West	31 acre office complex
New Orleans	Lakewood Plaza	77,000 square foot shopping center

Florida Only

Location and Name	Use	Sq. Ft.	Completion Date	% Interest
Broward County:				
Broward Business Park	Industrial warehouse, office	560,000	1983	75
Broward County:				
Headway Office Park	Office park	540,000	1983	100
North Dade County:				
California Club Mall	Shopping center	197,000	1982	100
Jupiter: Jupiter Mall	Shopping center	190,000	(summer, 1981)	100
Palm Beach County:				
Sandalfoot Plaza	Shopping center	150,000	1982	50
Hobe Sound: The Market Place	Shopping center	145,000	(summer, 1981)	50
Palm Beach County:				
Boca Lyons Plaza	Neighborhood center	116,000	(fall, 1981)	75
Palm Beach County:				
Shoppes of Rainberry	Specialty center	86,000	1982	50
Deerfield Beach:				
Shoppes of Hillsboro I	Shopping center	43,000	(spring, 1981)	100

Olympia & York

As of End of 1981

Completed	Sq. Ft.
Total	50 million
Total Canada	21 million
Total U.S.	approx. 22 million
Total Europe	approx. 7 million

Completed (By Size)

Canada

Location	Name	Floors	Sq. Ft.
Toronto	First Canadian Place I	72	3,500,000
	II	36	1,500,000
Ottawa	C.D. Howe Building	12	1,130,000
Ottawa	Place Bell Canada	26	1,000,000
Ottawa	L'Esplanade Laurier	21	1,000,000
Toronto	York Centre	28	910,000

U.S. New York

Address	Core Tenant	Floors	Sq. Ft.
55 Water Street	Chemical Bank	53	3,500,000
1290 Avenue of the Americas	Sperry Rand	43	2,000,000
245 Park Avenue	American Brands	47	1,600,000
2 Broadway	Citibank	32	1,600,000
60 Broad Street	RCA, Drexel Burnham	39	1,000,000
320 Park Avenue	ITT	34	700,000
850 Third Avenue	Western Publishing	21	550,000
10 East 53rd Street	Harper & Row	37	360,000

Europe

Location	Name	Floors	Sq. Ft.
London	Peterskill House	6	175,000
Paris	La Boursidière	6	50,000

Office Towers Under Development (By Size)

	Location	Name	Completion Date	Floors	Sq. Ft.
Canada	Calgary	Esso Plaza	1981	35	2,000,000
U.S.	Dallas	Arco Tower	1982	49	1,300,000
	Boston	Exchange Place	1982	40	1,200,000
	New York	Park Avenue Atrium	1981	21	1,100,000
	Dallas	Bryan at North Harwood	1982	36	760,000
	Los Angeles	400 South Hope	1982	26	710,000
	Hartford	One Commercial Plaza	1983	26	676,000
	Hartford	One Corporate Center	1982	16	425,000
	Springfield	One Financial Plaza	1982	17	380,000
	Boston	One Liberty Square (Restoration)	1982	13	150,000

Integrated Developments

	Location	Name	Description	Time Span
U.S.	New York	Battery Park	Four office buildings. Total of six million square feet on 91 acres. Cost: $1 billion.	Start date 1983
	San Francisco		Office space: 1,000 condominium units; 1,500 room hotel; shopping and recreation. 1 million square feet on 25 acres.	Five year program
	Portland	Fountain Plaza	Office and retail space; 285 room hotel; cinemas; condominium apartments.	Two years; to be completed by 1983 or 1984.

Oxford

	Sq. Ft.
Completed	
Canada	7,588,000
U.S.	4,225,000
Under Construction	Sq. Ft.
Canada	786,000
U.S.	4,367,000

Completed (By Size)

	Location	Name	Office Sq. Ft.	Retail Sq. Ft.	Total Sq. Ft.	% Interest	Year Completed
Canada	Edmonton	Edmonton Centre	1,219,000	633,000	1,463,000	40%	1975-1978
	Calgary	Toronto Dominion Square	768,000	217,000	985,000	51%	1977
	Toronto	Continental Bank of Canada (Head Office)	605,000	15,000	620,000	100%	1980
	Toronto	Richmond-Adelaide Centre	422,000	39,000	461,000	100%	1978
	Edmonton	Imperial Oil Building	366,000	23,000	389,000		1969
	Kitchener	Market Square	92,000	290,000	382,000	51%	1974
	Toronto	390 Bay Street	355,000	16,000	371,000	100%	1978 (Acquired)
	Toronto	Guardian of Canada Tower	284,000	18,000	302,000	100%	1975
	Halifax	Bank of Commerce Building	206,000	1,000	207,000	50%	1977
	Winnipeg	Royal Bank Building	156,000	3,000	159,000	100%	1966
U.S.	St. Paul	Town Square	431,000	231,000	662,000	100%	1979
	Denver	Anaconda Tower	646,000	11,000	657,000	70%	1978
	Denver	Great West Plaza	653,000	—	653,000	70%	1980
	Minneapolis	Multifoods Building	329,000	49,000	378,000	100%	1977 (Acquired)
	Minneapolis	Cargill Building	329,000	41,000	370,000	100%	1977

Location	Name	Office Sq. Ft.	Retail Sq. Ft.	Total Sq. Ft.	% Interest	Year
Phoenix	United Plaza (Phase I)	324,000	—	324,000	100%	(Acquired) 1979
Minneapolis	Pillsbury Building	258,000	22,000	280,000	100%	(Acquired) 1977
Minneapolis	Peavey Building	249,000	27,000	276,000	100%	(Acquired) 1977
Colorado Springs	Colorado Square	173,000	21,000	194,000	70%	(Acquired) 1977

Under Construction

	Location	Name	Office Sq. Ft.	Retail Sq. Ft.	Total Sq. Ft.
Canada	Edmonton	Edmonton Centre West	411,000	—	411,000
	Toronto	National Bank Building	375,000	—	375,000
U.S.	Minneapolis	Minneapolis City Center	1,429,000	591,000	2,020,000
	Denver	Republic Plaza	1,230,000	55,000	1,285,000
	Louisville	Louisville Galleria	830,000	232,000	1,062,000

Hotels

	Location	Name	% Interest	Rooms
Canada	Edmonton	Four Seasons Hotel	40	314
U.S.	Denver	Fairmont Hotel	70	550
	Minneapolis	Marquette Inn	100	277
	Minneapolis	Northstar Inn	100	226

Trizec

	Canada	U.S.
Office Buildings		
Completed (Sq. Ft.)	13,386,000	6,865,000
Planned (Sq. Ft.)	3,400,000	2,300,000
Shopping Centers		
Completed (Sq. Ft.)	6,663,000	22,437,000
Under construction (Sq. Ft.)	—	6,428,000
Planned (Sq. Ft.)	—	19,023,000
Retirement Lodges		
(Guest Capacity)	1,690	277
Nursing Homes		
(Guest Capacity)	1,867	—
Mobile Home Parks	1 park—364 trailer sites	31 parks—743 trailer sites

Office Buildings

	Location	Name	Sq. Ft.	% Interest
Canada	Montreal	Place Ville Marie	3,052,000	100
	Toronto	The Atrium on Bay—Phase I	942,000	40
	Vancouver	Royal Centre	893,000	100
	Quebec City	Place Quebec	790,000	100
	Calgary	Calgary Place	735,000	50
	Winnipeg	Winnipeg Square	625,000	100
	Calgary	Scotia Centre	616,000	100
	Calgary	Fifth and Fifth	571,000	75
	Montreal	2020 University	534,000	100
	Montreal	BCN Building	511,000	100
	Halifax	Maritime Centre	446,000	100

U.S.

Detroit	New Center One	1,032,000	67
Detroit	First National Building	944,000	100
Detroit	Fisher Building	920,000	100
Los Angeles	Marina Towers	669,000	40
Los Angeles	Encino Gateway	643,000	100
Atlanta	Peachtree Center Tower	428,000	100
Kansas City	One Pershing Square*	236,000	50

*Hotel and second office building planned.

Under Development

Canada

Location	Name	Description
Calgary	Bankers Hall*	1,800,000 sq. ft. (Two 50-floor towers for Royal Bank and Canadian Imperial Bank of Commerce.)
Calgary	Western Canadian Place	1,100,000 sq. ft.
Montreal	Place Beaver Hall	500,000 sq. ft.

*First project in Canada to have two banks on same site.

U.S.

Denver		460 acres: 1,000,000 sq. ft. Shopping center with 5 department stores, 10 office buildings (1,500,000 sq. ft.), 1 hotel—250 rooms.

Hotels

Canada

Location	Name	Rooms	% Interest
Quebec City	Quebec Hilton	572	50
Richmond, B.C.	River Inn	373	100
Saint John	Brunswick Square Hotel	260	100

Shopping Centers

	Location	Name	Sq. Ft.	% Interest
Canada	Toronto	Yorkdale	1,206,000	100
	Toronto	Scarborough Town Centre	1,110,000	100
	Winnipeg	St. Vital	627,000	50
	Halifax	Halifax Shopping Centre	558,000	100
	Calgary	Southcentre	544,000	50
	Vancouver	Lougheed Mall	493,000	50
U.S. Completed	City of Industry, Calif.	Puente Hills Mall	1,188,000	100
	Cerritos, Calif.	Los Cerritos Center	1,169,000	100
	Thousand Oaks, Calif.	The Oaks	1,107,000	100
	Dallas	Prestonwood Town Center	1,074,000	100
	Modesto, Calif.	Vintage Faire	1,059,000	100
	Albuquerque	Coronado Center	999,000	100
	Arcadia, Calif.	Santa Anita Fashion Park	978,000	100
	Murray, Utah	Fashion Place	967,000	100
U.S. Under Construction	Portland	Clockamas Town Center	1,200,000	100
	Memphis	Mall of Memphis	1,000,000	100
	San Mateo, Calif.	San Mateo Fashion Island	891,000	100
	Las Vegas	The Fashion Show	815,000	100
U.S. Planned	Woodbridge, Va.	Woodbridge Mall	1,350,000	100
	Houston	Northeast Mall	1,253,000	100
	Rancho Cucamonga, Calif.	Rancho Cucamonga Center	1,160,000	100
	Bridgewater, N.J.	Bridgewater Commons	1,141,000	100
	Escondido, Calif.	North Country Fair	1,110,000	100
	San Antonio	San Antonio Center	1,000,000	100

Appendix C

Five Year Review of Holdings

Notes:

(1) All tables are based on the companies' annual reports.

(2) There is no table for Olympia & York, which does not disclose such data. However, the bulk of its expansion has been since 1976, when the company acquired 11 million square feet of office space in New York City.

(3) The quantity of space may decrease from year to year as properties are sold.

Bramalea

	1976	1977	1978	1979	1980
Shopping Centers (Sq. Ft.)					
Canada	5,250,500	5,094,300	5,175,300	5,555,000	5,707,200
U.S.	—	—	—	—	3,055,700
Industrial (Sq. Ft.)					
Canada	1,514,500	1,444,300	1,857,000	2,473,100	3,013,050
U.S.	—	—	—	272,900	270,800
Office Buildings (Sq. Ft.)					
Canada	193,000	316,900	1,093,500	1,458,000	2,013,000
U.S.	—	—	—	586,000	1,111,700
Hotels (Rooms)					
Canada	1,172	1,172	1,172	1,316	1,689
U.S.	—	—	—	—	—
Rental Apartments (Units)					
Canada	1,369	1,369	1,739	1,556	1,755
U.S.	—	—	—	—	—
Condominium Apartments					
Canada	—	—	—	—	—
U.S.	—	—	—	—	—
Townhouses					
Canada	192	192	192	375	375
U.S.	—	—	—	—	—
Land Holdings (Acres)					
Canada	5,883	5,350	5,492	4,783	4,226
U.S.	55	50	—	1,087	1,117

Cadillac Fairview

(**Note:** *Cadillac Fairview's year end is the end of February. Thus, figures in these tables are for the calendar and not fiscal year.*)

	1976	1977	1978	1979	1980
Rental Apartments (Units)					
Canada	14,997	14,997	14,997	14,841	15,107
U.S.	—	—	—	2,927	2,927
Housing Sales (Units)					
Canada	655	666	823	757	483
U.S.	38	39	80	2,985	2,976
Condominium Sales (Units)					
Canada	492	538	533	796	108
U.S.	61	—	85	660	761
Shopping Centers (Sq. Ft.)					
Canada	7,552,000	7,593,000	8,405,000	8,345,000	8,761,000
U.S.	—	—	—	8,646,000	9,394,000
Office Buildings (Sq. Ft.) Mixed Use Commercial/Retail					
Canada	6,927,000	8,435,000	9,233,000	9,142,000	10,067,000
U.S.	—	—	1,356,000	1,782,000	2,109,000
Industrial Space (Sq. Ft.)					
Canada	1,274,000	1,536,000	1,621,000	1,854,000	2,152,000
U.S.	2,815,000	2,645,000	2,645,000	6,332,000	4,919,000

Campeau

	1976	1977	1978	1979	1980
Shopping Centers (Sq. Ft.)					
Canada	3,873,078	4,825,312	5,592,494	5,577,000	5,709,000
U.S.	—	—	—	442,000	60,000
Office Buildings (Sq. Ft.)					
Canada	196,250	247,209	257,596	4,963,000	5,325,000
U.S.	—	—	—	404,000	293,000
Hotels (Rooms)					
Canada	1,922	1,922	2,165	2,165	2,165
U.S.	—	—	—	—	—
Rental Apartments (Units)					
Canada	2,788	2,789	2,778	3,061	3,200
U.S.	—	—	—	4,363	1,052
Land Holdings (Acres) (Segmented only in 1979 and 1980 Annual Reports)					
Canada				10,715	10,342
U.S.				5,545	5,600
Industrial Properties (Sq. Ft.) (Segmented only in 1979 and 1980 Annual Reports)					
Canada				149,000	149,000
U.S.				1,478,000	1,189,000

Carma

Land Holdings (In Acres)

	1975	1976	1977	1978	1979	1980	Land Under Development 1980
Canada							
Alberta	10,523	11,032	11,911	10,077	9,293	13,604	419
British Columbia	1,248	1,189	1,181	1,303	1,404	1,570	48
Ontario	465	416	386	343	326	1,484	68
Saskatchewan	—	—	—	—	—	9	—
Total	12,236	12,637	13,478	11,723	11,023	16,667	535
U.S.							
Arizona	—	—	—	—	—	1,787	—
California	—	—	—	177	659	3,660	—
Colorado	—	—	—	—	2	—	24
Florida	—	—	—	—	666	667	—
Georgia	—	—	—	—	—	750	—
Nevada	—	—	—	—	—	605	—
Texas	—	—	1,517	1,709	1,568	1,382	101
Washington	—	—	—	325	228	88	105
Total	—	—	1,517	2,211	3,123	8,939	230
Mexico							
Puerto Vallarta	—	—	—	—	—	37	—
Total	—	—	—	—	—	37	—

Number of Lots Sold

	1975	1976	1977	1978	1979	1980
Canada						
Alberta	1,273	1,162	1,136	2,011	1,348	1,635
British Columbia	165	281	172	69	486	594
Ontario	—	164	8	15	171	258
Total	1,438	1,607	1,316	2,095	2,005	2,487

U.S.

California	—	—	—	—	191	384
Texas	—	—	34	94	119	104
Washington	—	—	—	—	130	122
Total	—	—	34	94	440	610

Shopping Centers

Location	Name	Sq. Ft.	Year Opened	Year Sold
Calgary	Silver Springs	78,000	1977	1980
Edmonton	Lakewood	20,000	1978	1979
Edmonton	Belmead	20,000	1978	1979
Edmonton	Blue Quill	30,000	1979	1979
Calgary	Braecentre	50,000	1978	1979
Hamilton	Albion Plaza	10,000	1978	—
Edmonton	Clareview	18,500	1981	1981
Denver	Marketplace	205,000	1978	—

Office Buildings

Location	Name	Sq. Ft.	Year Opened	Year Sold
Calgary	Deerfoot Business Centre	160,000	1980	—
	Carma Building*		1978	
Denver	Marketplace Complex			
	Office Tower 1	134,700	—	—
	Office Tower 2	134,700	—	—
	Fountainhead	54,800	—	—
Seattle	Plaza	250,400	1980	—
	Arcade	90,500	1980	1980

*Located on land leased from a partnership in which the Carma Group holds a 50% interest.

Daon

Shopping Centers Acquired & Developed
(Net Sq. Ft.)

CANADA	1975-79	1980	1980 Held*	at Oct. 31/80 Under Development
ALBERTA	593,000	—	145,000	1,860,000**
B.C.	637,000	—	604,000	—
MANITOBA	190,000	—	190,000	—
ONTARIO	—	285,000***	285,000	—
Total	1,420,000	285,000	1,224,000	1,860,000

U.S. SOUTHERN CALIFORNIA	46,000	15,500	15,500	—
Total	46,000	15,500	15,500	—

*As of year end, October 31, 1980.
**Subsequent to October 31, 1980, company marketed limited partnership units.
***Subsequent to October 31, 1980, purchased partners interest to hold 100%.

Commercial/Industrial Acquired and/or Developed (Net Sq. Ft.)

CANADA	1975-79	1980	1980 Held*	Under Development
ALBERTA				
Edmonton	1,806,000	386,000	427,000	246,000
Calgary	—	50,000	50,000	—
B.C.				
Vancouver	81,000	—	—	—
Total	1,887,000	436,000	477,000	246,000
U.S. SOUTHERN CALIFORNIA	53,000	308,000	50,000	125,000
Total	53,000	308,000	50,000	125,000

*As of year end October 31, 1980.

Residential Units Sold (Net)

	1975	1976	1977	1978	1979	TOTAL	1980**	At Oct. 31/80 For Sale
CANADA								
ALBERTA	735	346	249	579	124	2,033	303	—
B.C.	652	1,040	728	404	730	3,554	475	110
MANITOBA	—	—	—	121	363	484	22	—
Total	1,387	1,386	977	1,104	1,217	6,071	800	110
U.S.								
SOUTHERN CALIFORNIA	—	—	499	1,403	2,589	4,491	1,213	1,065
NORTHERN CALIFORNIA	—	—	—	167	386	553	1,685	1,114
WASHINGTON	—	—	—	839	170	1,009	250	42
NEW MEXICO	—	—	—	—	71	71	515	79
TEXAS	—	—	—	—	386	386	441	178
ARIZONA	—	—	—	666	112	778	—	—
MARYLAND	—	—	—	—	—	—	57	307
FLORIDA	—	—	—	—	—	—	170	695
ILLINOIS	—	—	—	—	—	—	136	154
Total	—	—	—	3,075	3,714	7,288	4,467	3,634

*Includes bulk sales.
**As of year end October 31, 1980.

Land Sold (Net Acres)

	1975	1976	1977	1978	1979	TOTAL	1980*	At Oct. 31/80 Under Development For Sale
CANADA								
ALBERTA	1,123	421	269	250	495	2,558	595	443
B.C.	1,769	87	68	47	79	2,050	294	132
Total	2,892	508	337	297	574	4,608	889	575

U.S.

SOUTHERN CALIFORNIA	140	559	780	1,479	386	1,154
NORTHERN CALIFORNIA	—	5	—	—	—	—
WASHINGTON	13	—	104	122	204	201
OREGON	155	—	39	194	17	56
TEXAS	—	—	81	81	75	13
Total	308	564	1,004	1,876	682	1,424

*As of year end October 31, 1980.

Office Buildings Acquired and/or Developed (Net Interest)

CANADA	1975-79	1980	1980 Held*	Under Development
ALBERTA				
Edmonton	629,000	—	66,000	—
Calgary	274,000	—	167,000	267,000
B.C.				
Vancouver	579,000	207,000	396,000	—
ONTARIO				
Toronto	401,000	—	401,000	—
Total	1,883,000	207,000	1,030,000	267,000
U.S.				
WASHINGTON				
Seattle	—	—	—	262,000
S. CALIFORNIA				
Orange County	196,000	—	20,000	—
Los Angeles County	200,000	—	—	—
N. CALIFORNIA				
Contra Cosa County	241,000	67,000	67,000	—
Marin County	—	59,000	59,000	—
Sacramento	—	—	—	228,000
San Francisco	87,000	303,000	390,000	107,000

COLORADO				
Denver	—	—	—	201,000
OTHER				
Phoenix	19,000	—	—	—
Total	743,000	424,000	536,000	798,000

*As of year end October 31, 1980.

Genstar

Land Acreage (As of December 31, 1980)

	Owned	Optioned	Held in Partnership	Total
Canada	15,263	969	11,067	27,299
U.S.	8,165	7,281	592	16,038

Housing Sales (Units)
(As of December 31, 1980)

	1976	1977	1978	1979	1980
Canada	2,446	2,707	2,534	2,199	1,757
U.S.	797	997	945	1,178	954

Note: *Land and housing located primarily in Alberta and San Diego, but also in Dade County, Florida; Houston; State of Washington; and other parts of California around Los Angeles and San Francisco. Until 1977, only in California. In 1978, moved into Texas. In 1979, extended into Washington, Oregon, and Florida.*

Nu-West

(As of December 31)

Housing Sales (Units)

	1976	1977	1978	1979	1980
Canada	3,515	4,737	4,930	4,221	4,918
U.S.	—	230	411	1,738	1,454

Land Holdings (Acres)

Canada	10,791	11,428	11,881	12,986	13,060
U.S.	334	621	7,882	10,014	4,421

Housing Sales (Units): Key Cities

	1976	1977	1978	1979	1980
Canada					
Calgary	1,108	1,654	1,523	1,655	2,056
Edmonton	786	1,008	1,075	1,219	1,737
Ontario	166	43	99	140	297
Regina	553	758	512	364	295
Saskatoon	183	380	296	394	191
Vancouver	302	243	496	228	163
Red Deer	104	89	126	96	118
Lloydminster, Sask.	—	—	27	37	19
Kamloops, B.C.	16	36	20	2	—
Resale	—	175	102	86	42

U.S.

Phoenix	—	—	47	1,280	1,091
Denver	—	57	146	173	185
Seattle	—	187	261	285	178

Major Land Holdings (Acres)

	1976	1977	1978	1979	1980
Canada					
Edmonton	3,769	4,740	5,165	6,623	6,818
Calgary	3,977	3,668	3,785	2,699	1,690
Regina	1,478	1,518	1,344	1,467	1,409
Northern and Northwest Ontario	—	—	—	—	838
Winnipeg	—	—	487	674	483
Kamloops	256	256	—	—	400
Southern and Eastern Ontario	79	254	47	317	349
Saskatchewan (Except Saskatoon and Regina)	—	—	—	182	289
Saskatoon	470	400	316	310	292
Vancouver Pacific Region	459	599	502	495	185
Kelowna, B.C.	—	—	—	—	138
Red Deer	303	249	128	103	110
Nanaimo, B.C.	—	—	—	—	59
U.S.					
Southern California	—	—	6,105	6,361	2,374
Phoenix	—	—	357	1,263	899
Seattle	193	286	385	692	784
Denver	141	335	1,035	1,060	364

Oxford

	1976	1977	1978	1979	1980
Office and Mixed Use (Commerical/Retail) (Sq. Ft.)					
Canada	3,872,000	4,405,000	7,889,000	7,770,000	7,588,000
U.S.	—	196,000	1,579,000	3,180,000	4,225,000
Shopping Centers (Sq. Ft.)					
Canada	5,986,000	6,734,400	7,139,400	7,834,000	SOLD
U.S.	—	—	—	—	—
Hotels (Rooms)					
Canada	1,460	2,037	2,164	151	314
U.S.	—	—	496	536	1,053

Trizec

	1976	1977	1978	1979	1980
Office Buildings					
(Sq. Ft.)					
Canada	13,493,000	11,224,000	11,818,000	13,705,000	13,386,000
U.S.	3,370,000	5,490,000	5,806,000	6,339,000	6,865,000
Shopping Centers					
(Sq. Ft.)					
Canada	4,511,000	4,500,000	5,565,000	6,344,000	6,663,000
U.S.	876,000	868,000	868,000	868,000	22,437,000
Retirement Lodges					
(Guest Capacity)					
Canada	3,358	3,463	3,393	3,425	3,557
U.S.	—	—	180	277	277
Mobile Homes					
(Sites)					
Canada	364	364	364	364	364
U.S.	11,302	10,984	10,564	10,863	743
Hotels					
(Rooms)					
Canada	1,185	1,185	1,185	1,445	1,205
U.S.	—	—	—	—	—
Apartments					
(Units)					
Canada	763	761	761	761	761
U.S.	—	—	—	—	—

Index